Socialism and the Literary Imagination

Edited by Martin Kane

The contributors to this volume – distinguished scholars from Britain, the United States and Germany – are all enthusiasts of East German literature who feel that the literary and artistic qualities of East German writing are all too often lost sight of in the debate about censorship, cultural control, dissident writers and related issues. Each contributor selects a particular East German writer and explains why the work of their chosen author deserves to be considered alongside the best in contemporary European and world literature.

Martin Kane is Senior Lecturer in German and European Studies at Darwin College, University of Kent

Socialism and the Literary Imagination

Essays on East German Writers

Edited by Martin Kane

BERG

New York / Oxford

Distributed exclusively in the US and Canada by
St Martin's Press, New York

First published in 1991 by
Berg Publishers Limited
Editorial offices:
165 Taber Avenue, Providence, RI 02906, USA
150 Cowley Road, Oxford, OX4 1JJ, UK

© Martin Kane 1991

British Library Cataloguing in Publication Data

Socialism and the literary imagination: Essays on
East German writers.
  I. Kane, Martin
  830.9
  ISBN 8–85496–643–9

Library of Congress Cataloging-in-Publication Data

Socialism and the literary imagination: essays on East German
writers
    /edited by Martin Kane.
        p.   cm.
    Includes bibliographical references and index.
    ISBN 0–85496–643–9
      1. German literature—Germany (East)—History and criticism.
    2. Socialism and literature—Germany (East)   3. German
    literature—20th century—History and criticism.   I. Kane, Martin.
    PT3705.S66   1991   91–17769
    830.9'9431—dc20   CIP

*(The publishers have attempted to observe the legal requirements with respect to the rights of
the suppliers of copyright materials; nevertheless persons who have claims are invited to apply
to the publishers.)*

Printed in Great Britain by
Billing and Sons Ltd, Worcester

Contents

Contents

Foreword

The ways in which the literary imagination has responded to the visions and aspirations, the achievements and the failures of socialism have been the topic of perennially intriguing investigation. This whole issue, however, takes on a new significance in the context of the German Democratic Republic, a self-proclaimed socialist state which, over the course of some forty years, has seen the emergence of a literary culture independent of and quite distinct from that of its West German neighbour. But what, in the light of the demise of the GDR as a separate political entity, will be the status of the culture it has produced? Will, in the process of future evaluation, its literature be worthy – as Stefan Heym has cryptically remarked of the East German state itself – of no more than a brief historical footnote?

When the first drafts of the pieces which make up this volume were presented at a small conference at the University of Kent at Canterbury in April 1989 these were not questions which in any way occupied the attention of those present. Now, in their final form, they constitute a response to them. In their examination of a range of East German writers of vastly different background, approach and interests, these essays set out to demonstrate that the literature of the GDR has succeeded in establishing a rich and varied identity for itself which will continue to engage the interests of the scholar, critic and general reader. In what ways the future in a unified Germany will shape this identity in the work of those writers who hitherto have been identified with the now defunct GDR must, of course, remain a matter for speculation.

During those initial discussions none but the most clairvoyant of participants could have foreseen the sequence of events which would take the two Germanies down the road of social and monetary, and eventually, full political union, or have been led to speculate about where this would leave the two respective German literatures. They would certainly not have been encouraged to anticipate the sheer unstoppable momentum with which the events of autumn 1989 would come to such a dramatic head.

Nevertheless, and certainly with the wisdom of hindsight, it is possible now to look back and – against the background of Gorbachev's attempts to introduce reforms in the Soviet Union and, more crucially, his obvious intention not to intervene in the internal affairs of the satellite communist states – to interpret a series of developments in the GDR in the late 1980s as pointing to the dramatic *Wende*, the revolution which was to come.

A number of very different factors might be singled out here. The establishment of a small but steadfast critical presence in the forums provided by the Protestant Church; the disgruntlement expressed by writers such as Christoph Hein at the Tenth Writers' Congress of November 1987; the growing exodus of the most skilled sections of the work force. But perhaps most important of all, one would wish to focus on what is at the heart of all these various phenomena – and what East German writers have done much over the years to articulate – the yawning gap between the image emanating from the GDR media of a society at harmonious ease with itself and the daily realities which any casual visitor to the country might register: the ubiquitous look of blank resignation in the press for tram or S-Bahn, for instance, or the snap of frustration to be observed as this or that trivial but basic commodity was not to be found on its customary spot on the *Kaufhalle* shelf. Common to all of these elements is that they are the product of that gulf in understanding and expectations between rulers and the ruled which is nowhere better demonstrated than in the response of the SED's chief ideologue Kurt Hager to a query, in 1987, about the possibility of Soviet style reforms in the GDR: 'Würden Sie, nebenbei gesagt, wenn Ihr Nachbar seine Wohnung neu tapeziert, sich verpflichtet fühlen, Ihre Wohnung ebenfalls neu zu tapezieren?'[1] Or which, to give a literary example, was caught so hauntingly in Monika Maron's novel *Flugasche* where the sense of a government remote from the people, of authority impervious to the feelings and needs of those it controls are perfectly pinned down in the image of a ministerial limousine sweeping past halted traffic as if through a silent vacuum: 'Die Stille war es, dachte Josefa, die Totenstille. Sie schoben die Stille vor sich her; wohin sie auch kamen, die Stille war vor ihnen da. Sie müssen taub sein davon . . .'[2]

This passage, with its demonstration of the role that the poetic sensibility, the literary imagination have in the illumination of

---

1. *Neues Deutschland*, 10 April 1987. Quoted here from 'Kurt Hager beantwortete Fragen der Illustrierten *Stern*' in *Deutschland Archiv*, 20, no. 6, June 1987, p. 656.
2. Monika Maron, *Flugasche. Roman*, Frankfurt am Main, 1981, p. 176.

social and political realities, illustrates not only one of the points of departure for the essays in this volume but also how historical developments have ensured an inevitable shift of emphasis in the way they will be read. Originally conceived as a project to demonstrate what literature might contribute – creatively and with credibility and in spite of a climate of cultural restrictiveness – to the understanding of a society in which official sources of information and comment have always been propagandistic and manipulative, the volume now becomes, inadvertently perhaps, a drawing up of account, a reminder, at a time when the political, economic and cultural merging of the two Germanies is in process, of the specific contribution which writers whose intellectual, emotional and artistic roots are in the GDR have made to the development of post-1945 German literature.

It must be stressed, however, that *Socialism and the Literary Imagination* aims neither in the direction of literary history, nor does it attempt to establish some sort of league table of literary achievement. Rather, it is born of the wish of a group of enthusiasts of GDR literature from very different quarters – the USA, Germany East and West, Great Britain – to attempt to avoid the usual debates about censorship, cultural control, dissident intellectuals and related issues and instead to explain their enthusiasm for particular writers. And, in doing this, to demonstrate that East German literature deserves to be read and appreciated not only for its relevance within a particular literary and social context, but also – although the extent of this will inevitably vary from author to author – for reasons, aesthetic and artistic, which go far beyond this. It was felt by those involved in the initial discussions for the project that the work of GDR writers was too frequently read not as literature but either for the embattled position it occupied in the continuing, niggling conflict between the artists and the ideologues, or as the only authentic source of insight into life in a society where official channels of information could not be trusted. Both these approaches are, of course to some extent inevitable. One would hardly be able to ignore, to take one example amongst many, the prolonged wrangles over the publication of a second edition of Erich Loest's novel *Es geht seinen Gang* which found their documentation in his classical account of the convoluted mechanisms of censorship in the GDR, *Der vierte Zensor*.[3] Nor would one wish to dispute the claims made by one of the GDR's most

3. Erich Loest, *Der vierte Zensor. Vom Entstehen und Sterben eines Romans in der DDR*, Edition Deutschland Archiv, Cologne, 1984.

distinguished intellectuals, Jürgen Kuczynski, for the superiority of the creative writer over the social scientist as a documenter of the strengths, weaknesses and contradictions of the development of socialism in the GDR. One recalls his comment, in a review of Dieter Noll's novel *Kippenberg*, that: '. . . die Aneignung der Realität mit der Perzeption des Künstlers im allgemeinen immer noch die Widersprüche und die Einheit der Realität besser erfaßt als die wissenschaftliche Perzeption'.[4] And yet to regard the GDR's novelists, poets and playwrights and what they have written either as pawns and pieces in a cultural and political debate, or, to use a scathing expression of one of the distinguished East German contributors to this volume, as 'Zeitungsersatz', would be deeply insulting and a severe diminishment of what individual writers have achieved. All of those discussed here illuminate for us the social context of the GDR, dramatising its strengths and shortcomings, helping us to fathom and understand them. But what is also common to them all is that they are able to transcend local particularities, reaching out to those emotions and experiences which bind or concern all human beings: the robust belief of an Anna Seghers or a Jurek Becker, for instance, in the indestructibility, throughout even the harshest of times, of the human spirit; the emphasis (to which Agnès Cardinal draws our attention) in the work of Irmtraud Morgner on the potential salvation which liberation of the imagination and creativity may bring; or the discussion in Ricarda Schmidt's essay on Christa Wolf of the resistance of subjective insight to ideological and historical certainties and the way in which fiction may create its own authenticity in the troubled nexus between language and reality. It is the universality of intellectual and spiritual concerns such as these which all of the authors discussed in this volume share.

Why this particular selection of authors? Broadly speaking, and notwithstanding an occasional element of overlap, they have been chosen to represent three generations of GDR writers. Those such as Johannes R. Becher, Anna Seghers and Stefan Heym, whose formative experiences were in the struggle against fascism and the years in exile and who brought with them, in their decision to return to what would become the GDR, high expectations of socialism. Secondly, those such as Franz Fühmann, Christa Wolf and Jurek Becker whose childhood and youth were spent under and

4. Jürgen Kuczynski, 'Ein Wissenschaftsbetrieb in künstlerischer Perzeption. Dieter Noll: *Kippenberg*' in *Neue Deutsche Literatur*, vol. 27, 1979, no. 6, pp. 93–9.

Foreword

shaped by National Socialism and for whom a conversion or
commitment to the values of the new society were closely bound
up with the need to evaluate and come to terms with their own past
and with the baleful paradox of '. . . wie man zugleich anwesend
und nicht dabeigewesen sein kann, das schauerliche Geheimnis der
Menschen dieses Jahrhunderts'.[5] And finally, those writers – Helga
Königsdorf, Volker Braun, Christoph Hein – the children of the
new state, the product of ideological and educational values which
they come increasingly to scrutinise, question and in some cases to
reject. Firmly in this last category are the handful of young poets
discussed by Ingrid Pergande in the final chapter of *Socialism and the
Literary Imagination*. This essay breaks with the pattern of the book,
but deliberately so. Although none of these writers have produced
a sufficient body of work to justify a separate essay, it was felt that
since what they had published – often either privately, in esoteric
magazines or in small editions – constituted some of the most
challenging and innovative writing to be produced in the GDR
over the last decade, some account of their vital contribution
should be made. History here has served only to justify this
decision. Expressed, albeit in frequently outlandish form, in the
thematic and aesthetic preoccupations of these young, culturally
and politically alienated poets is all that social and ideological
disaffection which would culminate in the events of November
1989.

In conclusion, grateful thanks must be extended to the generous
patrons of this project. The British Academy enabled the editor to
undertake a three week study visit in East Berlin in the summer of
1988 during which contacts with two of the contributors to this
book were made. Michael Holcroft, Cultural Attaché at the British
Embassy in East Berlin, very kindly smoothed the way for Ingrid
Pergande, Reinhard Hillich and Hans Richter to attend the conference at the University of Kent in April 1989 and also secured
financial support from the British Council, without which their
participation would not have been possible.

Martin Kane
Canterbury, June 1990

5. Christa Wolf, *Kindheitsmuster*, Darmstadt and Neuwied, 1977, p. 51.

–1–

'Vollendung träumend . . .':

Johannes R. Becher's Later Writing

Hans Richter

When, in May 1945, the Hitler regime had been defeated and the Second World War was at an end, German writers who had been driven into exile were faced with the decision of whether to return to Germany and to what part. Many, such as Lion Feuchtwanger or Oskar Maria Graf for instance, remained in their country of exile. Thomas Mann did not leave the USA until 1952 and went to Switzerland, while his brother Heinrich accepted the invitation of the GDR government to become President of the East Berlin Academy of Arts but died in March 1952 before taking up the post. Those authors who had played an active role in the German working class movement or had been in sympathy with its aims returned home as fast as possible, eager to participate in the renaissance of intellectual life. Most of them – Friedrich Wolf, Erich Weinert, Anna Seghers, Bertolt Brecht, Arnold Zweig, Ludwig Renn and many others – made for Berlin or other cities in the Soviet Occupied Zone. Communist authors such as Hans Marchwitza, Stephan Hermlin and Eduard Claudius who had initially settled in the Western Occupied Zones soon found themselves so restricted by the outbreak of the Cold War against the Soviet Union that they moved to what was to become the GDR.

Johannes R.Becher was the first of these significant writers to return to Germany from exile. Just a few weeks after the capitulation of Hitler's *Wehrmacht* he found himself on German soil again for the first time since 1933. He was both deeply moved and shaken by the experience. He wrote to his wife Lilly in Moscow that the eerie sight of mile after mile of ruined buildings on the verge of collapse and gigantic mountains of rubble were 'wirklich zum Heulen'; but at the same time he admits to being overjoyed:

'Kinder singen deutsch, Mütter sprechen deutsch . . .'[1]
Who in fact was this Johannes R. Becher, then fifty-four years old? Despite the fact that he had made a name for himself at the beginning of the second decade of the century with publications which indicated an unusual poetic talent, he was unknown to most Germans. The blossoming of Expressionist writing coincided with his first period of fame. Kurt Pinthus, the editor of the classical anthology of Expressionist poetry *Menschheitsdämmerung* (1920) gave this retrospective view of Becher after his death:

> Einer der Unruhigsten, zwischen Städten und Verlagen rastlos sich hin und her bewegenden, aber zugleich einer der als außerordentliche, wenn auch wilde Begabung am frühesten Anerkannten dieses Jahrzehnts war Johannes R. Becher [. . .] Schon zu Beginn des ersten Weltkriegs bewarben sich mehrere große Verlage um seine Bücher. Sein erstes zweibändiges Hauptwerk, *Verfall und Triumph*, war im traditionsbewußten Hyperion-Verlag (1914) erschienen, andere wurden nun in dem führenden Verlag expressionistischer Literatur von Kurt Wolff (*Verbrüderung, An Europa, Päan gegen die Zeit*), veröffentlicht und gleichzeitig wieder andere in dem klassisch-konservativen Insel-Verlag (*Das neue Gedicht, Gedichte für ein Volk*).[2]

It was a quite different Becher, however, who returned to Germany in 1945. Not only did his Expressionist epoch lie a quarter of a century back in the past, but he had come in the meantime to regard it as an aberration. The activist Expressionist who had undergone a period of crisis after the failure of the November Revolution in 1918 before publicly expressing his allegiance to communism in 1922, had become the leading advocate of a literature which expressed its passionate hostility to capitalism and which wished to prepare the way for socialism. He had become a member of the KPD, the German Communist Party, immediately after its foundation and, from 1922 on, had put himself at the service of the marxist-leninist workers movement as a party worker, literary politician, publicist, a writer of fiction and, above all, as a lyric poet. In the eyes of the judiciary of the Weimar Republic, the son of the steadfastly loyal Munich *Landgerichtsdirektor* Dr Heinrich Becher had become a traitor to be hauled before the courts. The charges levelled at him on 12 October 1927 used as evidence his prose writings *Vorwärts, du Rote Front* (1924), the

1. Quoted from Horst Haase, *Johannes R. Becher. Leben und Werk*, Berlin, 1981, p. 209.
2. *Sinn und Form*, Zweites Sonderheft Johannes R. Becher, Berlin, p. 117.

drama *Arbeiter, Bauern, Soldaten* (1924), the poem 'An Hinden-
burg', which was printed in the party newspaper *Rote Fahne* of 3
May 1925, the volume of poetry *Der Leichnam auf dem Thron* (1925)
as well as the militantly anti-war novel *Levisite*, seized immediately
after its publication in 1926, which warned of the dangers of a new
war fought with the weapons of mass destruction. Only the massive protests by German authors and also internationally-known
writers of diverse outlook and political persuasion such as Maxim
Gorki, Romain Rolland and Henri Barbusse prevented the case
from coming to trial. As a leading figure in the 'Bund proletarisch-
revolutionärer Schriftsteller', founded in 1928, Johannes R. Becher
made a considerable contribution to the development of a vigorous
socialist literature in Germany and to ensuring that it reached a
wide audience. Becher understood his own proletarian and revolutionary writing as something which offered vital support to the
working masses in the class struggle, but he did not regard it as
fulfilling his most intimate dreams as a poet. In 1928 he told Hans
Lorbeer, a proletarian writer who worked in the chemical industry:
'Wir trommeln und werben für unsere Sache. Doch wir werden
mit uns und dem Geschriebenen nicht fertig. Wir sind sozusagen
nur der Schotter, über den einmal die neuen Dichter schreiten
werden. Ein bitterer Gedanke.[. . .] Wenn von mir nur drei Gedichte vom Klang des Abendlieds des alten Matthias Claudius
bleiben, so habe ich als Dichter nicht umsonst gelebt.'[3] When the
Nazis seized power and Becher was forced to flee Germany, a
change was already underway in his work. The appeal inherent in a
return to the great artistic traditions of the Renaissance and to the
democratic German heritage of Classicism and Romanticism, along
with his work on the poetic conception of a non-fascist, humanitarian Germany – all of which bore fruit in the impressive maturity
of the volume of poems *Der Glücksucher und die sieben Lasten* (1938)
– were a product of the practical goal of uniting writers in a broad
popular front against Hitler and fascism. In reviewing this book for
the *Neue Weltbühne*, Berthold Viertel noted: 'Becher sagt wieder
"Ich" und gibt sein Ich, dessen innere und äußere Kontinuität,
dessen intime Erfahrung als eine gesetzmäßige Entwicklung, als ein
Beispiel und Vorbild für alle Menschen.'[4] Viertel views the author
as a 'Dichter der Deutschen [. . .], die da kommen werden – und

3. Hans Lorbeer, 'Die Reise nach Carona. Erinnerungen an Johannes R.
Becher', *Neue Deutsche Literatur*, 12, 1958, p. 15.
4. Berthold Viertel et al (eds), *Erinnerungen an Johannes R. Becher*, Leipzig,
p. 137 ff.

der Deutschen, die heute in Deutschland wie in einem Ausland leben und arbeiten.'[5] The revolutionary dimension was not to be articulated in anarchic destruction of form as it had been in the Expressionist period, nor was it to be found in the strident drumming up of support and propaganda for the Revolution, but, as Becher put it to Heinrich Mann on 9 March 1938, in something which the Germans had only rarely managed to achieve, the 'Verbindung des Freiheitlichen mit dem Heimatgefühl' (GW 4, p. 890). As a German poet in exile in Moscow after Stalin's pact of non-aggression with Hitler, and particularly after the fascist invasion of an unprepared Soviet Union, Becher had great difficulties in carrying out his plan to create a 'Deutschland-Dichtung'. He nevertheless clung tenaciously to the project. With strenuous, even over-strenuous efforts, he strove to assert himself as a poet in three ways: as 'der Deutschlandsucher, der Deutschlandkünder, der Deutschlandstreiter' (GW 16, p. 360). It was with this sense of himself and his mission that Becher returned to his home country when it had been finally liberated from Nazi rule.

Happy to be back in Germany, he felt simultaneously unhappy to find Germany and the Germans in a situation which he had previously, and all too optimistically, thought they had overcome. In order to prove himself as a poet for Germany, he was forced to summon up the requisite 'Vorstellungskraft [. . .] für den tatsächlichen Zustand der Menschen und Dinge'.[6] Becher's work of the time, more than that of any other comparable poet, is an act of mourning. The first of his postwar volumes, *Heimkehr* (1946) and *Volk im Dunkel wandelnd* (1948), are dominated by elegaic tones, expressions of grief at the destruction and suffering which fascism had wrought and a lament for the dead of the Second World War. Becher seeks to empathise profoundly with his fellow countrymen, to interpret their plight and urge them to reflection and change. In this process, the lyrical 'I' takes on an astonishing character; it participates unconditionally in the suffering, even acknowledging complicity in the guilt: 'Vor Deutschland sind wir schuldig allesamt' (GW 5, p. 415). It repeatedly, and with great urgency, takes itself to task, as for instance in the poem 'Die Asche brennt auf meiner Brust'.

Becher would, however, not be Becher if he indulged only in gloomy lament. He also writes verse of cathartic intent, aimed at

5. Ibid., p. 138.
6. Becher, *Der Aufstand im Menschen*, Berlin and Weimar, 1983, p. 5.

consolation, transformation and resurrection. Taking his cue from the Rilke of the *Sonette an Orpheus* ('Nur im Raum der Rühmung darf die Klage/gehen'[7]), he revives his former penchant for the hymnic. But these new beginnings (see GW 5, p. 501 ff.) initially remain very abstract and pale when set against the powerful landscape and nature poem 'Ahrenshoop'[8] which comes close to being a metaphor for life, or the sonnet 'O Acker, mein Gesicht!' which is one of the homecomer's most successful poems:

O Acker: mein Gesicht! Du aufgepflügte,
Durchwühlte Fläche Leid! In dir, dem alten,
Pflügt fort die Zeit, als ob ihr nicht genügte,
Gesicht, das Faltenspiel in deinen Falten.

O Acker: mein Gesicht! Was sät das Leid?
O furch noch tiefer, Leid! In deinem Pflügen
Reiß aus den Selbstbetrug, das Selbstgenügen –
Pflügt mit, ihr alle, die ihr leidend seid,

Und pflügt das Umgepflügte nochmals nach
Und senkt in mein Gesicht des Leidens Samen.
O Acker: mein Gesicht, lang lagst du brach,

Bevor die Pflüger und die Säer kamen . . .
Und tief aus deiner Tiefe wächst ein Licht,
Und wird Gesicht . . . O Acker: mein Gesicht!
(GW 5, p. 522)

The poem follows the author's well-tried principle of encompassing himself and the world in one. It is characterised by a firm, concentrating focus and dense language. It rigorously avoids what is always a latent danger in Becher; the tendency to slip into the rhetorical and general. At work at the heart of the poem is an old motif of central importance to Becher, one which is deeply rooted in his personality and experience of the world and still vitally intact despite the suppression of his early Expressionist phase. In the famous opening poem of the book of pacifistic revolt *An Europa* (1916) we read:

Ich lerne. Ich bereite vor. Ich übe mich.
Wie arbeite ich - ha leidenschaftlich! -

7. Rainer Maria Rilke, *Sämtliche Werke*, Frankfurt am Main, 1962, vol. 1, p. 735.
8. Opening line: 'Vom Meereshimmel wehend überdacht', GW 5, p. 486.

Gegen mein noch unplastisches Gesicht -:
Falten spanne ich.
Die Neue Welt
(- eine solche: die alte, die mystische, die Welt der Qual austilgend-)
zeichne ich, möglichst korrekt, darin ein.

(GW 1, p. 173)

Looked at from a poetological point of view, these lines by the already famous but still very young Becher represent an early version of his conception of lyrical self-presentation. They are linked to the late sonnet by the verbal motifs of 'Gesicht' and 'Falten' and, on a deeper level, also by the dynamic verb *arbeiten*. In the lines of Becher the Expressionist, the motif of suffering is to be found only in embryonic form (in the work 'gegen' the 'noch unplastisches Gesicht'). But now it is developed and raised almost to the point of self-torment: the 'world of pain', multiplied rather than eradicated, stamps itself on the face of the lyrical 'I' and the torment of suffering is poetically affirmed. This is made possible by linking the motifs of ploughing and sowing, ancient symbols of productivity which now also encompass and enhance the frequently recurring motifs of justice, guilt, shame, atonement and resurrection which one finds in the volume *Heimkehr*. The disturbing switches in the object of address that one sometimes finds in Becher are responsible in this sonnet for its multi-layered and dramatic quality: proclamation, invocation, question, entreaty and challenge blend persuasively to a single whole in a process of inexorably rising tension which culminates in a lyrical vision beyond all conceptualisation. It is in this that we find the rich significance of the poem: if tragedy has left its mark, it has not extinguished hope and potential for the future.

As an example of concentrated poetic strength, the sonnet 'O Acker, mein Gesicht' rises head and shoulders above the occasionally flat and superficial rhetoric of many of Becher's postwar poems. One can of course observe a certain unevenness in Becher's verse at every stage of his development. He is constantly driven to write and publish in order to extend and exploit to the full all the poetic possibilities at his disposal. Hanns Eisler, not only extraordinarily gifted and discerning as a composer, offers the following comment: 'Er wußte, was er machte; er mußte sehr viel schreiben, damit vieles eine hohe Höhe erreichte, das wußte er und war gelangweilt, wenn ihn irgend ein Plattkopf auf irgendwelche Verse aufmerksam machte, die ihm nicht gelungen schienen.'[9] The less

9. *Sinn und Form*, Zweites Sonderheft Johannes R. Becher, p. 218.

discerning reader, confronted with the quantity, the pace and the predominant simplicity of Becher's postwar lyric poetry might have the impression that he was lacking in self-criticism or even poetic substance and ability. But in evaluating this phase of his development it is vital to see it evolving as part of a great experiment. Having been guided since his last years in exile by the example of Puschkin and Eichendorff, Becher is striving to write in a popular classical manner. Having made a decisive break with his Expressionist as well as with his proletarian mode of writing, he is aiming for simplicity, for 'Meisterschaft' (see GW 5, p. 521) as well as for the joy, 'Als namenloses Lied durchs Volk zu gehn' (GW 12, p. 270 and GW 6, p. 136). This goal has its dangers, but also yields significant results. Becher's text for the national anthem of the GDR is, in the maturity of its thought and expression, inconceivable without the long years of attempting to create a simple mode of poetic expression which would have relevance and appeal for all Germans. One of the fruits of these efforts was his greatest success of the postwar period, the *Neue deutsche Volkslieder* which were set to music by Hanns Eisler, first performed by Ernst Busch and the radio children's choir of Leipzig, and enjoyed considerable popularity and influence. Many of these texts were also read and recited, especially the poem 'Deutschland, meine Trauer' written in spring 1949. The celebrity of the poem was enhanced not inconsiderably by the fact that Bertolt Brecht, in the little essay 'Wie man Gedichte lesen muß' which he had written for schoolchildren in 1953, produced an affectionate interpretation of its first stanza in order to demonstrate the beauties of a good poem and the necessity for careful reading.[10]

Becher's will to write poetry and his love of it determined his whole life. But already as a young poet, and as a result of his experience of the murderousness of the First World War, writing poetry is for him a political question. His letter of 9 August 1916 to the wife of the Insel-Verlag publisher Kippenberg demonstrates this with shattering clarity.[11] His conviction that the word must become deed, that books (in the sense of his beloved Hölderlin) should come alive, determines not only his understanding of what poetry is, but also spurs him directly to political activity. After

10. See Bertolt Brecht, *Schriften zur Literatur und Kunst*, vol. 2, Berlin and Weimar, 1966, pp. 309–11.
11. See Rolf Harder and Ilse Siebert (eds), *Becher und die Ilse. Briefe und Dichtungen 1916–54*, Leipzig, 1981, pp. 25–8.

joining the KPD he carried out, in the 1920s, many different forms
of party work. In exile he took over a number of important tasks,
among them the editorship in chief of the journal *Internationale
Literatur*, which he performed judiciously and with courage from
1935 to 1945. Having played a vital part in Moscow in shaping the
programme for the political and moral eradication of German
fascism (see particularly GW 16, pp. 403–36), he was numbered
among the most significant and cultured personalities with whom
the KPD would – after its licensing as the first political party in
postwar Germany – undertake the monumental task of bringing
about a thorough intellectual renewal. Ready to act, to take on
responsibility and to exercise political power he was soon plunged
into a complicated web of demanding social obligations:

> Er war Präsident des Kulturbundes und Mitglied des ZK der SED. Er
> wurde in das Parlament der DDR, die Volkskammer, gewählt und 1954
> als erster Minister für Kultur eingesetzt. Der Schriftstellerverband und
> die Akademie der Künste beriefen ihn in ihre Präsidien, von 1953 bis
> 1956 war Becher Präsident der Akademie. Im Weltfriedensrat und im
> PEN [. . .] leistete er wertvolle Arbeit. Das war fast zuviel für einen
> Menschen.[12]

But Becher did not allow these testing circumstances to keep him
from his literary activity. Understandably this led to crises and
conflicts and the proportions change in the genres he uses; speeches
and essays abound, for several years lyric poetry takes on a secondary role. An extra source of irritation and burden were the Cold
War attacks and calumnies from the West to which he, as a
prominent GDR public figure in the forefront of the all–German
intellectual dialogue and – a result of what he had written in exile –
as someone who enjoyed a larger audience than ever before in
Germany, was subjected. Some fifty-three thousand copies of his
autobiographical novel *Abschied*, which had first appeared in
Moscow in 1940, were published by the Aufbau-Verlag between
1946 and 1949. There were three printings in 1945/46 of
Ausgewählte Dichtung aus der Zeit der Verbannung 1933–1945, in 1946
the Aufbau-Verlag reprinted the collection *Romane in Versen* twice and
the following year an edition was published in Baden-Baden. Hans
Carossa, an author not exactly in sympathy with communism, wrote
to Becher on the 14 February 1947: 'Wochen lang hab ich nun mit
Ihren Heimkehr-Gedichten gelebt und mich oft gefragt, warum sie

12. See Haase, *Johannes R. Becher*, p. 264.

mich so stark angehen . . .'[13] Responses such as this which Becher's poetry aroused were, however, far outstripped by his public resonance as president of the 'Kulturbund' and his forceful promotion of an anti-fascist Germany, international understanding and peaceful co-operation in Europe and the world at large. This is the cause of the repeated, organised campaigns of malice against Becher in the western press, as for instance in spring 1947 and after the founding of the GDR.

What could the poet who now saw himself at a barrier[14] imposed by age still achieve in the last decade of his life, given the conditions already indicated? After he had established in his speech 'Vom Willen zum Frieden' at the first German Writers Congress on 7 October 1947 that 'Politik verschlingt die Literatur, wenn nicht die Literatur auf eine ihr eigentümliche und selbständige Art politisch wird' (GW 17, p. 170), he began in the same month to work on a manuscript which would occupy him until June 1948, but which, under the title *Der Aufstand im Menschen*, would not be published until 1983 (!) and be received with great interest by discriminating readers of all ages. This work, a cycle of 102 predominantly essayistic prose pieces, is an intensive, penetrating reflection on Man, a response to Becher's experience of his epoch, of wars, of fascism, of the acute crisis in the world situation. The author does not shy away from asking questions of an existentialist nature. Addressing himself to an audience in both Germanies, he avoids the stock vocabulary of marxism even in his critical discussion of capitalism and fascism. Philosophical, sociological, psychological and poetological elements fuse to form an offering which is as unsystematic as it is stimulating. It is the fruit of a complex search for answers to questions of great urgency, posed in the form of narrative texts which are more important to the author than over-hasty and easy solutions. One of Becher's central questions would be used twenty years later by Christa Wolf as the motto for her book *Nachdenken über Christa T.*: 'Was ist das: dieses Zu-sich-selber-Kommen des Menschen' (AiM, p. 116). Becher's answer is testament to his faith in the communist utopia; the vision before him, 'ist die Erfüllung aller der Möglichkeiten, wie sie dem Menschen gegeben sind' (AiM, p. 116). Anyone seeking to find a convenient formula for Becher's complex and fragmentary book should consult the final lines of the poem 'Hiob' which he wrote at the same time: 'Das Unerträgliche, das wir ertragen,/ Ist Menschenwerk und

---

13. Ibid., p. 218.
14. See Becher, 'Die Grenze und der große Mangel' in GW 12, pp. 600 ff.

müßte nicht so sein' (GW 6, p. 43). It is true that Becher did not have *Der Aufstand im Menschen* published but he also did not keep it a total secret. In a reduced and edited form, most of the texts in it were included a few years later in the literary diary *Auf andere Art so große Hoffnung.* This account of the year 1950, the first full calendar year after the founding of the GDR, is Becher's largest prose work (695 pages in the original), and is born of the wish to bear authentic witness in as comprehensive a manner as possible to the changes in the East of Germany where the attempt had begun to build a society from entirely new beginnings. Becher does not succeed, however, in making the diary a work of lasting value. Contemporary critics found much to take issue with, although not always with justification. But whatever its shortcomings, it has an important place in the history of GDR literature.[15] For the author himself it becomes 'ein großartiges Mittel zur Selbstverständigung' (GW 12, p. 21). Working on it, noted Becher, 'fördert eine Masse Unterirdisches zutage, konfrontiert mich mit mir selbst und erinnert an vieles, was ich schon immer auf dem Herzen hatte und sagen wollte' (GW 12, p. 87).

The lyric poetry which found its way into the diary for the year 1950 makes up the main substance of the little volume *Glück der Ferne – leuchtend nah* (1951) which was soon reprinted and, for its third edition, enlarged. This first lyric poetry which Becher produced in the GDR, is in lighter, more relaxed vein than the 'Heimkehr' poems; sometimes song-like, sometimes aphoristic, it is written in simple rhymed lines or in sonnet form. Alongside discreet or emphatic hymnic elements one finds a contemplative note, a lingering sorrow, but also a new source of lament: the double sonnet 'Auf den Mann mit dem Goldhelm' uses the painting, allegedly by Rembrandt, as a cue for tackling the problem of fame which now very much preoccupies Becher. A much-honoured man, he is regarded by friend and foe as the representative of the GDR. The sense in which he might be understood as a *Staatsdichter* emerges in the words of Thomas Mann which reveal a deep understanding of Becher and genuine sympathy for him:

Als sein Wesen empfand ich eine Selbstlosigkeit, rein wie die Flamme und verzehrend wie sie; eine bis zum Leiden inbrünstige Dienstwilligkeit, die sein Dichten und Schreiben ganz und gar durchdringt; ein Gemeinschaftsethos, das ihn seelisch zum Kommunisten prädisponiert und im Politischen denn auch zum kommunistischen Bekenntnis ge-

---

15. See Hans Richter, *Verwandeltes Dasein*, Berlin and Weimar, 1987, pp. 287–305.

worden ist. Dieser sein Kommunismus ist durchaus patriotisch gefärbt, er erfüllt sich im Patriotismus, und sein Drang zum Dienst an der Gemeinschaft, dem Volke, ist – man lese nur seine Gedichte – zuerst und zuletzt der heiße Wunsch, seinem Volke, dem Deutschen, zu dienen . . .[16]

This character portrayal helps to explain why Becher not only actively supported the Stalin cult, but also did so more intensively and extensively than many of his contemporaries. But it would be erroneous to presuppose from this that Becher had at all times without any conflict of conscience and even unthinkingly concurred readily in the Party's day to day policies and postulates. The idiosyncratic mournfulness of his postwar poetry, which fell far short of official expectations, disqualifies supposition of this kind. In the diary postscripts of 1951, Becher, the former swimmer and now a devotee of a new kind of sport, pokes fun at a standard saying of one of the political hard-liners: '"Du liegst schief" kann mich nicht schrecken, denn ich bin Segler. (Und liebe jede Schräglage.)' (GW 12, p. 701).

In a self-critical note in his diary, Becher observed that the manner of writing which Nietzsche had 'zur Meisterschaft entwickelt' (GW 12, p. 43), and which he himself was wont to use, encouraged the temptation to indulge in a detached mode of observation free of any sense of responsibility. But this observation did not signal a change of method. On the contrary. In the following period, it is this very same unsystematic and elliptically aphoristic approach to pondering things and thinking them through which Becher cultivates and pursues in the grand manner. The publicly conducted process of philosophical and aesthetic self-understanding, begun in *Aufstand im Menschen* and continued in the diary of 1950, was now single-mindedly developed as a special genre which he calls 'Denkdichtung in Prosa' (GW 13, p. 508). This marks his claim to be a serious thinker and at the same time the right to exercise poetic freedom. He was working at a point where dogmatism was at its height. At the beginning of the 1950s there was an increasing growth in the Soviet Union – and therefore also in the GDR, its friend and ally – of doctrinaire tracts and critiques which were the product of the cultural and political rigour of Zhdanov and his adherents. Becher, in declaring his intention to pursue 'Denkdichtung (see GW 14, p. 449), is withdrawing to a large extent from the pressure to maintain

---

16. Berthold Viertel et al. (eds), *Erinnerungen an Johannes R. Becher*, p. 296.

contact in thought and language with the propagandistic aspects of publishing current at the time. He is, of course, himself not entirely free of doctrinaire views. But the genre 'Denkdichtung in Prosa' makes possible a fruitful self-understanding which encourages intellectual flexibility and ensures that his thought does not become fossilised. In this way, there follow in quick succession the four separate volumes of *Bemühungen* whose titles indicate the main themes and most important intellectual preoccupations of Becher's late work: *Verteidigung der Poesie* (1952), *Poetische Konfession* (1954), *Macht der Poesie* (1955) and *Das poetische Prinzip. Mit einem Anhang: Philosophie des Sonetts oder kleine Sonettlehre und 'Ein wenig über vier Seiten . . .'* (1957). Although the justification, explanation and defence of his own poetic conception forms the real centre of the work, the horizons of the *Bemühungen* are very wide. No writer in the GDR at this time reveals a more catholic range of interests and concerns. He writes about Man, his origins and destination; about literature and poetry, their essence and influence; about tradition and innovation; about individual texts and authors. Undoubtedly they also contain – although to a lesser degree than the diary – much which is of casual interest, is imprecise and sometimes eccentric. All this ballast has certainly detracted from the productive content of the work, preventing it from showing to the effect it so clearly deserves. It has nevertheless exercised considerable influence on subsequent generations of writers.

The publication, three decades later in the journal *Sinn und Form* (no. 3, 1988) under the title 'Selbstzensur', of passages from the book *Das poetische Prinzip* which the author had removed when correcting the galley proofs, caused a sensation. They revealed Becher's strong reactions to Khrushchev's denunciation of Stalin's serious crimes and derelictions. It is certainly to be regretted that the author found it necessary at the time to exercise self-censorship. But despite the cuts he made, the attentive reader can, to a large extent, deduce from the last volume of the *Bemühungen* as it was published at the time that Johannes R. Becher was sensitively receptive to, and productively assimilated, the impulses which emanated from the twentieth Congress of the Communist Party of the Soviet Union. No other printed text in the GDR from those years contained so many and such differentiated starting points for fresh thinking as *Das poetische Prinzip*. The book reveals that Becher understood the Soviet Party Congress as the signal for a promising new departure. It contains clear reflections on the movement of socialism into a new phase in its history which, however, just a few years after the death of the poet on 11 October 1958, was to end in stagnation.

Johannes R. Becher's Later Writing

The intellectual scope of *Das poetische Prinzip* is especially appealing to the reader of today, particularly since it throws its net much wider than the title would lead one to believe. 'Wenn die Geschichte eine Frage aufwirft und diese wird nicht beantwortet,' writes Becher, 'so entsteht durch die Verzögerung solch einer Antwort unübersehbarer Schaden, und eines Tages muß die geschichtliche Frage beantwortet werden, und dann unter weitaus ungünstigeren Voraussetzungen als vorher' (GW 14, p. 521). He does not want to see the hard-won power relationships in the GDR changed, but he acknowledges from experience that 'Es ist schwer für die Mächtigen, die Macht so auszuüben, daß sie dem Leben zugute kommt und das Volk erfreut' (GW 14, p. 322). From this he concludes that high moral demands must be made of those who exercise power. And yet at the same time he recognises that, 'Der, der Macht ausübt, widersteht nur selten der Versuchung, diejenigen Menschen, die ihn umgeben, nicht als seine ihm untergebenen zu behandeln' (GW 14, p. 323).

Becher is critical of the fact that literature frequently 'das, was uns bedrängt, [. . .] verdrängt' (GW 14, p. 289), and he demands that the artist should have the courage, 'das zu sagen, was notwendig ist' (GW 14, p. 415). He draws attention to the situation where 'die Unterschätzung des Privaten im Menschen' has 'schon mancherlei Unheil angerichtet' (GW 14, pp. 301 ff.). Addressing himself to literary scholars, he defines the goal of his *Bemühungen* as being to 'nicht in erster Linie Lösungen bringen, sondern Fragen aufwerfen, schwierige, peinliche mitunter' and to 'Anregungen geben' in order that 'man sich mit der Problematik auseinandersetzt, wie sie sich uns aufgedrängt hat oder uns allen aufgedrängt ist – seit langem . . .' (GW 14, p. 364). He denounces with sharpness and perception those who merely make an appearance of attacking 'Schönfärberei'; he reveals their programme as one in which: 'Wir wünschen eine Schönfärberei, die nicht allzu schöngefärbt ist. Wir wünschen Pappfiguren in lebensechten Farben' (GW 14, p. 303). He criticises those who in 1951 had begun a campaign against formalism for, in the most part, fighting 'Formalismus mit formalistischen Mitteln' (GW 14, p. 314) and reinforces his argument with a drastic example from the sphere of architecture. He warns that making cultural and political demands too prematurely could mean that later, when their time had come, they could not be fulfilled (see GW 14, p. 381).

He sets himself against the expectation of a uniform literature in the GDR with the comment: 'Die Literatur bestand zu allen Zeiten aus verschiedenen Schulen, miteinander wetteifernden Richtungen und auch aus Persönlichkeiten, die keine Schule gebildet und keiner Richtung angehört haben' (GW 14, p. 353). Becher directs his polemic far into the future in resuming, strengthening and constructively developing his earlier criticism of the slogan 'Kunst ist Waffe!' (conducted in section 206 of the book *Macht der Poesie*); using metaphors which pull no punches, he wades in against a restriction of artistic freedoms and hammers the 'Kunstwaffenbesitzer und Waffenkünstler' with the declaration that, 'die ästhetische Aneignung der Welt [. . .] das eigentliche poetische Anliegen ist' (GW 14, p. 359 ff). Aesthetic theory in the GDR would not adopt this approach until very much later.

Becher emphatically rejects the excessive demands made on the artist; they have always been a particular threat to the creative process. Indignantly, he declares that 'der künstlerische Alltag, der eigentliche Schaffensprozeß verlaufen entgegengesetzt dem fordernden Gerede, das aus Anlaß von Konferenzen und Festlichkeiten offeriert wird und das so fern jeder Realität ist, daß es nicht einmal zum Widerspruch zu reizen vermag' (GW 14, p. 466). The question remains, however, whether he would like every one of his own speeches to be excluded from this criticism. By means of bold simplification he utterly dismisses the usual strained essays of the time on the subject of socialist realism. Guided as always in his activity as a poet by the necessity to look to the future, and taking as his support just a handful of lines from Schiller (from the poem 'Die Künstler') and from Brecht (from the poem 'Die Erziehung der Hirse'), he defines as the sole and deciding criterion for socialist realism the need 'realistische Visionen zu schaffen' in which 'das kommende Jahrhundert' would 'aufdämmern' (GW 14, p. 395). This is certainly not an ultimately valid definition, but one which serves as a usefully offensive defence against the scholastic prescriptions of theoreticians and politicians.

Also worthy of note is that Becher, long before the aesthetics of literary reception, discovers the reader as a topic and reflects on the art of reading. In this, he strikes a note of warning: 'Wer mit der Leserschaft als einer stabilen Größe rechnet, der wird sich sehr leicht mit billigen und ungekonnten Produkten zufriedengeben, in der Meinung, das entspräche dem Geschmack des Lesers und sei gerade genug für ihn' (GW 14, p. 514). His considerations of the effect of literature reveals Becher the dialectician; in response to a frequent question of the time about what a book could offer, he gives the answer: 'Ein Buch kann auch etwas geben, indem es uns etwas nimmt' (GW 14, p. 348). Without wishing to deny or diminish the repeated demands of politicians and cultural officials that literature should play its part in the formation of public consciousness, Becher nevertheless emphasises – against all orthodoxy, and for years as an isolated voice – how vital it was for literature to concern itself with the *whole* human being, because it also 'an der Bildung des Unbewußtseins (!) und Unterbewußtseins mitarbeitet' (GW 14, p. 407).

With reference to the author himself, the four volumes of his *Bemühungen* from the 1950s are an effective means of gradually freeing himself from the old handicaps with which he had been burdened in the struggles and debates of the preceding decades, as well as from the particular restrictions which had arisen in the first difficult years of the construction of socialism under the conditions of the Cold War and the Stalin cult. The liberating effect on Becher of this process of self-understanding manifests itself most clearly in his fresh re-evaluation of Expressionism. He is now able to affirm to his old and revered friend Georg Lukács that he had labelled this literary movement 'allzu gewalttätig mit einem politischen Etikett' (GW 14, p. 443). Rimbaud, one of the young Becher's most important idols but who more recently had been pushed into the background, now resumes his place in the firmament and even provides a proud motto for the whole volume (see GW 14, p. 332 ff. and p. 253). With astonishing passion, the figure of Jakob van Hoddis is evoked, one of the most fascinating members of the Becher generation from before the First World War (see GW 14, pp. 339–43). In other words, shortly before his death Johannes R.Becher revokes his damnation and denial of his early Expressionist period. The ideology of 'correcting' his own poems which had driven him for decades to vandalise his poetry to self-mutilatory effect is now expressly abandoned and he acknowledges that he must 'meine Gedichtkorrekturen korrigieren und die Gedichte wieder dorthin zurückführen, wo sie entstanden sind' (GW 14, p. 281).

The readiness and ability to see himself historically, renewed, in tendency at least, the possibilities for the poet Becher. This can be seen too in the fragments of *Wiederanders*, the result of an attempt, in narrative form, to take stock of his life. These beginnings of a novel are vastly different from other prose being written in the GDR at the time. Instead of following a strict plot, Becher constructs a series of relatively open-ended episodes in which the central figure appears in two guises, as a young man remembered, and as an old man remembering. While Becher does not choose the first person form, the innovatory narrative method differs considerably from that adopted in *Abschied* and is already leading towards that developed by Bobrowski in his novel *Levins Mühle*.

In his book *Das poetische Prinzip* Johannes R.Becher challenges himself to embark on a 'Heimkehr ins Reich der Poesie' (GW 14, p. 601). Having neglected poetry for some years, he now, at the age of sixty-five, has the urge once again to try his hand at it. The numerous lyrical texts which he now writes find their way, for the most part, into the last collection which he would see published. It appeared in August 1958, a few weeks before his death. This book, entitled *Schritt der Jahrhundertmitte*, distinguishes itself quite clearly from the mass of early GDR literature. The volume could never-theless still not aspire to the aesthetic niveau and the compositional balance of the most significant lyrical work of his exile period – *Der Glücksucher und die sieben Lasten*. Illness had already marked out the author for death, and his struggle to find literary expression for the historical conflicts of the age with their flood of new experiences called out for experiment rather than favouring the production of works of maturity.

After long being of the opinion that what is new does not initially express itself in new forms, he now declared in the prog-rammatic poem 'Von einer neuen Versart': 'Aber was neu ist,/ Will auch neuartig gesagt sein,/ In der Dichtung vor allem.' (GW 6, p. 303). The text is the first of a series of free verse poems which make up a fifth of the entire volume (one must remember that since the 1920s Becher had made a principle of totally eschewing free verse). The next text, again programmatic, discovers and demands 'Themen-Unendlichkeit': 'Ich muß dem Blick standhalten,/ Wenn ich aus dem Fenster schaue,/ In die Themen-Unendlichkeit hinein' (GW 6, p. 313). It is true that Becher, in his last volume of poetry, is far from having only fresh things to say and that he is also not entirely original in the way he says them. Yet again, almost half of the texts are sonnets and many of the titles alert us once more to a familiar range of Becher motifs ('Neugeburt', 'Reich des Mens-chen' and 'Macht der Poesie' amongst others). But there is also an unmistakably fresh multiplicity and sobriety of perspective on Man and the world, on his own poetic 'I' along with its history and situation. Many different factors and causes come together to produce this: the various experiences which Becher had had in his capacities as functionary and minister, sickness and the process of ageing and, not least of all, the twentieth Soviet Party Congress with all its revelations.

Experience had taught Johannes R.Becher that with every will in the world poetry and politics could not be successfully fused and he now (under the title 'Staatsmann und Dichter') comes to the following sarcastic conclusion:

Wären ihre Rollen
Miteinander vertauscht,
Würde der Staatsmann als Dichter
Die Dichtung zugrunde richten,
Und er, der Dichter als Staatsmann,
Würde den Staat vernichten.

(GW 6, p. 425)

At the same time he feels challenged to react with satirical verses to aspects of an evolving socialist society which are deserving of criticism. Texts such as 'Ballade von der Beschallung', 'Haus des Gähnens', 'Der ganze Mensch' or 'Sagenhafte Stadt' which are directed against the shortcomings of political culture in the GDR are admittedly of no great aesthetic consequence, but they are of importance in encouraging the future generation of lyric poets who would emerge in the 1960s to try their hand at socialist self-criticism.

Something new in these poems is the theme of space flight. Becher celebrates the pioneering efforts of the Soviet Union as a sure sign of a socialist future for humanity. (Autumn 1957 saw the launching of the world's first earth satellites.) One of the most important new features of Becher's last volume of poetry however is the frequency of the motif of death. The poet focusses on the end of his own life, human mortality, the memory of the victims of fascism, the early death of his fellow poets Bertolt Brecht and Louis Fürnberg. He grieves deeply for the many innocent lives lost at the hands of Stalin. Experiences in soviet exile (1935–45) which were incomprehensible at the time now find their poetic expression:

Sein oder Nichtsein war auch unsre Frage,
Und unsre Frage hieß auch: Wer ist wer?
Ist er des Nachts derselbe wie am Tage?
Wohin geht er? Er kommt des Wegs – woher?

In welchem Auftrag? Und im Dienste wessen?
Fragwürdig jeder und befragenswert.
Vielleicht kann mancher selber nicht ermessen,
In welchem Spiel man seinen Dienst begehrt . . .

(GW 6, p. 405)

These new motifs – along with many others – are also incorporated into the long poem 'Das Atelier' in which Becher succeeds in reviewing the rich panorama of his whole life. Much less inhibited in the use of biographical detail than he was in his earlier writing,

Becher has succeeded in creating a poem of powerful and radiant poetic aura. This is due not least to the choice and treatment of the central motif. In four chapters the poet describes his studio as the centre of his existence and as a recurrent stopping point on his way through life from Munich to Berlin, Moscow and Bad Saarow. The passage of time is both mirrored in his workshop and at the same time characterised by the lyrical 'I'. In this autobiographical poem Becher's concept of poetic self-portrayal (see GW 14, pp. 452–4) finds its fullest realisation. A poem of this kind however presumes interest in the personality of the poet and a good deal of knowledge about his life. Becher's poems are probably guaranteed a greater impact when they avail themselves of subject matter which is linked less to his personal concerns and aims only indirectly at self-portrayal. As for instance the sonnet 'Größe und Elend' which deals with Man as such, and only obliquely bears reference to Becher's own situation. It is true that the poem 'Windflüchter' gives voice to the poet's personal experiences, but they are objectified in the powerful nature metaphor and thereby given general validity. The fine poem 'Das weiße Wunder' is testament to Becher's love of Utrillo, but achieves much more than this: it discovers manifold variety where only sameness seems apparent, and praises in the painter's art the plenitude of what is real.

One of the most striking examples of the maturity of Becher's late art is the sonnet 'Auf einen französischen Dichter'. As we can see from a passage in *Das poetische Prinzip* (see GW 14, p. 596 ff.), the poem, which refers to someone completely unknown, is rooted in Becher's renewed and deepened understanding of the particular and the concrete. The sonnet has more than a little to tell us about its author despite being not about him, but a soldier who fell in the First World War:

Es war ein Sommertag, für den er fiel
Am Chemin des Dames, er fiel für seine Straße,
Für sein Geburtshaus, für die kleine Vase
Am Fenstersims und für der Kinder Spiel.

Für einen Ausflug und für das und dies,
Wovon er wünschte, daß es bleibe leben,
Für Tauben, Bienen, Wiesenhang und Reben,
Und auch für dich fiel er, Place Saint-Sulpice.
Er fiel für ihn auch, für den weichen Rauch
Der Zigarette, und er ist gefallen

Für Sacré-Coeur und die geliebten 'Hallen'
Und eines Mundes zauberhaften Hauch –

Er fiel mit einem Buche in der Hand
Und für Paris et pour la France, sein Land.
(GW 6, p. 404)

This sonnet, which is in stark contrast to the abstract rhetoric and
excessive pathos to which the poet was given on occasion, is
nevertheless a highly characteristic Becher poem. It is testament to
that love of literature and of France which he had strongly pro-
claimed as early as his Expressionist period; it is a quiet confirmation of his old hostility to nationalism and chauvinism; an expression
of his constant negation of war and his passionate commitment to
peace; it offers insistent praise of what he had dreamed of all his life –
happiness and harmony between men as well as between men and
nature.

Poems of this kind are of great help in understanding and
justifying the lofty words of the four line poem which Johannes
R. Becher used as the motto for a selection of his older texts and
which, since autumn 1958, may be read on his gravestone:

VOLLENDUNG TRÄUMEND, hab ich mich vollendet,
Wenn auch mein Werk nicht als vollendet endet.
Denn das war meines Werkes heilige Sendung:
Dienst an der Menschheit künftiger Vollendung.
(GW 6, p. 459)

Translated by Martin Kane

Author's Note

The following editions and abbreviations are used for Becher's works:
GW: Johannes R. Becher, *Gesammelte Werke*, vols 1–18, Berlin and Weimar, 1966–1981.
AiM: Johannes R. Becher, *Der Aufstand im Menschen*, Berlin and Weimar,
1983.

Secondary Material

Hans Richter, 'Johannes R.Bechers *Der Aufstand im Menschen*' in *Weimarer Beiträge*, 32, 1986, pp. 181–95.

Michael Rohrwasser, *Der Weg nach oben. Johannes R. Becher. Politiken des Schreibens*, Frankfurt am Main, 1980.

Ilse Siebert, 'Johannes R.Becher', in Geerdts et al. (eds), *Literatur der Deutschen Demokratischen Republik in Einzeldarstellungen*, Berlin, 1974, vol. 1, pp. 23–43.

Alexander Stephan, 'Johannes R. Becher and the cultural development of the GDR' (translated from the German by Sara Lennox and Frank Lennox), in *New German Critique*, 2, spring 1974, pp. 72–89.

–2–

Laudatio for Anna Seghers

Walter Jens

It is said that following a period of imprisonment, about the duration of which as little is known as the reasons for her release, Anna Seghers, hounded as both a Jew and a communist, fled via Switzerland to France. The only thing of which we can be certain is that she lived with her children and husband Laszlo Radványi (known in the Communist Party as Johann Lorenz Schmidt) in the environs of Paris, moved in conspiratorial circles, pushed ahead with the refounding of the Association for the Protection of German Writers, was a strong advocate of the Popular Front at the Congress for the Defence of Culture in 1935 and, in poetic pursuance of the view that only a broad alliance of liberals, social democrats and communists could rid the world of fascism, wrote *Das siebte Kreuz*, a novel about two Germanies – the one brutally triumphant, the other defeated, but which also depicted a Germany which ultimately would remain invincible. We are told, that in 1940 as German troops advanced ever closer, Anna Seghers burned the penultimate copy of her epos while the final remaining copy found its way to America to be published in English translation in 1942.

We learn further that Netty Radványi (Anna Seghers was her *nom de plume*) was separated from her husband in autumn 1940, fled Paris but quickly returned to the capital, attempting to continue working there under very difficult circumstances ('ich hatte die Kinder bei mir, lebte in größter Unsicherheit, schlief jede Nacht woanders'): underground, always on the move, constantly changing lodgings, 'in irgendwelchen Löchern versteckt' and at the same time, in an act of foolhardly provocation, engaging in conversation on the streets in broad daylight with German soldiers whose thoughts, dreams and wishes she sought to grasp as exactly as possible:

Walter Jens

Ich habe selbst, als ich mich in Paris verstecken mußte, mit vielen deutschen Soldaten gesprochen. Ich habe mich früher oft gefragt, wie ein Soldat Hitlers denken und aussehen mag, aus welchem Stoffe dieser Mensch gemacht ist, der sein Leben für den Faschismus aufs Spiel setzt . . . Sie fühlten sich als Sieger, sie, die daheim nicht in dem kleinsten Lohnkampf gesiegt hatten, sie fühlten sich als Herrscher von Ländern, sie, die daheim kaum Zweikuhbauern waren. Sie, die daheim armselig . . .dahingelebt hatten, wurden plötzlich dringend gebraucht mit Leib und Seele, sie, die in Deutschland nichts von sozialer Gleichheit gesehen hatten, sahen plötzlich die unbezweifelbare Gleichheit vor dem Tod. In ihnen war jene große Bresche gewesen, die der Faschismus aufgefüllt hatte, hier hatte er zaubern und hochstapeln können . . . Etliche aber, wenn der französische Wein sie etwas gelockert hatte, äußerten unverhohlen den brennenden Wunsch, heimzukehren in ihre Familie, in einen ordentlichen Beruf, in eine 'andre Welt'; äußerten unverhohlen Haß, Ekel, Todesangst . . .Was ist Deutschland? Alle diese Soldaten? Einer von ihnen? Keiner? Welcher hat für Deutschland gesprochen? Geflucht? Geschwiegen?[1]

This is moving to behold: in the middle of the war a writer who has been harassed into exile is speaking to her 'own people', or rather those to whom she has long since ceased to belong, and it is not hatred, emphatic self-righteousness and the determination to summarily condemn the murderers which govern the flow of her sentences, but careful differentiation, a measured and sobre distinguishing between what is arrogant in the victors and what is merely pitiable. How characteristic of Anna Seghers that the portrayal of the boys who carry the picture of the Führer next to their hearts should be followed by the insistent description of the one among them who at the moment of personal devastation should be vouchsafed insight into the misery induced by the appeal to great and general ideals: 'In einem Dorf bei Paris stürzte ein Soldat, laut Hitler verfluchend, auf die Gasse. Eben hat er heim auf Urlaub fahren wollen, da kam die Nachricht von dem Tode seiner Frau bei einem Fliegerangriff. Sein Fluch war vielleicht der erste laute in der Armee.'[2]

The émigrée Anna Seghers on the avenues of Paris in conversation with her persecutors: a snapshot, gone in a flash, briefly illuminating the dark years marked by the deprivations of exile and the will, under adverse and often degrading circumstances, to

1. In 'Deutschland und Wir', Anna Seghers, *Gesammelte Werke in Einzelausgaben*, vol. XIII, *Aufsätze, Ansprachen, Essays 1927–1953*, 2nd edition, Berlin and Weimar, 1984, p. 92ff.
2. Ibid.

furnish exemplary documentation of what she had suffered.

And what then, after the summer of 1940? We are faced here with a dearth of personal testimony, there are no diaries or correspondence to show us the way. As when in search of Netty Radványi's unknown companions, the literary sleuth has to rely on the contemporary account of those who shared her fate – fellow exiles or French friends such as Jeanne Stern who took Anna Seghers to the unoccupied South – or one is dependent on unknown documents of the importance of those found in an American archive by Hans Albert Walter, made accessible to a West German readership and which demonstrate that Anna Seghers, together with other writers whose lives were endangered, had received a Mexican visa which waited to be collected at the consulate in Marseille.

The stages of the journey to the Mexican consulate from Paris, where the émigrée apparently received the news of her imminent deliverance in a café in the midst of German officers, are not known. Just how Anna Seghers, a Mother Courage who had been plunged into the turmoil of the Second World War, managed to get her husband out of the infamous internment camp of Vernet in the Pyrenees has also not been established. How she survived the winter in the tiny village of Pamiers near Vernet (see Hans Albert Walter's superb reconnoitering work in connection with his deciphering of the novel *Transit*); what the nature of the support was, filed under '1065: Radvan, Ladislas et Anna', which she received from the Centre Américain de Secours, how she, together with her family and a fellow passenger by the name of Alfred Kantorowicz managed to secure a passage to Martinique and under what circumstances, via the Dominican Republic and the United States, she managed to reach Mexico City, one of the most important centres for literary emigrés, and how she survived the year between fleeing from Paris and arriving in America – all this is uncertain: 'Ich habe das Gefühl', she writes in 1941 in a letter to Bodo Uhse, 'ich wäre ein Jahr lang tot gewesen.'[3]

Anna Seghers's first years in exile between 1933 and 1941 are, at first sight, shrouded in a darkness which sets the author of *Das siebte Kreuz* alongside those nameless refugees, some thirty thousand in number, who, in French internment camps, were left to the mercy of the occupiers; at second glance however we are, thanks to *Das siebte Kreuz* and even more to the novel *Transit*, no less informed about Anna Seghers's experiences, meditations and

---

3. Letter to Bodo Uhse quoted in Kurt Batt, *Anna Seghers. Versuch über Entwicklung und Werke*, Leipzig, 1980, p. 135.

Walter Jens

memories than we are about those sufferings of an unpolitical man
to which Thomas Mann bears witness, day by day, in his diaries.
How she lived, among the 'abgeschiedenen Seelen' of emigré
circles, driven by the 'einzige[n] Wunsch: abfahren' and pursued by
the 'einzige[n] Furcht: zurückbleiben', how she attempted to assert
herself in a world which was half 'Hafen der Freiheit' and half
'homerisches Totenreich', how she learned to think 'in Konsultats-
fristen', tried to counteract the 'blöde Ordnung der Dossiers',
constantly in desperate search of short cuts which could lead more
quickly, but all the more riskily, to the ship which would take her
to safety – Anna Seghers, articulating the plight of thousands, has
described all this in that archetypal document of emigration, the
novel *Transit*. Here a perceptive if somewhat strange old man
comments:

> . . . durch irgendeinen Glücksfall, durch eigene Kraft . . . vielleicht
> durch die Vorsehung selbst, vielleicht durch ein Komitee, erhalten Sie
> ein Visum. Da sind Sie einen Augenblick lang glücklich. Doch sehr
> rasch merken Sie, daß damit gar nichts getan ist. Sie haben ein Ziel – das
> ist wenig . . . Sie brauchen ein Transit . . . Sie dürfen nur an Ihr Transit
> denken. Sie müssen . . . Ihr Ziel eine Zeitlang vergessen, jetzt gelten nur
> die Zwischenländer, sonst wird aus der Abfahrt nichts . . . Nun nehmen
> wir einmal den Glücksfall an, der ein Wunder ist, wenn man bedenkt,
> wie viele abfahren wollen auf wie wenig Schiffen, Ihr Schiffsplatz als
> solcher, die Fahrt als solche sei gesichert . . . glauben Sie ja nicht, . . .
> daß damit Ihr Transit schon sicher sei, und selbst, wenn es sicher wäre!
> Inzwischen ist so viel Zeit vergangen, daß wieder das erste, das Haupt-
> ziel entschwunden ist. Dein Visum ist abgelaufen, und wie auch das
> Transit notwendig war, es ist wieder gar nichts ohne das Visum, und
> so immer weiter, immer weiter . . . Nun stell dir vor, du hast es
> erreicht . . . gut, träumen wir jetzt gemeinsam, du hast es erreicht, dein
> Visa de sortie. Du bist reisefertig . . . Du denkst jetzt nur an das Ziel.
> Du willst endgültig an Bord gehen –

The old man continues, still addressing the narrator:

> Ich sprach gestern einen jungen Mann . . . Der hatte alles. Doch als er an
> Bord gehen wollte, verweigerte ihm das Hafenamt den letzten
> Stempel . . . Er war aus einem Lager entflohen als die Deutschen
> kamen . . . Er hatte keinen Entlassungsschein aus dem Lager – so war
> denn alles für ihn umsonst."[4]

4. Anna Seghers, *Transit. Roman*, in *Gesammelte Werke in Einzelausgaben*, vol. V,
2nd edition, Berlin and Weimar, 1982, p. 47ff.

This is Kafka's *Der Prozeß* re-enacted in Marseille. We watch as what art had forseen is fulfilled in the misery of our century with its persecution, the anguish of exile and the absurdity of life robbed of meaning – of a life, of course, which, in the case of Anna Seghers, is characterised not only by general *tristesse*, but also by the private interplay of great sorrow and modest happiness, of desolation and rare moments of security: reversals of fortune, heaven changing in a flash to hell, the mingling of ancient doubts and blood-young courage, of tireless search and the losing, finding and losing again of one's way, hideous rumours cheek by jowl with the glorious, timeless gossip of the dockside, one moment absorbed in the life of a stranger, the next assuming dogged responsibility for oneself – each of these opposites complementing the other, happiness in the realm of the dead and despair in a hell which, revealing its kafka-esque absurdity, does not of course present itself as hell: 'Sie kennen vielleicht das Märchen von dem toten Mann' says one of the persecuted in the novel who is no longer able to tolerate the waiting and sets off towards the Germans, going home to certain death.

> Er wartete in der Ewigkeit, was der Herr über ihn beschlossen hatte. Er wartete und wartete, ein Jahr, zehn Jahre, hundert Jahre. Dann bat er flehentlich um sein Urteil. Er konnte das Warten nicht mehr ertragen. Man erwiderte ihm: 'Auf was wartest du eigentlich? Du bist doch schon längst in der Hölle.' Das war sie nämlich: ein blödsinniges Warten auf nichts. Was kann denn höllischer sein? Der Krieg? Der springt auch über den Ozean nach. Ich habe jetzt genug von allem. Ich will heim.[5]

Indeed. Anyone, who would like to know how Anna Seghers *lived*, on a knife edge between great despair and inextinguishable hope, somewhat privileged among the refugees (but only somewhat), should read *Transit*, an account of the gates to hell, which, with its indications of fatalism and resignation, already points from afar to the submissive condemned of Treblinka and Birkenau. Anyone, however, who would like to know how she, the Jew and communist from Mainz, *thought*, how she saw Germany, the Reich of banished poets and a country of a handful of righteous men amidst countless rogues, henchmen, traitors, blind fellow travellers and cunning opportunists, should read – how often will they have already read it? – *Das siebte Kreuz*. Since it is written with an incorruptible yearning for home, this is the fairest book about the

5. Ibid., p. 211.

Germany of National Socialism. It describes a country which, from the perspective of the Resistance is condemned, but one which will also, in its inviolability, outlive fascism.

By his very existence, one single individual, Georg Heisler – a fugitive who anticipates the fugitives of Marseille and Nice (the one standing for the many) – helps those he meets to find themselves, arouses the inner strength of the resolute, arouses the all but forgotten dream of a better world which steadfast solidarity can create, arouses memories of days of struggle and hope, arouses the courage of the weak as well as the resolve, in a time of great challenge, to reflect upon that iron reserve of humanity which provides the same communal sustenance as did the breaking of the bread at the Last Supper, and, in the face of an all powerful enemy, encourages a composure and even an almost cheerful superiority: 'In seinem Innern', we read of Georg Heisler, persecuted and amongst murderers, 'erhob sich, leise und rein und klar, eine unverletzbare, unüberhörbare Stimme, und er wußte, daß er sofort bereit war zu sterben, wie er zwar nicht immer gelebt, aber immer zu leben gewünscht hatte, kühn und ruhig.'[6]

Das siebte Kreuz is a gentle, not an angry book; its dominant note is not accusation but sorrow and tenderness, a sympathy with the victims along with the will – accompanied by anger at the traitors (from among their own ranks to boot) – to absolve the weak who, in moments of danger, develop a humanity and, something Anna Seghers discovers again and again, a very individual form of tender courage, be it a simple woman spreading a cloth over the face of a dead circus artiste, a peaceable man who became a martyr – 'man sah ihr an, daß sie diesen Dienst nicht zum ersten Mal leistete';[7] a minor Nazi fellow traveller Paul Röder offering refuge to an old companion; or an old man from the country who, beyond all fear and reproach, conquers the dangers around him with a simplicity and humility upon which power cannot impinge.

Anna Seghers's heroes are not heroes in the conventional sense, but reflective people, constantly embattled and marked by the sorrow they feel at being excluded. They are ordinary people inclined by nature to timidity; they are disunited, morally ambivalent even, but when things become serious, are able to challenge the apparently omnipotent, whose fallibility a single lapse may expose: a gardener's apprentice siding with the persecuted may make the mighty feel insecure.

6. Anna Seghers, *Das siebte Kreuz. Roman*, Berlin, 1962, p. 48.
7. Ibid., p. 211.

The *other* Germany conjured up so often in exile, the Germany of Bertolt Brecht in America and of Ricard Huch back at home, has been depicted by many writers perhaps more emphatically, but by none more calmly, more justly and, thanks to a humane dialectical method, more generously than by the exiled Netty Radványi from Mainz, a writer who all her life sided with the victims, took the side of the martyrs, the side of the upright in the struggle against the tyranny of fascism. In the essay 'Köln' published in 1942 in the journal *Freies Deutschland* we read: 'Die barbarische Hinrichtung von vier Kölner Arbeitern erfüllte die Stadt mit Haß und Schrecken. Aber die große, die entscheidende Demonstration, auf die die in der Todeszelle eingeschlossenen Männer ihre letzte Hoffnung gesetzt hatten, die blieb aus . . . Der katholische Priester, der eine Messe für die Hingerichteten lesen ließ, kam ins Konzentrationslager.' Seghers relates further how one of the men, his name was Engel, a window cleaner by trade, had written on the eve of his execution: 'Hör auf mich, SA-Mann! Dein Weg ist falsch'. She continues:

> Engel bekam auf sein Grab einen Stein, in den eine Uhr eingeschnitten war, deren Ziffer die Hinrichtungsstunde anzeigte. Jetzt liegt auch dieses Grab unter den Trümmern, die das furchtbare Gericht hinter sich läßt, das Hitler über das Volk beschworen hat, weil das Volk nicht rechtzeitig sein Gericht über Hitler beschworen hat. Wir aber denken mit Trauer und Achtung, daß jede deutsche Stadt, auf die jetzt Bomben fallen, solche Gräber enthält . . .[8]

Justice united with compassion: Anna Seghers's socialism, broadly and undogmatically exemplified in both novel and essay, awaits, in the spirit of glasnost, courageous and careful reconsideration – in honour of writers who, from Shanghai to New Mexico during the years of National Socialism made clear to the world that the Germany of Goethe was being preserved not in the Reich Chancellery but in the barracks of Buchenwald.

'Was hat unsere Freiheit für einen Sinn, wenn wir nicht immer die Namenlosen nennen, wir, die wir reden und schreiben können': words of Anna Seghers which it is our duty as writers – today as then – to make serve as the motto for responsible writing.

Translated by Martin Kane

8. Anna Seghers, *Gesammelte Werke*, vol. XIII, pp. 110ff.

Author's Note

This paper was delivered at the annual conference of the West German PEN, Cologne, May 1989.

–3–

Visions for a New Society:
Anna Seghers in the GDR

Martin Kane

As Walter Jens has so eloquently reminded us, when Anna Seghers died in Berlin on 1 June 1983 at the age of eighty-two, the German Democratic Republic lost one of the most eminent of that group of writers and artists who returned from exile after 1945 to what was then the Soviet Occupied Zone, convinced that their work would have a vital role to play in the creation of a new socialist society. Unlike fellow marxists such as Brecht, however, who soon found a gap between their expectations and reality and discovered that the relationship between the SED and its intellectuals did not always run smoothly, Anna Seghers's attitude to the GDR as it manifested itself in her essays and fictional writings was, throughout all its crises and teething troubles, one of unswerving commitment. If she ever had any doubts about the system, they were never expressed openly; she never deviated from the notion that to offer personal misgivings and reservations for public consideration is merely to hand ammunition to those whose social and political ideals one has spent a lifetime combating. Or, to express this viewpoint in a different, more positively vigorous way, she returned to live and work in the GDR because she could, in her own words, 'hier ausdrücken [. . .], wozu ich gelebt habe'.[1]

While this energetic loyalty played no small part in the rapid establishment of her reputation in the GDR as an author of classical proportions, it has often led to her work being the subject of bitter controversy in the Federal Republic, controversy which recently – as a consequence of the publication in 1989 of Walter Janka's

---

1. Anna Seghers, 'Ansprache in Weimar', in *Aufsätze, Ansprachen, Essays 1954–1979. Gesammelte Werke in Einzelausgaben*. vol. XIV, 2nd edition, Berlin and Weimar, 1984, p. 308.

Schwierigkeiten mit der Wahrheit[2] – has been refuelled. When one looks back, it is easy to see for instance that the poet Peter Jokostra, the principal orchestrator of the campaign of protest which greeted the Luchterhand Verlag's initial attempt to publish an edition of Seghers's work in the West, is typical, in his comment that she had purchased her fame and reputation with 'Verrat und Korrumpierung',[3] of those whose Cold War postures in the 1950s and 1960s blocked any serious evaluation of her literary achievement. As Frank Benseler notes in his introduction to the first representative and widely available collection of Anna Seghers's essayistic writings to be published in the Federal Republic, anyone who opted to live in the socialist part of Germany was, from a West German point of view, an 'Unperson'.[4]

More recently, Walter Janka's autobiographical revelations have lent some substance to the accusations levelled by individuals such as Peter Jokostra against Anna Seghers. Janka is one in a long line of favoured socialists to have fallen from grace; one of the select band (Robert Havemann is the most distinguished), who under National Socialism found themselves in prison for being communists, and under communism found themselves incarcerated for being 'counter-revolutionary fascists'.

His socialist credentials were seemingly impeccable. Born in 1914 of working-class parents, persecuted for his politics by the Gestapo, three times wounded fighting with the International Brigade in the Spanish Civil War, founder of the exile publishing house El Libro Libre, head of the Aufbau-Verlag and publisher of, *inter alia*, Anna Seghers and Heinrich Mann, why was it that he could be sentenced in 1957 to five years in prison for supposedly conspiring to overthrow the State? His crime was to participate in the renaissance of new thinking about the nature of socialism which had arisen after the death of Stalin. It was to endeavour – at the suggestion of Anna Seghers and with the connivance and encouragement of Johannes R. Becher – to bring the Aufbau Verlag's 'most important author' (Seghers) out of Hungary at the time of the 1956 uprising. The second and third chapters of Janka's essay which are written from the distancing perspective of the third

2. Walter Janka. *Schwierigkeiten mit der Wahrheit*. Reinbek bei Hamburg, 1989.
3. Peter Jokostra, 'Offener Brief an einen Verleger' (*Die Welt* 1 August 1962), reprinted in Peter Roos and Friederike J. Hassauer-Roos (eds), *Anna Seghers. Materialienbuch*, Darmstadt/Neuwied, 1977, pp. 11–14.
4. Frank Benseler in his foreword to Manfred Behn (ed.), *Anna Seghers. Woher sie kommen, wohin sie gehen: Essays aus vier Jahrzehnten*. Darmstadt/Neuwied, 1980, p. 5.

person and deal with his arrest, trial and the initial stage of his imprisonment, represent an at times terrifying account of the ruthless disregard for judicial procedures of a paranoid political apparatus bent on preserving its position by making deterrent example of those who cross it, even, as is the case with Janka, in the mildest of forms and with the best of intentions. What is most remarkable here, what made the most sobering impact on Janka, was not however the injustice inflicted on him, but that in the inhumane manner of his trial and treatment a crime was being perpetrated against socialism itself: 'Er empfand Scham darüber, daß solche Prozeduren im Sozialismus möglich sind'. It is this perhaps which explains why Janka did not turn his back on the GDR and its political system when he was eventually released and which helps us to unravel the somewhat tantalising final paragraphs of his essay. In an elliptical, all-too-brief account of the years of reflection in the solitary confinement of a filthy, airless and virtually unlit cell he finds no harsh words for socialism itself, only for those who have perverted its ideals; a perversion in which Seghers – present at his trial and silent witness to its savage injustice – is clearly implicated. We will return to this episode and the shadow it throws over Seghers's reputation at the end of this essay.

Anna Seghers was born Netty Reiling in Mainz on 19 November 1900. Her *nom de plume* is derived from a minor seventeenth-century Dutch painter whose work she encountered in the course of her doctoral thesis studies on Jews and Jewry in the work of Rembrandt. During the years in exile from 1933 to 1947 Anna Seghers was to return to her birthplace and its location on the Rhine in two of her most impressive works: her finest novel, *Das siebte Kreuz* and arguably the most powerful and accomplished of her shorter prose pieces, *Der Ausflug der toten Mädchen*, written 1943/44.

In *Das siebte Kreuz* – the story of Georg Heisler, the only one of seven prisoners who manages to escape the concentration camp at Westhofen and survive – Mainz and the territory which stretches in a rough triangle to Worms in the south and Frankfurt am Main in the north is invested at points with a mythical dimension vital to the meaning of the novel. The vista, for instance, surveyed by the shepherd Ernst in the opening chapter, is made to yield up the two thousand years of history it had witnessed and given setting to. The vision of passing Roman and crusader armies, successive wars and revolutions is reduced to moments of fleeting turmoil when viewed against the recurrent rhythms of nature and the seasons. It is as if the present horror of Nazism is, by implication, also no more than a fleeting excrescence on the passage of history; as if this landscape, evoked from afar and in exile, and representing that third Germany – neither defeated or fascist – of which Walter Jens has spoken, prefaces and supports in its reassuring constancy the perspective of hope spun out through the characters and events of the novel. The sense of permanence which radiates from it here as the story begins finds its human counterpart in the tribute to the indestructibility of the human spirit expressed in the lines which bring the novel to a conclusion: 'Wir fühlten alle, wie tief und furchtbar die äußeren Mächte in den Menschen hineingreifen können, bis in sein Innerstes, aber wir fühlten auch, daß es im Innersten etwas gab, was unangreifbar war und unverletzbar'.[5]

In *Der Ausflug der toten Mädchen*, Mainz and the Rhine again have a vital part to play. The description of the blistering heat and glaring sunlight of an isolated Mexican village with which the story opens induces a vision of childhood friends on a schooltrip on the Rhine some three decades before. In this rare autobiographical work from an author notably reticent about her own life, Anna Seghers uses her real name. The narrator, Netty, recalling the essay she had, as a young girl, been required to write about the excursion, describes not only the day's events – an evocation of idyll – but intercuts her account from the perspective of grim hindsight with the contrasting, developing destinies of her former classmates. She moves in elliptical flashback through the 1920s and 1930s and into the Second World War when all of them had perished. It is a moving, melancholic tale of individual but, we are made to feel, representative lives, which, in this context of Germany and Germans between the wars, brings fatal overtones to a traditional theme of crumbling childhood innocence. Leni and Marianne, two of Netty's close friends whom we see at one moment arm in arm will become bitter political enemies: Leni is starved and tortured to death in a concentration camp; Marianne marries a high Nazi official and is eventually killed in a bombing raid on Mainz; the Jewish schoolmistress we see happily shepherding her high-spirited charges on the Rhine excursion, will later, we learn, be reviled and spat upon by one of these same girls. If this story seems to offer, in its fragmented view across three decades of German history, a foretaste of the ground covered so exhaustively in *Die Toten bleiben jung*, first published in 1949, it differs totally in its style and technique. Whereas the much longer novel makes its mark because of the attempt to grasp in comprehensive narrative form and

5. Anna Seghers, *Das siebte Kreuz*, Darmstadt/Neuwied, 1985, 23rd edition, p. 288.

through a bewildering array and variety of different characters the totality of social, political and economic factors which make up the history of Germany from 1918 to 1945, what is memorable about *Der Ausflug der toten Mädchen* is its atmosphere. The magical effects of light and heat evoked in the opening sequence establish precisely the right mood for the sense of what the narrator calls 'einen unermeßlichen Strom von Zeit, unbezwingbar wie die Luft',[6] out of which she summons the phantasmagoria of places and figures from the past which make this story so intensely haunting.

Both here and in *Das siebte Kreuz* we lose sight of Anna Seghers the communist writer who had joined the KPD in 1928, the same year she had won the prestigious Kleist prize for her tale *Aufstand der Fischer von St. Barbara*. Just as Anna Seghers's autobiographical story is more memorable for its mood, the ease with which it moves back and forth in time, than for the political perspectives it brings to bear, so does *Das siebte Kreuz*, in its description of the effect Georg Heisler has on the people he meets in the course of his flight to freedom, rise above schematic presentation of communist activists engaged in the struggle against fascism. The matter of fact courage and heroism displayed by those who, at great risk to themselves, help Georg Heisler along his way, are a testament not to Party ideology but to the resilience of the human spirit. The conscious use of Christian symbol to render the social and political message – as long as one of the seven crosses erected by the Westhofen Camp Commandant remains unoccupied the spell of Nazi invincibility will remain broken – also steers the book away from a simple communist interpretation. Whether consciously or not on Anna Seghers's part, this undoubtedly helped to strengthen the impact of the novel and its subsequent film version in America where it became a powerful reminder that it was not just the world at large, but first of all the Germans themselves who had suffered at the hands of National Socialism.

From this brief confrontation with *Der Ausflug der toten Mädchen* and *Das siebte Kreuz*, it would seem that the circumstances in which Anna Seghers found herself for a brief period from the late 1930s onwards considerably extended the metaphysical range of her work. This impression is reinforced by *Transit*, a novel set in Marseille in 1940 and describing events which Anna Seghers was herself experiencing almost as she was setting them down. The main thread of the novel – two men are in love with the same

---

6. In Anna Seghers, *Erzählungen 1926–1944*, 2nd edition, Berlin and Weimar, 1981, p. 362.

woman, who herself loves a third who is dead – which Seghers
claims she derived from Racine's *Andromache*, is interwoven with
the plight of refugees from Hitler desperately caught up in the
nightmarish bureaucracy bedevilling the procuring of exit permits
and travel and transit documents. What is totally unexpected in a
writer who as a member of the 'Bund proletarisch-revolutionärer
Schriftsteller' in the late 1920s and 1930s, as well as in her celebrated
exchange of correspondence with Georg Lukács, had been at the
centre of the animated discussions among marxist intellectuals
about socialist realism, and who, in the GDR, would be so in tune
with what the ruling SED required of its writers, is that *Transit* is
close to a brand of despair associated more with certain kinds of
existentialism than it is with the sustaining tenets of marxism. Its
optimistic conclusion (the narrator/hero decides not to seize his
hard-won opportunity to escape to exile, but stays in France to take
his chances in the resistance struggle against the Nazis) seems
artificial and contrived when set against the bulk of the book
which, like Kafka's *Das Schloß*, raises despairing confrontations
with a wilfully uncomprehending officialdom to a metaphor for the
false starts and frustrations of the human condition. Is it justifiable
to detect here the beginnings of a personal, ideological crisis? It
seems not unreasonable to speculate that private anguish at the
German-Soviet pact of 1939 and the apparently inexorable advances being made on all fronts by the Nazis may have temporarily
shaken the resolute faith in revolutionary socialism which
forms the backbone of the novels she had written in the 1930s: *Die
Gefährten* (1932), which pressed the cause of worldwide revolution
through the depiction of the struggle of communists in Europe and
China; *Der Kopflohn* (1933), which dealt with the hostilities between communists and fascists in the early 1930s as they manifested
themselves in a small village in Hesse; *Der Weg durch den Februar*
(1935), a novel about the attempt to topple the Dollfuss regime in
Austria in February 1934; and *Die Rettung* (1937), about the repercussions on a small Upper Silesian mining community of a pit
disaster, economic crisis and rapidly nascent fascism. With the
exception of *Die Gefährten* these are all novels written in exile and
are free of the doubts and uncertainties which beset so many of
Seghers's fellow writers who had been forced to leave Germany.
Frequently to be seen in the 1930s at a table outside the Café de la
Paix in Paris writing for long stretches in totally self-absorbed
fashion in school exercise books, she was a source of astonishment
at this time to other exiles who were too unstable, because of the
fraught and uncertain political climate, to settle to creative work.

Her own crisis of resolve and belief – if we may describe in these terms the undercurrent of despair in *Transit* and, in different vein, the search for consolation in the consciously affirmative, almost Christian view of the tenacity of the human spirit we find in *Das siebte Kreuz* – comes later. The closest she comes, however, to voicing it in any overt way, is in a letter dated 1 June 1941, to Bodo Uhse when she says 'Ich habe das Gefühl, ich war ein Jahr lang tot gewesen'.[7]

The collapse of the Third Reich, and with it the end of her exile in Mexico, saw a revitalisation of spirits for Anna Seghers. She returned to East Berlin determined to be, in Christa Wolf's description, 'Lehrer für ein ganzes Volk'.[8] What this might mean in terms of her writing is exemplified by the story 'Die Rückkehr' (1949).[9] This is the tale of a soldier Werner Funk who returns totally disillusioned from the war and in a state of political apathy and uncertainty about his ideological allegiances. He leaves his family to go to work in the West, seduced by the relatively higher living standards, but soon meets with virulent anti-communism and ruthless treatment of the labour force at the hands of reinstated capitalist reactionaries. The story documents a gradual process of political awakening; Werner Funk's initial feelings of wanting to be merely left in peace are disturbed by a succession of experiences and confrontations which call upon him to opt for one system or the other. Like so many of Anna Seghers's stories and novels, 'Die Rückkehr' turns on an individual at a point of decision in his life. When presented on the one hand with the equation potato salad, plus sausage, plus exploitation in the West, and on the other with that of potato salad, plus no sausage plus no exploitation in the East, he plumps for the latter. 'Die Rückkehr' is an unashamedly didactic story. And yet, as Gerd Fuchs's novel *Stunde Null*, published in 1981, clearly corroborates,[10] in its much more comprehensive account of the manipulation of the labour force in the West in this immediate postwar period by unscrupulous industrialists with fascist pasts, it in no way distorts the alternatives the two already rapidly bifurcating social and political systems had to offer.

When at the end of the story, Seghers has her hero say that to

---

7. Quoted in Kurt Batt, *Anna Seghers. Versuch über Entwicklung und Werke*, Leipzig, 1980, p. 135.
8. Christa Wolf, 'Glauben an Irdisches', in *Lesen und Schreiben*, Darmstadt/Neuwied, 1981, p. 131.
9. In Anna Seghers. *Der Bienenstock. Gesammelte Erzählungen in drei Bänden*, vol. 2, Berlin and Weimar, 1963, pp. 285ff.
10. Gerd Fuchs, *Stunde Null*, Munich, 1981.

have stayed in the West would have been tantamount to selling his future for 'Bohnenkaffee' (to a nation heartily sick by this time of *Ersatz*, the notion of real coffee and the standard of living it implied would have had very special connotations), she is clearly giving outline in very partisan fashion to her belief in the moral and social superiority of the system in the East. It is this taking up of cudgels on behalf of the new society in the making which is the predominant characteristic of her work from the late 1940s through to the end of the 1960s. She does not always do it, however, in the very straightforwardly realistic style of 'Die Rückkehr' which, with its very precise account of bombed urban landscape and grim living conditions, is typical of the *Trümmerliteratur* of the immediate postwar period. In the six vignettes, for instance, which make up the *Friedensgeschichten* of 1950[11] and where Seghers turns her attention to the land and the problems of the agricultural, peasant milieu, she introduces an element of almost woodcut stylisation and simplicity. In one story, 'Die Umsiedlerin', a woman refugee billeted on an avaricious farmer who ill treats and exploits her, finds justice at the hands of the new regime: in another, 'Der Traktorist', a tractor driver whose leg is blown off when he ploughs up an unexploded shell inspires, with his eagerness to get back to the harvest, the beginnings of a change of heart in a colleague much less committed to the aims and ideals of the new system. While these sparse, economically narrated tales may fall short of grappling fully with the frequently harsh measures which accompanied the process of land reform and collectivisation in the GDR, neither do they see this difficult period through rose-tinted spectacles – they all have figures who are less than enthusiastic for the social revolution going on around them. In the story 'Der Landvermesser', for instance, Seghers portrays and, more surprisingly leaves undetected, an official who works opportunistically for the new society while hankering passionately for his old, feudalistic master who has been swept away. But it would in any case not be taking these stories on their own terms were one to reproach them for failing to mirror in sufficiently grim detail the real harshness and bitterness engendered by early policies of land reform. In her essays and speeches on the function of the writer, Anna Seghers frequently stresses – in clear echo of Marx's eleventh thesis on Feuerbach – that she does not write in order to describe, but in order, by describing, to change things. The veracity and the enlightening impact of these stories lies not in their ability to mirror society

11. Anna Seghers, *Bienenstock*, vol. 3, pp. 5ff.

faithfully, but in the vision they present of human possibilities, in their dramatisation of a humanity which is just emerging.

If the *Friedensgeschichten* may be described as miniatures, *Die Enstcheidung* of 1959, the centrepiece of a trilogy begun with *Die Toten bleiben jung* and concluded with *Das Vertrauen* of 1968, is to be seen as painting on a vast, panoramic canvas. It is also that among Anna Seghers's works which has aroused most critical animus. Marcel Reich-Ranicki, in remarks which in their outright hostility are almost counterproductive, provoking rather than deterring the reader's curiosity (could the authoress of *Das siebte Kreuz* ever produce a novel which was quite that bad?) wrote 'Der Roman *Die Entstehung* dokumentiert den Zusammenbruch eines großen Talents, die vollkommene Kapitulation einer Schriftstellerin. Sie, die Jahrzehnte um die Synthese von epischer Kunst und kommunistischer Ideologie gekämpft hat, ist dem Dogma und der 'scholastischen' Schreibart zum Opfer gefallen'.[12] What we have here is an unmistakable whiff of bad faith; the whole trend of Reich-Ranicki's piece up to this point is to single out for praise those aspects of Anna Seghers's writing which transcend the political and to denigrate those which grapple with it. To give positive emphasis in this concluding sentence to her supposed struggle to synthesise her art and her ideological beliefs is little short of dishonest. Reich-Ranicki's objections to *Die Entscheidung* – schematic or insufficiently differentiated characterisation, lack of central focus, an excess of inadequately developed sub-plots – have their roots essentially in the fact that he is totally out of sympathy with the political and ideological perspectives which Anna Seghers brings to her subject matter in this novel. What has annoyed him (but fascinates the Western reader unused to such perspectives) is that Seghers has attempted across a Tolstoyan range of characters (some eighty of the novel's main figures are detailed at the outset in a list of *dramatis personae*), and settings (Germany East and West, the USA, Paris, Mexico and, in retrospect, Spain) to give an account of the diverging development of the world into capitalist and socialist camps and particularly as it is reflected in the split, often between families and friends, in the two Germanies. It is not just about divisions, however, but, as was the case with Werner Funk, about decisions. Seghers writes, with respect to *Die Entscheidung*:

---

12. Marcel Reich-Ranicki, 'Die kommunistische Erzählerin Anna Seghers', in *Deutsche Literatur in Ost und West*, Munich, 1963, p. 385.

Mir war die Hauptsache zu zeigen, wie in unserer Zeit der Bruch, der die Welt in zwei Lager spaltet, auf alle, selbst die privatesten, selbst die intimsten Teile unseres Lebens einwirkt: Liebe, Ehe, Beruf sind sowenig von der großen Entscheidung ausgenommen wie Politik und Wirtschaft. Keiner kann sich entziehen, jeder wird vor die Frage gestellt: für wen, gegen wen bist du?[13]

The novel hinges on the depiction of two separate industrial milieux. In the West, the Bentheim industrial complex owned by a family who, while too fastidious ever to associate directly with the Nazis, had, for their commercial advantage given Hitler financial and political support; in the East, the Kossin steel works, a former subsidiary of Bentheim's, now named after the town where it is located and run as a VEB, or people's collective. As with 'Die Rückkehr' this novel is an act of partisan commitment. The Bentheim works in the West (a thinly disguised Krupp/Thyssen amalgam) is seen as locked into a capitalist, imperialist system directed from the USA and whose survival depends on the armaments industry and nurturing the notion of a Soviet threat. What we have here, in other words, is the tracing of the roots of an economic and political development which would rise to a frantic head in the nuclear escalation of the postwar world.

While she never reaches for the grotesquely satirical images of George Grosz's industrial barons in her portraits of the Bentheims and their hangers-on, Anna Seghers fixes her characters as class representatives. Psychological complexities are of secondary interest to her; she does not venture, for instance, when dealing with Western capitalists, into that tempting area of contradiction which would allow personable and appealing individuals to be shown administering a deplorable system. Character is similarly equated with social function in her presentation of those engaged in the reconstruction of the Kossin steel works along progressive, socialist lines. The image she gives us of the steel worker Robert Lohse and of the Party activist Richard Hagen – both veterans of the Spanish Civil War and now key figures who are better able than their less convinced workmates to see the way through present difficulties and aggravations to a vision of wider socialist goals – has few of the flaws and weaknesses which make Georg Heisler in *Das siebte Kreuz* such a fascinating character. What seems to have been sacrificed here in the fertile creation of incident and the rapid

13. Interview with Christa Wolf, in *Aufsätze, Ansprachen, Essays 1954–1979*, p. 400.

switches between a multitude of different venues in different corners of the globe is a concern for the psychological complexities of those involved. In her eagerness to set forth her enthusiasm for the social experiment in the East and to lay bare the industrial and political mechanisms of the Cold War from an unambiguously socialist point of view, she has relegated the subtleties and contradictions of character to a secondary role. This will disturb some readers. Anyone, however, looking for a vigorously narrated account from the other side of the ideological divide of the social and economic basis to East-West relations in the period 1947 to 1951 will respond positively to *Die Entscheidung* and its sequel *Das Vertrauen* which covers the years 1952 to 1953.

These two novels are a robust gesture of support for the GDR. They are Anna Seghers's attempt to write on a monumental scale about the Germany she had chosen to live in. But she also, in the final period of her life, produced shorter work in less combative vein which casts its net wider, in time and geography, than the immediate reality of the GDR. Particularly outstanding here is *Die Kraft der Schwachen* (1965),[14] a collection of nine short stories in which, as their title implies, testament is given to the ability of the materially and spiritually disadvantaged to assert themselves. Or 'Das wirkliche Blau' (1976),[15] which depicts the persevering search of a Mexican potter to find the lost colour ingredient vital to his work. And finally, *Sonderbare Begegnungen* of 1973,[16] a collection of three fantasies in the most memorable of which Seghers assembles Kafka, E.T.A. Hoffmann and Gogol for a meeting and literary discussion in Kafka's Prague. All of these pieces would seem to be markedly different in scope and approach from her two great socialist realist novels, but they nonetheless bear the unmistakeable mark of that restrained but confident belief in the human spirit which characterises all of Anna Seghers's work. But how, to return to what was broached at the outset of this discussion, are we to respond to this high-mindedness in the knowledge of Seghers's involvement in the Walter Janka episode? For all its detailing of Stalinist excesses, what will most stick in the gullet of students of GDR cultural and intellectual life is the opening chapter of *Schwierigkeiten mit der Wahrheit* and its pondering of the reasons for the failure of Seghers and Becher to speak out at Janka's trial against

14. In Anna Seghers, *Gesammelte Erzählungen 1963–1977*, 2nd edition, 1981, pp. 5–185.
15. Ibid., pp. 187–275.
16. Ibid., pp. 413–529.

what they knew to be blatant untruths and distortions. The tale of their utterly spineless conduct raises many nagging questions. Should the spectacle of writers guilty of the ethically reprehensible be allowed to affect the reception of their work? Are the claims which are made for the inherent moral superiority of socialism in the writings of these two celebrated GDR authors fatally undermined by knowledge of their conduct in the Janka affair?

Walter Janka himself is magnanimous in this respect. Towards the conclusion of his opening chapter he writes: 'Mit diesem Rückblick mache ich keinen Abstrich an Bechers poetischem Werk . . . Und Anna Seghers? Ich habe sie immer als Schriftstellerin geachtet'.[17] Will future readers of their work, one wonders, feel able to extend so much generosity to Johannes R. Becher and Anna Seghers?

Suggested Further Reading

Anna Seghers's novels are published in volumes I–VIII, her stories in volumes IX–XII and her essays and speeches in volumes XIII and XIV of the *Gesammelte Werke in Einzelausgaben*, Aufbau-Verlag, Berlin and Weimar.

A West German edition of the work, *Werke in zehn Bänden*, has been published by the Luchterhand Verlag.

Secondary Material

Heinz Ludwig Arnold (ed.), *Anna Seghers*, in *Text + Kritik*, no.78, 2nd revised edition, September 1982 has a very detailed listing of primary and secondary material.
Heinz Neugebauer, *Anna Seghers. Ihr Leben und Werk*, Berlin, 1970.
J.K.A. Thomanek, 'Anna Seghers', in Ian Wallace (ed.), *The Writer and Society in the GDR*. Tayport/Fife, 1984, pp. 67–82.

17. Walter Janka, *Schwierigkeiten*, pp. 41–2.

–4–

Erwin Strittmatter:
A Poetical Philosopher from the Land of *Naivitas*

Reinhard Hillich

I have three caricatures of Erwin Strittmatter in front of me. The oldest, from the 1950s, depicts the author as a farmer. Leaning on his spade, he stands there sucking reflectively on his pipe and seems to be using the break from work to think and compose. Pigs, chickens and geese are cheerfully milling around him while he does so. The second has him astride a lofty steed, engaged in alfresco studies in the forest. He is peering over the top of his glasses at the world which lies at his feet (a pinewood clearing) and is recording his observations on a typewriter which is lodged on the neck of his Pegasus. The third caricature, which appeared in 1974, is a portrait. The author has his eyes closed and is apparently deep in contemplation. On his head is a bird whom those in the know will recognise as a nightingale; it must be blue since it is Strittmatter's symbol for poetry.

Whether depicting the author as countryman, observer of nature or as seeker after poetry, these interpretative drawings are both witty and apposite. They point to concentrations of emphasis and changes in Strittmatter's work over more than forty years of creative activity which have made him one of the most distinctive and frequently read authors in the GDR.

Tales from the Countryside

When, in 1951, Erwin Strittmatter made his debut with the novel *Ochsenkutscher* he was thirty-nine years old, no longer a beginner and had already largely broken free from his early literary mentors (L. Tolstoy, H. Laxness, M. Andersen-Nexö). He had more than twenty years of trying to write as well as an extraordinarily varied life behind him.

He grew up in modest circumstances in a village in the Niederlausitz. His parents sent him to the grammar school in Spremberg, but he left at the age of sixteen before completing his education. He was destined to become neither a teacher nor a clergyman but, like his father before him, a baker. His years of itinerant apprenticeship coincided with the period of mass unemployment at the beginning of the 1930s. He made his way with casual jobs as chauffeur, waiter, animal keeper, labourer and as a worker in the chemical industry. His early poetry articulates in elegaiac tones the experience of the social outcast: 'Müde bin ich und verlassen / bitter ist mein Leid und stumm / einsam such ich meine Straßen . . .'[1] Neither his lyric poetry nor his first novel were able to find a publisher. Having retreated into a kind of philosophical inwardness, he remained virtually silent, an author without audience. And so it was that 1941 saw him marching off to war with Schopenhauer and Rilke in his knapsack. He deserted at the beginning of 1945, went into hiding until the arrival of the Americans and then resumed his civilian life working as he had done before the war as a casual labourer and baker. But very soon new possibilities opened up for him. Totally without possessions or property, he received, as a result of the programme of land reform, a few acres of land; a process he describes as being responsible for restoring him to good health once again.[2] In 1947 he joined the SED, was appointed supervisor of seven villages and, at the end of the year, he became the editor of the daily *Märkische Volksstimme*. His newspaper work with its goal of influencing public opinion and establishing contact with a large readership was a new route to writing. In addition to reportages and stories of everyday life he produced the novel *Ochsenkutscher* which immediately enabled him to set up as an independent writer. In 1954 he confessed the following:

Ich bin jünger geworden, ich singe jetzt anders als früher. Ich möchte vier Hände haben, um alles das aufzuschreiben und tun zu können, was in dieser Zeit und dieser Republik, in der der arbeitende Mensch zu seinem Recht kommt, aufzuschreiben und zu tun ist. [. . .] Ich selbst habe in einem Alter, in dem man in einem kapitalistischen Land schon

1. Erwin Strittmatter, 'Man müßte vier Hände haben', in *Neues Deutschland*, 30 September 1954.
2. Cf. Willi Boelcke, 'Ein Schriftsteller des neuen Dorfes und sein Weg', in *Bauern-Echo*, 4 November 1951.

zum alten Eisen zu zählen beginnt, erst mein Talent entfalten, viele Erzählungen, zwei Romane und ein Theaterstück schreiben können.[3]

Strittmatter's literary debut is closely linked with the experience of social upheaval after the end of the war. There are biographical roots for the theme which we repeatedly find in his early works: social change and the releasing in so-called ordinary people of productive energies. In the initial phase of his writing which lasts until the early 1960s, Strittmatter sees himself as the committed chronicler of the new social circumstances in the GDR. His main focus is on the dynamics of these developments. Regardless of whether he is dealing with individual fates or social processes, man and society are depicted in a state of rapid change and development.

Strittmatter takes as his point of departure the programme of land reform which he celebrates in heady fashion in a number of newspaper stories published between 1948 and 1951. In 'Aus einem Kontobuch'[4] he describes how a farm labourer's dreams of owning his own property are fulfilled. One story, 'Mein erster Sägang'[5] depicts the feelings of joy experienced by one of the new farmers as he sows his plot of land; another, 'Das Jahr der kleinen Kartoffeln',[6] consists of a fictitious monologue directed at the estate owner who has fled to the West, in which the rhetoric of the basic situation – pride in one's new position and scornful rejection of the former master – has a clear affinity with Goethe's *Prometheus*. Moments of high emphasis point up the human and historical context in which the distribution of land to those who own nothing takes place: those affected follow the process with the same amazement as once the biblical shepherds tending their flocks had done; just like the Easter walk in Goethe's *Faust*, the inspection of the land they have received becomes an image of the awakening of fresh life and activity after a long winter.

Strittmatter intended to encompass the great historical dimension of land reform, which he could only indicate symbolically with the limited resources of the short story, in a novel trilogy of which only the first volume, *Ochsenkutscher*, was ever completed. In going back to the time when expropriation of Junker land 'noch ein Traum ist',[7] this novel constitutes an exposition of the theme. It sketches the panorama of a Lausitz village in the 1920s. The

3. Strittmatter, 'Man müßte vier Hände haben'.
4. In *Märkische Volksstimme*, 18 December 1949.
5. In *Märkische Volksstimme*, 30/31 October 1948.
6. In *Eine Mauer fällt. Erzählungen*, Berlin, 1953, pp. 5–11.
7. Anon., 'Unser neuer Roman', in *Märkische Volksstimme*, 23 February 1950.

villagers live in feudal dependence on a lord of the manor and mine owner who, in their influence over school, church and police, exercise total control. The village proletariat are so demoralised by their oppressive poverty that they are incapable of concerning themselves with anything but the naked anxiety about how to survive. It is a leaden time of stagnation, of semi-stupor in which the Nazis with their slogans 'Arbeit und Brot' and 'Brechung der Zinsknechtschaft' are very successful. All this is portrayed mainly from the naive perspective of the young boy, Lope Kleinermann, who works on the estate and struggles to understand the cause and effect of this complex world. At the end of the book he leaves his native village with his friend, the class-conscious worker Blemska. The planned second part was to deal with the period 1933–45 in which Lope would become a soldier and be captured by the Soviet army while his friend, now in the resistance, would be imprisoned in a concentration camp. Strittmatter intended that the third part should describe the experiences of Lope as a 'Neubauer' in the period from the redistribution of land up to the present.

Ochsenkutscher represented a narrative breakthrough for Strittmatter. The novel had several qualities which would be characteristic of his mode of writing: a naively unprejudiced perspective on the world, a playfully experimental way with language and an often salty and down-to-earth humour. A lively discussion was set in motion by the graphic language of *Ochsenkutscher* and by a frank depiction of misery and sexuality which was thought somewhat shocking at the time. Readers' reactions demonstrated how unusual the novel was in the literary landscape of the immediate postwar years which was shaped in the main by the work of writers returning from exile. Whereas these authors depicted the organised struggle against fascism (for instance, Anna Seghers's *Die Toten bleiben jung*) or made the politically aligned class of industrial workers the focus of attention (for instance, Willi Bredel's *Verwandte und Bekannte*), *Ochsenkutscher* demonstrated the failure of the industrial and rural proletariat to consolidate their alliance and the fateful consequences this brought with the rise of the Nazis.

Katzgraben, Strittmatter's first work for the stage, was directed by Brecht in 1953 but enjoyed little popular success. It is nevertheless worth looking at the play in some detail since it establishes the pattern according to which Strittmatter subsequently portrays the thematic connection between new social beginnings, change on the land and self-realisation of the individual. This pattern occurs again with only slight variations in the novel *Tinko* (1954) and in the play *Die Holländerbraut* (1959) until, in Strittmatter's most popular novel

Ole Bienkopp (1963), it is then turned virtually on its head.

As in the newspaper stories, the new circumstances which land reform has brought are seen as a new opportunity for the erstwhile agricultural proletariat. Strittmatter, however, avoids dealing merely with the ideological principle which is at stake (conveyed, in the stories, by the pathos of the symbolism) by leaving considerable leeway for the contradictions of the age. The play is constructed as a chronicle. It depicts the situation in the village of Katzgraben at four different points in time between 1947 and 1949. The focus of the plot is the building, under very difficult circumstances, of a road to the town, symbolising the advent of progress for the backwoods village. While the jumps in time between the acts convey with some verve the idea of progress (the principle behind the play), individual scenes demonstrate the crab-like speed of progress in practice.

The new farmer Kleinschmidt is spontaneously in favour of the road since it represents progress: 'Die Straße holt die Wissenschaft ins Dorf, und Wissenschaft und Wohlstand sind ein Paar.'[8] The large landowner Großmann is opposed to the road because it would threaten his position of supremacy – the new farmers have to borrow horses from him to plough their land. Steinert, the Party secretary at the nearby mine, urges the farmers to build the road. In fact this should be the task of the mine (which, in transporting its coal, has made the old road unpassable), but it is economically not in a position to do so. Steinert's thinking is as follows: if the farmers can demonstrate sufficient solidarity to take on the building of the road, he would regard this as proof of their political maturity and endeavour to ensure that the party sends tractors to Katzgraben (thereby, as it were, revolutionising backward conditions from outside). Before the referendum on the building of the road, the Katzgraben farmers receive the first economic plan for the village which Kleinschmidt again impulsively welcomes as progress. Both aspects of this progress however present him with a dilemma. He cannot both support the building of the road and fulfill his part in the agricultural plan since he is reliant on Großmann's horses. The plays begins with Kleinschmidt caving in – he votes against the road. His wife responds with the following comment: 'Gackert vom Fortschritt, aber legt kein Ei.'[9] The following year there is another referendum. The resourceful improvisor Kleinschmidt has, through improving his farming methods in a variety of ways, been

8. Erwin Strittmatter, *Katzgraben, Szenen aus dem Bauernleben*, Berlin, 1954, p. 13.
9. Ibid., p. 22

able to meet his quotas and is able to buy an ox. He now votes in favour of the road. Since, however, he has too little fodder for the ox he is once again in danger of becoming dependent on Groß- mann. Steinert offers the new farmers a political solution: give the ox over to the farmers co-operative and buy the fodder jointly. In the third act the building of the road is held up because the nearby mine has caused the level of the ground water to sink and the harvest is in danger of withering. At this point when Steinert is at his wits' end and begins to curse the wavering farmers as 'Ziegen- proleten', the women and young people in the village seize the initiative. They are more radical because as victims of the prevail- ing conditions they have nothing to lose and can afford to be a little more adventurous. They it is who suggest a solution to the water problem which the mine engineers then implement.

It should have become clear that this is not a traditional literary treatment of life on the land. Strittmatter presents the events in Katzgraben as the rural manifestation of movements and conflicts which are affecting the whole of GDR society at the time. In doing this he avails himself of several advantages which the rural setting has to offer: economic changes on the land evolve more slowly and less anonymously than in the industrial milieu. A more readily available overview of class struggles and conflicts of interest offers itself in the context of the village. Their effects are felt in each and every family (as is the case with the Kleinschmidts, for instance) and can therefore be dramatised in the more personal terms of love, marriage and the family.

The novel *Tinko* is the tale of an eleven year old boy in the postwar period (1948/49) who grows up with his grandfather, the new farmer August Kraske. His mother has been killed in the war, his father is released late from a prisoner of war camp, remarries and remains a stranger to his young son. The contradiction which Tinko experiences is – as was the case with *Katzgraben* – that as a result of the reforms the new farmers now own land, but they have hardly any machinery or the animals to operate their farming equipment. As a consequence much has to be done by hand. Tinko has to play his part working hard in the fields. The situation is aggravated by his grandfather's newly aroused pride of ownership which prevents him from participating in the collective. Tinko has insufficient time for his studies and he does badly at school. His whole development is jeopardised. Not until tractors arrive in the village (he calls them 'Kinderglückmaschinen') does he have the opportunity to live like a normal child. The film version of the novel (1957) ends with the line: 'Tinko, geh spielen!'.

The positive development of the young boy is contrasted with the stagnation and decline of old Kraske. The grandfather dies at the end of the novel, a tragic figure who cuts himself off from progress and has lost his way between two epochs:

> Die alten Zeiten? Meint der Meister die ganz alten Zeiten, als Großvater noch Hüttenmaurer war und jeden Morgen in die Glashütte trabte? Diese alten Zeiten kann Kimpel doch nicht meinen. Damals gab's keine Freundschaft zwischen ihm und dem Kahlwicht. Großvater kann nicht ergründen, welche alten Zeiten gemeint sind. Er für seinen Teil meint nicht die ganz alten Zeiten. Er meint mehr die neueren Zeiten, aber nicht die ganz neuen. (T, p.357)

In discussions about the book it was argued that the death of August Kraske was unnecessary since as a new farmer all possibilities had been, in principle, open to him. Here, Strittmatter links the theme of the general possibilities for emancipation with the particular historical individuality of a specific human being. Old Kraske does not react out of ideological principle to the new conditions, but as a human being who has been distorted by hunger for land and is virtually beyond help. This, for the literature of the early 1950s, rare perspective on a character represented a careful moving away from overly optimistic conceptions of change. Strittmatter's second agricultural drama *Die Holländerbraut* goes further in this respect. This somewhat melodramatic play about the unhappy love of a day labourer for the son of a large landowner may be understood as a variation on Brecht's *Der gute Mensch von Sezuan*. It poses the question of the extent to which a bad person may be improved by favourable circumstances, love and kindness.

Despite some modification of detail, the thematic constellation of social progress as the impetus for the development of personality remains constant in Strittmatter's work in the 1950s. Changes occur on the other hand in his aesthetic method and modes of presentation. The impulse for this comes on the one hand from his collaboration (and later close friendship) with Brecht, on the other from the events of 16 and 17 June 1953 which cause him to rethink, self-critically and in public, his contacts with the masses. His conclusion: 'Den faschistischen Provokateuren keine Gnade, aber mit den Menschen unserer Deutschen Demokratischen Republik müssen wir auf menschliche und nicht auf mechanisierte Weise zu reden beginnen.'[10] With this in mind he conducts, in speeches and

10. Erwin Strittmatter, 'Einige Lehren vom 16/17 Juni', in *Der Schriftsteller*, no. 7, 1953.

articles, a polemical case against the 'positive hero', a literary stereotype he deems to have outlived its use. He turns against 'ex cathedra' writers who talk down to the reader and characterises his concept of the writer as someone who would be the 'Mund für viele'. To articulate mass experiences for a mass public – this plebeian and democratic model for literary activity defines in essence Strittmatter's work and his practical approach to it. It leads to a particular kind of popular narrative which – anti-elitist in posture and anti-pretentious in form – appeals to readers with extremely varied literary tastes. This applies to the novel *Tinko*, the irresistible charm of which rests on the fact that all is portrayed from the childlike perspective of the eponymous hero. In his next novel *Der Wundertäter* (1957) Strittmatter, in using the structure and the popular diction of the picaresque form, is aiming at the broadest audience of readers. The most concentrated incorporation and deployment of the motifs and methods of popular literature however is in the novel *Ole Bienkopp* (1963). Very soon after it was first published, its universal appeal amongst readers of all kinds had secured it the status of a popular classic. It is not however merely the choice of particular narrative techniques which guarantees the success of Strittmatter's work with such a wide audience. In 1954 he took a practical step to ensure a level of shared experience between himself and his readers. He moved to a small village (where he still lives), participated in the harvest and, in 1957, became a member of the local agricultural co-operative. From this intimate contact with the village milieu Strittmatter drew the material for *Ole Bienkopp*, which utilises the changes which socialism had brought about on the land in order to draw up a historical balance of the development of the relationship between individual and society in the GDR.

Once again in his title character Strittmatter draws on the figure of the resourceful improvisor who is only fully able to develop his talents as a result of the acres he has received under the land reform programme and who, in the process, gradually comes to understand the pointers to socialist development and to follow them. What is new in the novel is that this figure from humble circumstances moves – due to the process of learning and emancipation – into the vanguard of social progress and wants to play a determining role in it himself. This represents a reversal of the original didactic model of socialist realism and opens up a view of completely new constellations of conflict.

Conditions in the village of Blumenau are portrayed at two different points in time by means of leaps in chronology similar to those used in *Katzgraben*. Firstly we have the situation in 1951. Since the implementation of land reform new inequalities and kinds of dependency have arisen among the new farmers because their fields have very different yields. The new farmer Ole Hansen – he is known as 'Bienkopp' because of his fertile imagination – searches for a way of removing this injustice. With the weakest farmers he founds a 'Neue Bauerngemeinschaft' in which work is organised communally and along communist and original christian principles and where profits are shared out equitably. This initiative is rejected by the authorities, Bienkopp is censured and driven to leave the Party. Shortly after, however, he is rehabilitated by the official decision of the SED to form agricultural co-operatives (LPGs). The second part of the novel which is set around 1958/9 deals with the economic viability of the Blumenau co-operative. Bienkopp, its chairman, devises a series of profit-making projects in order to do without state subsidies. As a somewhat prickly innovator however, his unconventional ideas bring him repeatedly into conflict with the local functionaries of the Party and state apparatus who stick rigidly to what has been laid down in the plan. In the end, Bienkopp is sacked. Whereupon he attempts to go it alone in an attempt to vindicate the feasibility of his innovatory project and, in doing so, loses his life in an accident.

That a figure who embraced socialism because he saw that it was a way of increasing productivity could also perish in the process, was something quite new in the literature of the GDR. What was also new was that the prevention of this increased productivity was brought about by resistance and stubborness from within. Attention was directed in the novel at inflexible leadership structures and dogmatic modes of behaviour which hampered socialist development. It was these points which stimulated the liveliest and most wide-ranging public discussion to date in the history of GDR literature.

Bienkopp is hindered from shaking off his reputation as a ridiculed eccentric and from becoming a pioneer for the new society by three functionaries who are working towards a static and regimented order of things. Their behaviour (like that of old Kraske) is a product of the way that history has moulded them, of the way in which they have become fossilised in their official functions. In the case of Simson the fault lies with her love of the military which she does not abandon even when, after doing purely administrative work, she begins to work for the Party. Once a secretary in an army barracks ('Sie leugnet nicht, daß sie die Uniformen liebte; je mehr Silbertressen und Blechsterne desto

Reinhard Hillich

heftiger'[11]), she is secretary to the local community after 1945, then becomes mayor but remains, despite all the efforts of her comrades to change her, the obedient receiver and transmitter of orders. The regional Party secretary Wunschgetreu also has to carry round with him a baggage of misdemeanours from the past. Among these is that in the effort to be a 'good comrade' he had once denounced a bookseller who had asserted that not all Soviet novels were good literature. Guilt about this makes him excessively careful. Kraushaar, a specialist in the local agricultural council, is a former activist, a worker whose health has been ruined driving a tractor and who now has an office job but has succumbed to the easy life, to a 'Sog zur Behäbigkeit'.

The contrast between the impatiently progressive Bienkopp and this dogmatic, anxious and bureaucratic trio who cling to the status quo is accentuated by Strittmatter to the point where it has tragic consequences. Dürrenmatt once remarked that a story has only reached its conclusion when it has taken its worst turn. It is on this note that Strittmatter ended his novel, declaring that, with Bienkopp's unexpected death, he had wanted to shake up the reader and cause him to reflect on the following problem: 'Wie bringen wir in unserer Gesellschaft den Neuerer, den Vorwärtsdränger, gut unter, so daß wir ihm nicht seinen Tatendrang beschneiden, aber auch so, daß wir ihn nicht nach der anarchischen Seite ausscheren lassen.'[12] In writing an end of this kind, Strittmatter went beyond his original intention of chronicling developments in the GDR. He now no longer regards literature primarily as the attempt to follow, comprehend and reflect upon what is happening in society but as something which may encourage public understanding of the problems of social practice.

Studies from Nature and Life

Between 1966 and 1970 Strittmatter published three volumes of short prose – *Schulzenhofer Kramkalender*, *3/4hundert Kleingeschichten* and *Ein Dienstag im September*. The first two of these volumes are characterised by a blend of nature observation and philosophical reflection. The third is a collection of stories which deal in a sober,

11. Erwin Strittmatter, *Ole Bienkopp. Roman*, Berlin and Weimar, 1972, 15th edition, p. 142.
12. Walter Nowojoski, 'Schriftsteller an der Basis. Interview mit Erwin Strittmatter', in *Neue Deutsche Literatur*, no. 6, 1965, p. 69.

Reinhard Hillich

terse and – as the subtitle '16 Romane im Stenogramm' suggests –
short-hand fashion with lives, and critical points in people's lives,
which have been beset with difficulty. At the heart of all three
volumes is a quality of analysis and a detailed accumulation of
reality which in neither Strittmatter's earlier or subsequent writing
have such a dominant position. He is in a period of transition in
which his literary programme is undergoing considerable change.

These are 'wichtige Jahre für Erwin Strittmatter, Jahre der Erkenntnisse, Krankheiten, Umbrüche, Reisen – nicht gerade leicht-
estes Leben'.[13] The public reception of *Ole Bienkopp* takes a
disappointing turn after 1964/65. The democratic appeal of the
novel to the basis of society for social change from below is
thwarted by cultural and political developments from above which
now want the writer to dramatise the statesmanlike perspective of
the 'Planer und Leiter' of society. The demand to view things from
this perspective is, very understandably, somewhat at odds with
Strittmatter's artistic disposition. His reluctance to implement it is
further aggravated by severe health problems which focus his
attention much more on problems of a purely existential kind. No
wonder then that his contribution to 'Planer-und-Leiter-Literatur'
is tinged by a somewhat grim irony. In the story 'Die Cholera' a
deputy minister returns ill from a trip abroad and, while in an
isolation ward, goes through a drastic process of disillusionment.[14]
The polemical implications of the story go even further. They
indicate that Strittmatter is turning away from the use of the
positive hero as a means of encouraging the enthusiastic identification of the reader. Instead, as was demonstrated in the case of the
tragic end of *Ole Bienkopp*, the emphasis now is much more on
shaking him up.

These volumes of short prose reveal Strittmatter in the process of
reasserting his grip on reality – gradually and by means of strenuous empirical and philosophical effort; they show him rebuilding,
brick by brick as it were, the entire edifice of his aesthetic *Weltan-
schauung*. This happens by virtue of the need to adjust to a long
period in which rapid and dramatic social changes are not on the
agenda. Symptomatic of the new situation is that the process of
revolutionising the ownership of the means of production on the
land, from which Strittmatter had taken the examples for his

13. Eva Strittmatter in 'Nachwort' to *Wahre Geschichten aller Ard(t)*. *Aus
    Tagebüchern*, Berlin and Weimar, 1982.
14. Erwin Strittmatter, 'Die Cholera' in *Neue Deutsche Literatur*, 1967, no. 11,
    pp. 64– 70.

conception of social progress and the development of personality, is now complete. The agricultural milieu as the stuff of literature also loses in a further respect its original exemplary value. In the 1960s, agriculture becomes increasingly dominated by the methods of large-scale industrial production and there is increasingly less room for specialisation and the division of labour. The possibility of participating in all levels, mental and physical, of farming work – which Strittmatter had depicted in *Ole Bienkopp* as a model for future communist working methods – has disappeared for ever. The only way now of becoming and remaining creative is in consciously resisting monotony and the narrowing down of one's working sphere. This is demonstrated by the story 'Der Stein'[15] in which a tractor driver relieves the tedium of ploughing by indulging in a 'verflucht privaten Spaß'. He interrupts his real work to deploy all of his imagination and resourcefulness to remove from his field a large boulder which for generations has been a great source of nuisance. The story 'Kraftstrom'[16] shows how social and technological progress does not automatically guarantee a meaningful and productive life. It deals with old Adam, a forester who associates the new order after the war with the electricity which it has brought to his village. Electricity makes his life easier but gradually robs him of all the tasks with which he could make himself useful in the village. It reaches the point where he is made to feel superfluous. He reacts by planning to smash an electrical motor and then kill himself. Only when he recognises that electricity is a harnessed force of nature and learns to control it does he recover his will to live. At the end of the story old Adam is put in charge of the electrical cattle fence and is once again 'mächtig am Leben'.

In the mid-1960s Strittmatter notes in his diaries (*Selbstermunterungen*, 1982): 'Für mich war's ein Fortschritt, als ich erkannte, daß der Fortschritt, von dem wir immerfort reden, Grenzen hat' (S, p. 95). In the philosophically accentuated prose miniatures of the *Schulzenhofer Kramkalender* and the *3/4hundert Kleingeschichten* the search for a comprehensive concept of progress plays a central role. Here, the notion of the unity of the universe is pressed with a particular urgency. Strittmatter traces the mutual interdependence of man and nature, clearly prompted in this by the destruction of the environment. Becoming aware of the ubiquitous circulation of

15. In *Ein Dienstag im September. 16 Romane im Stenogramm*, Berlin and Weimar, 1969, pp. 260–275.
16. Ibid., pp. 142–167.

atoms in material both living and inert gives him insight into the continuous process of transformation and renewal which connects the individual with the universe and the history of mankind. These global considerations extend Strittmatter's concept of the subject matter and influence of literary activity – from roughly 1970 on he believes that a genuine work of art should have an international resonance. On the other hand his studies of nature, for instance the observation that no leaf resembles any other, confirm the legitimacy and value of what is totally distinctive and unique, of his own individual voice as an author for instance. In 'Saubohnen', one of the sixteen novels in shorthand, he permits a writer the following thought:

> Jeder Mensch ist eine unwiederholbare Einmaligkeit, und es muß ihm gelingen, einen Punkt zu finden, seinen Punkt, von dem aus er zeigt, wie er die Welt sieht, wie nur er die Welt sehen kann. Es gehört Mut dazu, [. . .] eine Menge Mut, auf diesem Punkt, trotz aller sich anbietenden Vorbilder, zu verharren, auf diesem Aussichtspunkt. (DS, p. 111)

Strittmatter is seeking here to escape the relatively anonymous role of the 'Mund für viele'. Some points of reference in his writing however stand the test of this critical revision. In the 1960s, a period characterised by programmatic upheavals, there is one aspect of his work which gives it continuity – the tendency towards brevity and compression. Strittmatter offers two reasons for this emphasis on the laconic which is already visible in *Ole Bienkopp* and leads, with a certain logical inevitability, to his embracing of the short prose form. One is in line with the democratic aim of his writing. He draws here on the fund of shared social experience among the population of the GDR in the years of constructing socialism. This consensus of experience, he argues, permits direct and intimate communication between author and reader. A writer who, as it were, speaks from amidst his readers will always be understood even when – or precisely because – he avails himself of that eloquent abbreviation which is the expression of a shared communality. On the other hand Strittmatter sees literature as being in competition with television which, by the beginning of the 1960s, has become a mass medium in the GDR. Literature he believes can only compete for the favour of the public if it offers the reader entertainment in as compressed a form as television. This is not however a view which Strittmatter holds for very long. His theories about brevity and compression become increasingly less important for his later writing.

Reinhard Hillich

In search of 'Produktivkraft Poesie'

As a signal, so to speak, for the beginning of a relatively new phase in his writing, Strittmatter published in 1972 a book with the evocative title *Die blaue Nachtigall oder Der Anfang von etwas*. It contained four stories in which he portrayed episodes from his own childhood and youth. This autobiographical twist – something hitherto new for Strittmatter but which subsequently was to become a permanent feature of his writing – was not altogether unexpected in an author who was now in his sixties. Strittmatter stressed however that these were not memoirs written on the threshold of old age. In an afterword to the volume he stated that he was attempting a literary exploration of those moments of 'Poesie und Schwerelosigkeit' he had experienced in his youth and he asked: 'Sollte man nicht [. . .] solche reaktionslosen Augenblicke bewußt und mit dem Effekt von damals in sein Leben einbauen können?' In the meantime, two further volumes of *Nachtigall* stories have appeared. They are unsentimental recollections, Strittmatter's 'Forschungsberichte' about his search for a harmonious and productive attitude to the world. Above all they are reflections on writing, they deal with the 'Produktivkraft Poesie' which drives him on as a writer and which, as he noted in an interview, may be demonstrated in the positive attitudes of people who have permitted it to work its effect on them: 'Ein Künstler muß, so meine ich, die Wirklichkeit beständig auf Lebenshilfen für sich und seine Mitmenschen durchforschen.'[17]

Strittmatter now regards his literary programme emphatically as a response to the reality of the twentieth century which is characterised by a constantly increasing division of labour and specialisation, by a bewildering splintering of knowledge and of our grasp of the conceptual world. In contrast to the world of science which, with its analytical methods, furthers the fragmentation of reality and encourages myopic modes of behaviour (frenetic euphoria or psychotic anxiety about the future of civilisation), art must concentrate its efforts on seeing these scattered fragments as part of a single whole. Strittmatter couples this view of the synthesising function of literature with the hope 'unsere geistige Entwicklung zu beschleunigen'.[18] What for him is at stake here is human integrity

17. Heinz Plavius, 'Produktivkraft Poesie. Gespräch mit Erwin Strittmatter', in *Neue Deutsche Literatur*, 1973, no. 5, p. 12.
18. Ibid., p. 12.

and an intellectual attitude which enables him to get to grips with what threatens our reality.

Strittmatter's concept of a search for poetry as something which can help us to live fuses together knowledge of both self and of the world. The stuff of his literature is now his own biography, authentic life which is perused and subjected to philosophical evaluation. This process governs not only the *Nachtigall* stories but also Strittmatter's more recent writing – the two volume novel *Der Laden* for instance which tells of the childhood of the boy Esau Matt growing up in a Lausitz-Sorbian village between the First World War and the period of inflation. And also volumes two and three of the novel *Der Wundertäter* which depict the postwar experiences of the Simplicissimus-like hero Stanislaus Büdner, baker's apprentice and would-be writer, in divided Germany. Strittmatter here renews his interest in a period which he had already dealt with in literary form, but views it now with fresh insight and from a different perspective. He is now interested in the whole of life as the source of individual and general experience which has not yet been subjected to theoretical scrutiny. Certain things are now articulated which before, in the attempt to demonstrate the parallels between social and human progress, were passed over because they were untypical or could not be considered as valid evidence. Examples of more or less taboo subjects which *Der Wundertäter* (vol. 3) dramatises and moves into the public arena are: attacks by Soviet soldiers on the German civilian population at the end of the war, self-deception and the information policy of the daily press, questionable ideological campaigns, undemocratic exercise of power, fetishisation of political leaders, the collective, Party and state. Not exactly unproblematical phenomena of the age such as these are not treated as revelations – they are as familiar to the reader as they are to the author and would contribute to the cumulative sense of grievance which drove so many GDR citizens onto the streets in the last months of 1989. Strittmatter depicts them from the standpoint of Stanislaus Büdner, 'Schreibschwerarbeiter, beschäftigt beim Präsidialamt des Lebens', and how he is to get to grips with them. Strittmatter's published extracts from his diaries – *Selbstermunterungen* and *Geschichten aller Ard(t)* – also offer authentic testament to individual attempts to come to terms with life and are illustration of the way in which literature may be of help with the problem of living. Strittmatter intended to document a year of his life in the form of an 800 page diary. The manuscript was prepared for publication, but – 'aus vielerlei Rücksichten' – there seemed, when he wrote it, that there would be no possibility of it appearing in the forseeable future.[19] Circumstances have, of course, changed dramatically in the meantime.

In his autobiographical prose, be it in the form of short story, novel or diary entry, Strittmatter maintains a stubborn concern for existential questions – death, ageing, sickness and suffering – questions which have received scant attention from philosophers in the GDR. Strittmatter is one of the few East German authors who attempt to answer these questions on materialist grounds and are able to offer an element of consolation. In *Selbstermunterungen*, for instance, he notes: 'Alles in der Natur demonstriert mir: Du hast Zeit. Nichts geht zu Ende, nur die Formen wechseln. Ich aber bilde mir ein, nur die Form, in der ich jetzt existiere, sei gültig, und das Leben höre auf, wenn ich die Form wechsele' (S, p. 54).

Strittmatter's attempt to convey the individual experience of coping with life corresponds with a significant trend in GDR literature from the 1970s on which has found expression in aesthetically very diverse forms. In artistically structured memoirs and diaries (Stephan Hermlin: *Abendlicht*, 1979; Franz Fühmann: *22 Tage oder Die Hälfte des Lebens*, 1973), but also in relatively unpolished documentary literature. This development, which began with reportage interviews with women (Sarah Kirsch: *Die Pantherfrau*, 1973; Maxie Wander: *Guten Morgen, du Schöne*, 1977) and was continued with numerous books by younger authors in the 1980s, confronts us with very specific experiences of socialisation which are either individual or peculiar to particular groups. In general, the repeated use of the biographical or autobiographical subject seems to be an attempt to avoid fictional clichés about the changing individual and, through the use of the authentic voice, to intensify the quality of intellectual exchange with the reader.

Strittmatter's prose of the 1970s and 1980s differs considerably from that of his earlier writing, particularly in the increasing use of passages of reflection. He deploys the dual perspective of autobiographical narrative – levels of experience and consciousness in the past are contrasted with those of the writer in the present – in order to pass blunt and decisive comment on contemporary problems. Strittmatter's transformation from the plot-oriented narrator of the *Wundertäter* (vol. 1) or *Ole Bienkopp* to one who, in the manner of Goethe or Scott, repeatedly interrupts the action to blend in polemical or philosophical statements, met with a mixed reception. Many of his readers miss the narrative directness and exuberant inventiveness of the earlier work and believe something has been

19. Eva Strittmatter, 'Nachwort'.

lost. His increasing tendency to philosophise as well as his penchant for poetic generalisation have also been received very variously and, on occasion, have been interpreted as impermissible simplification. It is apparent that Strittmatter's concept of writing, operating as it does with an experience of life spanning more than seven decades, leads to opinions and an approach which are frequently irreconcilable with the reservoir of experience of younger generations. His sons, the author of *Der Laden* informs us, called him an 'alten Kacker, der nicht mehr ganz richtig tickt'.

Strittmatter himself does not regard the method which he is at present using to write about his life as the ultimate one. In his most recent *Nachtigall* story 'Grüner Juni' he comments:

> Im Augenblick scheint mir die Gefahr groß zu sein, daß ich, im Gegensatz zu früher in meinen Anfangsjahren, da ich nur das grob Äußerliche erfundener fremder Leben beschrieb, jetzt nur noch das fein Innerliche meines eigenen Lebens beschreibe, und daß ich mich in das Lager derer begebe, die mit Einseitigkeiten und Spezialitäten langweilen. Deshalb Schluß mit diesen Untersuchungen! (GJ, p. 58)

I cast my eye once again over the three Stittmatter caricatures. The country writer who gave valid formulation to the hopes and contradictions of the years of construction; the philosophising observer or nature and men who wrote prose poems of high succinctness; the seeker after poetry who, looking back at his childhood and youth with the clarity of his later years, is in search of the wisdom of his life. These rough structures of a lifetime of literary endeavour – what do they have to tell us? Months ago, when these three drawings lay together before me for the first time, I recognized in them the astonishing rigour with which Strittmatter had repeatedly liberated himself from the onset of routine, had overturned and reworked his artistic program. I now have the impression that he has remained true to the theme of his literary beginnings, by practising both change and being productive.

And does my affection for this author not stem in essence from that handful of qualities which, despite every metamorphosis in his literary activity, have remained constant and belong, as it were, to the solid core of his artistic temperament? I am thinking of that pinch of naivety which lends his perspective on the world a particular interest for the reader. This Strittmatter distancing effect, often created through childlike figures or adults who, in their unreserved and unprejudiced approach to the world react like children, provokes participation in the reader. One could perhaps describe this process as a pleasurable interchange between knowledge and experience or give it a much simpler formulation: even the most jaded of readers can, in confronting Strittmatter, recover the ability to marvel and to question. And I am thinking here too of Strittmatter's highly individual use of language (a challenge for any translator!), which has its roots in his half-Sorbian origins. In his childhood, Strittmatter spoke a mixture of German and Sorbian. It is this which explains the various models and patterns of language which he has at his disposal and which he utilises to create unique and experimental combinations and abbreviations of style, word and phrase. Some of this may, on occasion, appear somewhat mannered. But there is, after all, much to be said for writers who, with every word they use, defend themselves against frozen routine.

Translated by Martin Kane

Author's Note

The following editions and abbreviations are used for Strittmatter's works:
T: *Tinko. Roman*, Berlin, 1954.
S: *Selbstermunterungen*, Berlin and Weimar, 1982.
DS: *Ein Dienstag im September. 16 Romane im Stenogramm*, Berlin and Weimar, 1969.
GJ: *Grüner Juni. Eine Nachtigall-Geschichte*, Berlin and Weimar, 1985.

Suggested Further Reading

Other works by Erwin Strittmatter:

Prose

Ochsenkutscher. Roman, Potsdam, 1950.
Der Wundertäter. Roman, Berlin, 1957 (vol. 2:1973, vol. 3:1980).
Ole Bienkopp. Roman, Berlin, 1963.
Schulzenhofer Kramkalender, Berlin, 1963.
3/4hundert Kleingeschichten, Berlin and Weimar, 1971.

Die blaue Nachtigall oder Der Anfang von etwas. Erzählungen, Berlin and Weimar, 1972.
Meine Freundin Tina Babe. Drei Nachtigall-Geschichten, Berlin and Weimar, 1977.
Der Laden. Roman, Berlin and Weimar, 1983 (vol. 2: 1987).
Lebenszeit. Ein Brevier, selected by Helga Pankoke, Berlin and Weimar, 1987.

Plays

Katzgraben. Szenen aus dem Bauernleben, Berlin, 1954.
Die Holländerbraut. Schauspiel in 5 Akten, Berlin, 1961.

Secondary Material

Reso, Hillich et al. (eds), *Schriftsteller der Gegenwart. Erwin Strittmatter*, Berlin, 1984.
Ruth Rindfleisch, 'Erwin Strittmatter' in Geerdts et al. (eds), *Literatur der Deutschen Demokratischen Republik in Einzeldarstellungen*, Berlin, 1974, vol. 1, pp. 216–241.

–5–

Popularising Socialism:
The Case of Stefan Heym

Malcolm Pender

Speaking in Munich in November 1983 on the subject 'Deutschland', Stefan Heym reflected on the recent past, assessed the current state of divided Germany and speculated on the future[1]. Common to the forms of government in both East and West Germany was that they had been imposed on the Germans by the respective occupying forces. In the East, the continuing inability to produce a German socialist model had not only contributed to the division of Germany, but had also made the construction of the Berlin Wall inevitable. Moreover, since the GDR had competed on the terms of Western capitalism, this had been a further impediment to the development of a genuine alternative. Those in power there imagined that the present situation would persist – 'welch unmarxistischer Gedanke!'. For change would come, indeed there were signs that change was already under way. It would be absurd to think that reunification would take place wholly on the terms of East or West Germany, but each might move towards aspects of the other. Since, at the very least, the inhabitants of both states wished to survive, a start could be made by creating a nuclear-free zone in the two Germanies.

It was characteristic of Heym, by his own description 'die bekannteste Unperson' (N, p. 776)[2] of the GDR, that he should proclaim a vision which, although at odds with official orthodoxies, related to trends of thinking in the population at large. For Heym, in the course of a long and eventful career, has consistently sought to engage in public life, whether by journalism or by

---

1. The text is published in *Deutschland. Nachdenken über das eigene Land*, Munich, 1988, pp. 19–39; I am grateful to Frau Barbara Wahba, Munich, for establishing that the speech was given on 1 November 1983.
2. See Author's Note below for key to abbreviations.

fiction, in a manner which addresses current issues in clear and accessible form. Although it is obvious that he is fascinated by the craft of story-telling, his stories are like his journalism in the sense that they too aim to publicise. Interest in the figure of Heym derives in part from the position of his fiction in his wider concerns, and in part from his status in a divided Germany. As Egon Bahr said of him in the Federal Republic in 1988: 'Ohne sie [die deutsche Teilung] wäre er weder hier noch drüben so hörbar angeeckt'.[3]

Six years after the prescient Munich speech, Heym participates tirelessly in the momentous events of the autumn of 1989. He reminds his audiences, both by word and print, that German revolutions have up till now not worked, and he pleads energetically for 'ein demokratisches Deutschland mit sozialistischen Elementen'.[4] Yet towards the end of the year, as certain indications begin to emerge from the confusion, Heym is sounding a gloomy, if not a despairing note: 'Ich habe Angst, daß aus dem Traum ein Alptraum werden könnte'.[5] Despite a new sense of identity imparted to the people of the GDR by their achievement in removing the old order, he fears that the economic might of the Federal Republic will prove so strong that it cannot be resisted, and that reunification will be an exclusively economic matter: 'Ich bin Demokrat. Wenn die Leute ein vereintes Deutschland wollen – bitte sehr. Meine Ideale werde ich dennoch nicht ablegen'.[6]

It is a tribute to the strength of these ideals that they can still generate in Heym, at the age of seventy-seven, sufficient energy for him to be so active politically. This is all the more the case since his foreboding towards the end of 1989 would mark the third time in his life that political events had fallen very far short of realising his ideals. As an American citizen of decidedly left-wing view, he had in 1951 felt sufficiently disillusioned with American democracy and sufficiently threatened by McCarthyism to leave the United States with his wife. Later, as a citizen of the GDR and as a committed socialist, he had come to regard the structures of the GDR as inimical to the introduction of workable socialism on German soil.

3. Egon Bahr, 'Einer, der nirgendwo ganz dazu gehören konnte', *Frankfurter Rundschau*, 6 October 1988.
4. 'Es ging immer unmoralisch zu in dieser Partei. Interview mit Stefan Heym', *Süddeutsche Zeitung*, 25/26 November 1989; see also Stefan Heym, 'Zwischenbericht', *Der Spiegel*, 43, 1989 and Stefan Heym, 'Hurra für den Pöbel', *Der Spiegel*, 45, 1989.
5. '"Wir brauchen Boden unter den Füßen". Stefan Heym bei der IG Metall', *Frankfurter Rundschau*, 13 December 1989.
6. Fritz J. Raddatz, 'Das wehende Vakuum', *Die Zeit*, 15 December 1989.

It seems as if Heym's entire work, both 'Publizistik' and fiction, was created in spite of his political experience, as an act of faith in the eventual efficacy of his ideals. It is worthwhile considering some special features in his case, before discussing the books which he published after 1952, books which reflect his concerns both as a socialist living in the GDR and as a German living in a divided Germany.

Three features of the twenty years which Heym spent out of Germany as a result of his flight from the Nazis have a bearing on the views which he put forward after his return there in 1952. Firstly, during his period in the United States, he adopted attitudes from American culture. In the field of communication, these derived partly from his experience of the English language which he found advantageous 'because its strict rules of sentence structure require clear thought, German lends itself to muddleheadedness'.[7] English was also in the US the only medium for his activist intentions: 'Er wollte wirken, literarisch und politisch' (N, p. 207). To this end he drew on the techniques of market research when he tailored his first novel *Hostages* (1942) to the expectations of the American market.[8] His absorption of the entire range of methods employed in public relations is apparent to Heym himself many years later, when he asks himself how he managed to stand up to pressures in the GDR when others did not: 'S.H.s für Deutschland ungewöhnliche Verhaltensweise findet ihren Grund in seiner amerikanischen Zeit, da er lernte, daß man im Kampf gegen Mächtigere jede zur Verfügung stehende Öffentlichkeit und jede wie immer geartete Möglichkeit, die das Gesetz bietet, ausnutzen muß' (N, p. 716).

A second feature of Heym's years outside Germany is that he was one of the few exile Germans who actually fought against Nazi Germany, not primarily in a combat role but as a member of a psychological warfare team responsible for disseminating antifascist propaganda to the troops of the Wehrmacht. The strength and inventiveness of much of the material for which Heym himself was responsible can be gauged from what has been published,[9] and

7. Stefan Heym, 'I arrive at Socialism by Train', *The Nation*, 11 October 1965, p. 229.
8. See Stefan Heym, 'Es hatte keinen Zweck, deutsch zu schreiben', in Hans Daiber (ed.) *Wie ich anfing. 24 Autoren berichten von ihrem Anfang*, Düsseldorf, 1979, pp. 145–54.
9. See Stefan Heym, *Wege und Umwege. Streitbare Schriften aus fünf Jahrzehnten*, edited by Peter Mallwitz, Munich 1980 and *Reden an den Feind*, edited by Peter Mallwitz, Munich 1986.

clearly these pieces further honed his powers of communication. But there were two additonal consequences of his war experience. His view of the Germans was not improved by his experience of interrogating them in France and later in occupied Germany: no one had been a member of the party, all were subscribing eagerly to what they imagined the views of the victors to be, a situation to which Heym was to see parallels forty-four years later when the SED was dethroned in the GDR.[10] But his experience of the American army also opened his eyes to the nature of American society whose structures the army reflected, and he gave expression in his novel *The Crusaders* (1948) to his own disillusionment at the manner in which the ideals with which the battle against fascism was joined were betrayed to reinforce the existing capitalist order. *Goldsborough* (1953) followed, depicting the ruthlessness of American capitalism in seeking to suppress a miners' strike in Pennsylvania.[11]

A third feature of Heym's life away from Germany relates to his decision to go to the GDR. For at the end of the 1940s such roots as he had seemed to be in the United States: 'Wenn überhaupt irgendwohin, gehört er hierher, in dieses Land, diese Stadt [New York], hier hat er seine Bücher geschrieben, von hier aus zog er in den Krieg, unter anderem auch dafür, daß er jetzt sagen kann: hier gehöre ich hin' (N, p. 454). The description of this sense of belonging indicates the force of the pressures which McCarthyism was exerting by the beginning of the 1950s, when Heym took his decision to leave, but at the same time the impression is created that without these pressures he might well not have left. Interestingly, the description Heym gives in 1965 to American readers of the attraction for him of the GDR over a decade earlier is, even making allowances for his audience, redolent of a journalistic rather than an ideological interest: for Heym the abolition of capitalism on part of German soil 'was a highly interesting, new situation, a field untapped, pure gold if you only could dig it up'.[12] The upheaval in Heym's life caused by the decision to leave the United States should not be minimised and his motives should not be trivialised. At the same time, his own description of the various facets of the situation suggests that it was not primarily a driving sense of ideological

10. See 'Zwischenbericht'.
11. That *Goldborough* is, thirty years later, still relevant to conditions in the American mining community was shown by a report on a seven-month long strike in Virginia, 'Big Rock Union Mountain', *The Weekend Guardian*, 30/31 December 1989.
12. 'I arrive at Socialism by Train', p. 229.

commitment which made Heym, after unsuccessfully seeking residence in Prague, apply for entry to the GDR.

The fact remains, however, that Heym, resident in the GDR not many months before the events of 17 June 1953 posed the greatest test to the GDR, displayed exemplary commitment to the ideals of a socialist state in two articles written a very few weeks after these events, 'Beobachtungen zum Pressewesen in der DDR' and 'Beobachtungen zum literarischen Leben in der DDR'.[13] He has come to the conclusion that one of the major factors which gave rise to the crisis was a failure of communication, and in these two articles and in others in the mid-1950s, he sets forth what he considers to be essential guidelines both for reporting and commenting on current affairs and for imaginative literature. There are three main strands which are relevant in the present context. Firstly, the trust of the people in their leadership must be restored, a plea which Heym was to repeat thirty-six years later in 1989,[14] and to this end it is necessary for the press to be made reliable and for literature to be made truthful; and in the latter endeavour, the writer remains the conscience of the people, a view from which Heym was not to resile over the years despite the fact that it clashed with the doctrine of the infallibility of the party. Secondly, there was a great need in the GDR for 'Unterhaltungsliteratur', which, in an exciting, interesting fashion, could show the problems and difficulties of society and could portray the gradual changes in those living under socialism. Thirdly, it was essential, if literature was to play its role in the creation of a genuinely socialist society, to set credible situations before the reader: 'Unsere Leser haben [. . .] ein sehr feines Gefühl für die Wirklichkeit, denn sie leben darin'.[15] It was a programme which was bound to run into difficulties with developments in the GDR.

The novels published after 1952 can broadly speaking be divided into three groups. The first group, *Goldsborough* (1953), *Lenz* (1963), *Lassalle* (1969) and *Fünf Tage im Juni* (1974, but which relates conceptually to the 1950s) all deal with some kind of attempted change in the social order. *Fünf Tage im Juni*, arguably Heym's best-known book, was the first novel he wrote in the GDR and is one of only two set there, the other being *Collin*. Heym had already published a series of essays relating to the events of the 17

13. *Wege und Umwege*, pp. 209–17 and pp. 218–25 respectively.
14. See 'Hurra für den Pöbel'.
15. Stefan Heym, 'Der vergessene Konflikt' in *Offen Gesagt. Schriften zum Tage*, Berlin, 1957, p. 277.

June 1953, *So liegen die Dinge*, which had been widely distributed. The novel proved to have a much more difficult career, however, circulating in the mid-1950s in cyclostyled form, before being re-worked in the early 1970s and published in West Germany.

Fünf Tage im Juni purports to record, from Sunday 13 June to the evening of 17 June, the activities of a varied group of people. The narrative is interspersed with the text of speeches, broadcasts and public statements, and so provides a mixture of fact and fiction which Heym regards as being part of his American heritage.[16] The hero, the works trade union secretary Martin Witte, is one of the line of perceptive individualists with a highly developed sense of responsibility on whom the action of Heym's earlier novels centre and who are the precursors of the later writer figures. Largely through Witte's eyes, the 'Tendenzen, die wahrscheinlich [. . .] eine große Rolle gespielt haben'[17] in the events are observed: the dissatisfaction of the workers, especially with the work norms; the isolation of officials and functionaries (with the exception of Witte) from the feelings and aspirations of the work force; and the involvement of Western agents and unregenerate Nazis in fomenting the unrest. With hindsight, it is interesting to see that the first two at least of these three elements were in some form present in the events which led to the downfall of the Honecker regime in the autumn of 1989. In June 1953, towards the end of the most momentous day to date in the history of the GDR, Witte appears to be making a plea for reform: the GDR has scored a victory in that it has survived intact and it has suffered a defeat in that the events took place at all: 'Alles hängt davon ab, was wir aus unserem Sieg machen, und wieviel wir aus unserer Niederlage lernen' (F, p. 260). But the brief epilogue a year later is ambiguous, since it could indicate the continuing inflexibility of the party or the intransigeance of Witte.[18]

The literary quality of *Fünf Tage im Juni* has been widely questioned even when allowances are made for the fact that it is a 'Reportageroman', and it has been suggested that literary cliché implies political cliché. It is therefore interesting that Stephan Hermlin, on the occasion of Heym's seventy-fifth birthday should

16. Hans Wolfschütz, 'Gespräch mit Stefan Heym', *GDR Monitor*, no. 8, Winter 1982/3, p. 14.
17. Ibid, p. 7; see also Heinrich Mohr, 'Der 17. Juni als Thema der Literatur in der DDR', in *Die deutsche Teilung im Spiegel der Literatur*, 3rd edition, Stuttgart, 1981, pp. 71–2.
18. Pavel Petr, 'Stefan Heym and the Concept of Misunderstanding', *AUMLA*, 48 (1977), p. 219.

describe *Fünf Tage im Juni* as 'die bis heute beste und gerechteste Darstellung der damaligen Ereignisse' and that the novel, never published in the GDR, appeared there in December 1989 in an edition of thirty thousand copies.[19]

In the last two works which deal with change in the social order, *Lenz* (1963) and *Lassalle* (1969), the individualist central figure of the earlier novels is also a writer so that these novels form a bridge to the second group of novels, represented chiefly by *Der König David Bericht* (1973) and *Collin* (1979), in which the main theme is the relationship of the writer to the state. Heym claims to have been exercised since the mid-1960s by 'die Funktion des Schriftstellers und sein Verhältnis zur Macht' (N, p. 767) because the figure of the writer is 'für die Konflikte der Zeit . . . barometerartig empfindlich'.[20]

Certainly, the difficulties encountered by Ethan, the writer-historian in *Der König David Bericht*, who has been commissioned by King Solomon to write the official history of King David, offer many parallels between the totalitarian state of biblical times and that of the twentieth century.[21] Within this kind of political structure language, then as now, must be handled with the greatest care: as Ethan struggles to balance what should be said against what can be said, he reflects 'Das Wort[. . .] ist doppeldeutig, es verbirgt und enthüllt, beides; und hinter jeder Zeile lauert Gefahr' (K, p. 100). When Ethan, his self-appointed task of presenting the truth unaccomplished, leaves Jerusalem, the seat of power, the captain of the guard mocks his indeterminate status: 'Du zählst nicht zu den Herrschenden, und bei den Beherrschten findet man dich auch nicht' (K, p. 210). This expression of the social vulnerability of the writer relates to a perception of the writer in the GDR at the time, and severely relativises Heym's earlier assertion that the writer is 'das Gewissen des Volkes'[22] since his livelihood is shown to be wholly dependent on the benevolence of those in power. Moreover, Heym's claim in respect of the parallels drawn by the novel,

19. Respectively: Fritz J. Raddatz, 'Gruppenbild mit Genosse', *Der Spiegel*, 47, 1974; Stephan Hermlin, 'Arbeit und Konflikte. Glückwünsche an Stefan Heym zum 75. Geburtstag'. *Wochenpost*, 8 April 1988, quoted by Margy Gerber, '"Glasnost ohne Glasnost"'. Cultural Policy and Practice in the GDR', *Politics and Society in Germany, Austria and Switzerland*, vol. 1, no. 2 Winter 1988, p. 33.
20. H. Wolfschütz, 'Gespräch mit Stefan Heym', p. 9.
21. See Peter Hutchinson, 'Problems of Socialist Historiography: The Example of Stefan Heym's *The King David Report*', *Modern Language Review*, 81, 1986, p. 133.
22. 'Der vergessene Konflikt', p. 281.

'daß die Menschen sich damals ganz ähnlich verhalten haben, wie unsere Menschen sich heute und in unserer Zeit verhalten',[23] not only refutes his earlier assertion that literature in a socialist country should portray changes in Man but also is in conflict with marxist notions of historical development. Or, looking at the matter from another perspective, in the light of the parable of *Der König David Bericht*, 'the DDR, and the socialist bloc, cannot be seen as socialist'.[24]

Whereas *Der König David Bericht* is a depiction of biblical society which provides parallels to later societies, *Collin*, arguably the most interesting novel in the present context, is a highly specific portrait of a point in GDR history from which its development is reviewed. In the late 1970s the writer Hans Collin confronts his contemporary, Wilhelm Urack, head of state security, in the clinic for the privileged where they are patients. Both are veterans of the Spanish Civil War and both, sharply aware of their mortality, are exercised by their relationship to the past. Their common memory stretching over a period of almost half a century is of 'dunkle Erlebnisse [. . .], über die man sich ausschwieg' (C, p. 32), and Collin later refers to 'eine ganze Generation in Schuld verstrickt' (C, p. 155). In the case of Collin himself, the 'Klassiker' (C, p. 9) of GDR literature, he is increasingly troubled by what he now interprets as complaisance towards official thinking in his writing – a socialist von Aschenbach, he has suppressed his knowledge. To the doctor Christine Roth, a member of the younger generation who is seen acquiring a historical perspective from Collin's account of the Spanish Civil War, the writer seeks to explain the manner in which he played 'Verstecken vor sich selber und vor seinen Zweifeln' (C, p. 113) in order that his work acquire official approval. Were he now to write his memoirs without his customary self-censorship, he might redeem himself in his own eyes and leave a record which presents an alternative to the authorised version.

Collin's resolve to set forth a truthful account is given added relevance by the appearance of Havelka, who has come to visit his wife, also a patient at the clinic. Havelka, in command of troops of the International Brigade in Spain, had caused Collin to be withdrawn from the front-line so that he could record the struggle against fascism for posterity. But forty years later, Havelka has

---

23. 'Wahrheit als Ärgernis. Gespräch mit Stefan Heym', *Nürnberger Nachrichten*, 7/8 October 1972.
24. David Roberts, 'Stefan Heym, *Der König David Bericht*', *AUMLA*, 48, 1977, p. 209.

become for Collin a 'Leiche im Keller' (C, p. 213) since Collin is unable to forget his silence at the show trial in the GDR in the 1950s of the man who protected his life in Spain in the 1930s. Together with other literary figures and members of the intelligentsia, Collin had been present under duress at the contrived disgrace which led to Havelka's imprisonment. The course of the trial is described to Christine Roth partly by Havelka and partly by Collin himself, who seeks to explain his silence: at the trial intervention would not have altered the course of events and would have put himself at risk; there was a direct parallel to the situation in Spain and he had said to himself: 'Ich habe ja meine Aufgabe, meine höhere, ich muß schreiben, muß das alles aufschreiben, und um schreiben zu können, muß ich leben' (C, pp. 273–4). His silence at the trial, indelible in Havelka's memory, now causes Collin, as he confronts it openly after all this time, to call in question the validity of his achievements since. His sense of guilt towards Havelka is now compounded by his realisation that he has harboured self-delusions about his room for manoeuvre. The relationship of the writer to the state acquires a further dimension of ambiguity by virtue of his complicity in the actions of the state.[25]

Urack, aware of Collin's intention to write his memoirs, is anxious to thwart an undertaking which could lead to embarrassment and mobilises the pressures to which Collin might be susceptible. Since Collin, whatever his own thoughts might have been, has subscribed in his published work to the omniscience of the Party, Urack now seeks to demonstrate to him its omnipotence. In the 1950s, Faber had been a victim of the purges and had been coerced into giving false witness at the Havelka trial. Now, twenty years later, Urack implies that Collin's supineness then was justified since the transgression for which Faber was punished was not really of Faber's own doing: 'Der Faber hat nichts Böses getan [. . .] Seine Schuld ist, daß er da war und daß er war, wie er war. Daß er wie zugeschnitten war für den Rock, den wir ihm anzogen' (C, p. 212). The whole matter had in fact been stage-managed by the party: 'The nature of dissidence [. . .] is defined by the state and the party according to the situational, i.e. tactical and strategic,

25. A fresh interest was imparted to the story-line of *Collin* a decade after its appearance with the publication by Walter Janka, the model for Havelka, of his account of the trial and its attendant circumstances, *Schwierigkeiten mit der Wahrheit*, Reinbek bei Hamburg, 1989; at the beginning of 1990, the Supreme Court of the GDR quashed Janka's 1957 conviction, and accepted that he was due adequate compensation. See also Martin Kane's piece on Anna Seghers in this volume.

conditions which prevail'.[26] It is a point which is not without relevance for the perception of Heym himself.

Collin's suspicion that he is being told about this 'Vergangenheit, die, nie begraben, wie ein Alp hockte auf allem Geschehen im Lande' (C, p. 215) because Urack has discovered that Collin's situation is terminal, blinds him to the implications of Urack's revelations for his own situation as a writer. For, just as Faber the dissident was marginalised, so Collin the writer has been hopelessly compromised. What value would be attached to the memoirs of a writer who is perceived as a member of the élite? Significantly, the critic Theodor Pollock, who encourages Collin in the project of writing his memoirs, claims to have done so in terms of power, not of truth: Collin responded strongly to the suggestion that his total control over his material would make of him 'ein Urack des Wortes' (C, p. 50). And, taking the matter beyond the immediate confines of the novel, even the critical writer such as Heym enjoys the privileges of the élite so that, as was pointed out before the publication of *Collin*, his position is not that of a representative of 'Geist' opposing 'Macht' but 'that of an outsider of the ruling class'.[27] Such reflections on the situation of the writer in the GDR prior to 1989 are, in the aftermath of the events of late 1989, of crucial moment.

An equally direct, if more general, link to the problems of the 1990s is provided in the reflections of Christine Roth, through whom the older generation is assessed. When she reads of the unresolved political disputes relating to the Spanish Civil War which, as she knows professionally, still exercise the surviving participants to the detriment of their health, she is afflicted with a sense of foreboding at the possibility of a cyclical historical process: 'Wird das ewig so weitergehen, die Fragen von heute, zur Seite geschoben und unter den Teppich gefegt, in wiederum zehn, zwanzig, dreißig Jahren fortzeugend Infarkten gebärend?' (C, p. 56), again a question which acquires a particular resonance after 1989. *Collin* suggests that a contributary factor here is the position of the individual in socialist society which, as Heym asserted in 1974, is a 'Gesellschaft,. . . die mit dem Vorsatz antrat, die Interessen des einzelnen und der Gesellschaft in Übereinstimmung zu bringen'.[28] But the novel claims through Pollock, who at the close

26. Wilfried van der Will, 'The Nature of Dissidence in the GDR', in Ian Wallace (ed.) *The GDR in the 1980s*, Dundee, 1984, p. 39.
27. D. Roberts, 'Stefan Heym, *Der König David Bericht*', p. 210.
28. Stefan Heym, 'Vorwort' to *Ankunft. Neue Prosa aus der DDR*, edited by Stefan Heym, Munich, 1974, p. 10.

Popularising Socialism: Stefan Heym

appropriates the manuscript of the now dead Collin, that this is a
matter which is in fact ideologically unresolved: 'das Gewicht und
die Rolle des einzelnen' is 'ein Thema, [. . .] das von marxistischen
Aspekten her nie ganz durchdacht wurde' (C, p. 84). Clearly, this
lack of clear definition must create the acutest dilemma in the case
of the writer, 'das Gewissen des Volkes', and 'this structural
imbalance between the demands of the state and the integrity of the
individual viewpoint [. . .] is at the heart of Heym's concern'.[29]

The ambiguities surrounding the writer in the GDR as portrayed
in *Collin* – not least the ambiguity of which the novel does not seem
fully aware, namely the effect of his privileged position on the way
in which he and his work are perceived – are highlighted by events
following the novel's publication, without official permission, in
the Federal Republic. Heym had to pay a heavy fine, which he
regarded as 'die beste Investition' (N, p. 834) of his life since it
boosted sales in the West. But Erich Loest, who was one of the
eight signatories to a letter of protest to Honecker (his name and
that of Martin Stade are omitted in Heym's account (N, p. 834)),
lists the adverse fates which befell these writers and concludes:
'Wir acht haben, während Heym glänzend investierte, die Zeche
bezahlt'.[30]

In the two novels published in the 1980s, *Ahasver* (1981) and
Schwarzenberg (1984), Heym returns to the theme of change in the
social order. *Ahasver*, which takes place at four levels – outwith the
normal framework of time, at the time of Christ, in the sixteenth
century at the time of the Reformation and in contemporary East
Berlin and Jerusalem[31] – presents the widest-ranging examination
in Heym's writing of the forces of movement and inertia, order and
disorder in the body politic. In the view of the novel, Lucifer, far
from being the agent of disruption as traditionally perceived,
represents a major stabilising factor: because he regards the world
as organised in the worst possible way and hence propitious for his
work, he is a reactionary. The contrary principle is represented by
Ahasver, 'welcher die Welt verändern will, da er glaubt, sie
sei veränderbar und die Menschen in ihr desgleichen' (A, p. 76).
But the perennial problem of whoever sides with Ahasver and

29. Peter Graves, 'Authority, the State and the Individual: Stefan Heym's *Collin*',
    Forum for Modern Language Studies, 23, 1987, p. 348.
30. Erich Loest, 'Bastion Schreibtisch', *Frankfurter Allgemeine Zeitung*, 15
    October 1988; the full list of signatories to the letter is given in Manfred Jäger,
    Kultur und Politik in der DDR, Cologne, 1982, p. 165.
31. Rodney Fisher, 'Stefan Heym's *Ahasver*: Structure and Principles'. *Seminar*,
    22, 1986, pp. 232–4.

challenges and overthrows an order which he believes to be in some way unjust or wrong is that 'his wisdom is incomplete and inadequate for the inevitable disorder which follows such a challenge'.[32] Thus, in order to maintain what he might regard as at least a partial achievement, he must cause inertia to be restored, and so it comes about 'daß aus den lautesten Revolutionären die strengsten Hüter der Ordnung werden' (A, p. 176). In this situation of consolidation, explanations must be found which exculpate the particular revolutionary goal: 'Die Unvollkommenheit der Menschen ist die Ausrede einer jeden Revolution, die ihr Ziel nicht erreicht hat' (A, p. 211). Appeals to faith represent similar attempts to shirk responsibility, since 'die Wahrheit ist sichtbar [. . .] und [. . .] erforschbar' (A, p. 210). On none of the three levels of actual time in the novel is a situation depicted which contains productive disorder and movement and, significantly, the last words of Ahasver which close the novel are 'ein Traum' (A, p. 319).

Schwarzenberg, set at the close of hostilities in 1945 in the southern part of what is now the GDR, speculates on what might have been had the Germans been able to create their own social order after the Second World War. The area round about the town of Schwarzenberg, briefly unoccupied, serves as a 'Labor zur Entwicklung einer echten Demokratie' (S, p. 276) since the Germans do not have a political system imposed on them. Were the experiment in Schwarzenberg to succeed, it would act as a 'Präzedenzfall [. . .] und als ein bescheidenes Beispiel für künftige Versuche' since it is a historical fact 'daß es in Deutschland noch nie gelungen war, eine Revolution aus eigener Kraft zum Siege zu führen' (S, p. 67). The efforts to construct an alternative to American capitalism and to Russian socialism take place within the appalling problems of the aftermath of war, and a governing forum, consisting largely of Communists and Social Democrats, seeks to administer to the needs of the population and to establish its own legitimacy and authority. Simultaneously, a possible political framework is created as a constitution is drafted in accordance with the political ideals of Max Wolfram, the last of Heym's involved intellectual figures to date. He seeks a radical break with certain German traditions, as another central figure, the honest communist Ernst Kadletz also makes clear in the course of a speech: 'Niemals wieder dürften wir unser Gewissen betäuben und das eigene Denken einem höheren Befehl unterwerfen' (S, p. 207). Wolfram's plans would place all organs of the state under rigorously democratic control, but before the draft

---

32. Ibid, p. 241.

constitution can be put to the people, the world of power politics intervenes and the enclave ceases to exist. Kadletz is aware that his sorrow at the lost opportunity is not shared by all his fellow citizens when he says 'daß die fremde Macht ihnen die Auseinandersetzung mit sich selbst ersparte, indem sie ihnen einen neuen Kodex, den sie aus Eigenem hätten finden müssen, einfach auferlegte' (S, p. 246). Clearly, the implications of the novel, which contains many of Heym's known views, are intended to extend well beyond the limited area of Schwarzenberg.

The reader seeking help from the massive autobiography *Nachruf* (1988) with the paradoxes of the figure of Heym as a writer in the GDR is disappointed on two counts. Firstly, whereas Heym has spent almost exactly half his life in the GDR, just over a third of the volume is devoted to this period and that only up to the point of his expulsion from the Writers' Union in 1979. Against that, just under half the book deals with the sixteen years of his involvement with the United States. Secondly, and more importantly, there is very little of the inner man, of the tensions and pressures to which he must have been subject and which claimed three members of his family through suicide. Instead, there is a colourful presentation, told largely through the distancing mechanism of the third person, of the external life of a professional survivor. The constant skirmishing in various countries with officials whose patterns of expectation Heym never seems to fit, the ceaseless war with the faceless bureaucracy of the GDR from which Heym has the splendid knack of extracting embarrassed faces – the tactics of survival are well documented. But it is precisely here, where the reader wishes to know how this steadfast resistance is fuelled, that the author falls silent and so provides an ironic parallel to his novels in which Heym avoids depicting the wellsprings of human behaviour. If the abiding interest of *Nachruf* lies in the fact that it chronicles events in the odyssey of a German Jew who chanced to be born in 1913, it is perhaps fitting that its title should relate to the style and direction of an obituary tribute, albeit an interim one in this case.

The reader wishing to make his own interim assessment of Heym is faced with difficulties. The hope that the West German 'Werkausgabe', started in 1981, might disengage the figure of Heym from the political confrontation of the two Germanies and so promote 'eine wertfreiere, also mehr literarische Rezeption des Heymschen Oeuvres',[33] would not necessarily benefit Heym if it

---

33. Hartmut Panskus, 'Das Interview mit Stefan Heym zu seinem neuen Roman *Ahasver*', reprinted from *Börsenblatt für den deutschen Buchhandel*, 26 May 1981, Munich, 1981, p. 3.

were fulfilled. Almost twenty years ago, Heym was described as representing 'ein Desiderat der deutschen, nicht nur der ostdeutschen Literatur' because he deals with 'Themen des Tages' in a manner which is 'packend, rasant und direkt'; it was a moot point whether one might call his books 'glänzenden Journalismus oder tagespolitische Schriftstellerei'.[34] Certainly, the first part of this assessment corresponds with the professed aims of Heym when he arrived in the GDR, and the problem of categorisation raised by the second part is not dispelled by Heym's own description of the manner in which he seized on current events as stories for his novels (see, for example, N, p. 425, p. 474, p. 581). Thirty years later Heym was not only claiming that his particular style of writing was much more appreciated in the Anglo-Saxon world 'als bei diesen Snobs hier' but also that he was at that time probably the most popular author in the GDR.[35] In his own perception, therefore, he sits uneasily but successfully in the German tradition, although it might be felt that he fits easily enough into a popularising strand in postwar writing in German.

Heym has been at odds with orthodoxies in the GDR, moving from a position which sought to depict the changing individual to one which held that the individual remained unchanged, and his insistence at all times on the primacy of personal conscience conflicted with the notion of the supreme authority of the party. Yet one might ask, without calling in question for a moment the human feat of his survival, whether his opposition to orthodoxies was as outright and straightforward as it appears since if it had been – it is legitimate to speculate – he might not have survived as a writer. Egon Bahr sees Heym as a beneficiary of the division of Germany and certainly Heym's status cannot be separated from propaganda simplicities which mask more complex realities. In this respect, the case of Heym exemplifies wider problems of assessment.

Finally, it is striking, in view of his survival and his continuing unflagging activity, that Heym's novels, whether they deal with the past or the present, almost all portray failure, either political or personal. Perhaps this represents the honesty of the good reporter who is driven by a vision of what could be to report what is. At the beginning of the 1980s, Heym claimed that, in the irrepressible character of Ahasver who survives all manner of adversity with his

34. Fritz J. Raddatz, 'Zurück zu David und Salomon', *Süddeutsche Zeitung*, 27 January 1973.
35. H. Wolfschütz 'Gespräch mit Stefan Heym', pp. 1–2.

vision of ultimate justice on earth intact, 'steckt drin, was mich einen großen Teil meines Lebens bewegt hat. Eine Utopie vielleicht, nicht realisierbar. Aber im Grunde sind es immer die Utopisten gewesen, die die Welt vorwärtsbewegt haben. Zwar wurden sie alle am Ende enttäuscht, aber eine auf vielen Gebieten spürbare Wirkung hatten sie schon'.[36] At the beginning of the 1990s, it will be interesting to see what stories the political flux of central Europe will yield to Heym's literary imagination in the time which remains to him.

Author's Note

The following editions and abbreviations are used for Heym's works:
N : *Nachruf*, Munich, 1988.
F : *Fünf Tage im Juni. Roman*, Frankfurt am Main, 1977.
K : *Der König David Bericht. Roman*, Frankfurt am Main, 1974.
C : *Collin. Roman*, Frankfurt am Main, 1981.
A : *Ahasver. Roman*, Munich, 1981.
S : *Schwarzenberg. Roman*, Munich, 1984.

Secondary Material

Hans Wolfschütz's essay on Heym in the *Kritisches Lexikon zur deutschsprachigen Gegenwartsliteratur* offers an extensive list of reviews and articles on his work going back to 1942.

Werner Brettschneider, *Zwischen literarischer Autonomie und Staatsdienst. Die Literatur in der DDR*, 2nd edition, Berlin, 1974, pp. 78–85.

Melvyn Dorman, 'The state versus the writer: recent developments in Stefan Heym's struggle against the GDR's Kulturpolitik', in *Modern Languages*, 1981, no. 62, pp. 144–52.

Heinrich Mohr, 'Der 17.Juni als Thema der Literatur in der DDR' in Karl Lamers (ed.) *Die deutsche Teilung im Spiegel der Literatur*, Stuttgart, 1978, pp. 43–84.

Malcolm Pender, 'Stefan Heym', in Ian Wallace (ed.) *The Writer and Society in the GDR*, Dundee, 1984, pp. 34–51.

Arnim Stolper, '. . . als wäre der Juni nicht gewesen', review of East

36. H. Panskus, 'Das Interview mit Stefan Heym', p. 14.

German edition of *5 Tage im Juni* in *Neue Deutsche Literatur*, 38, no. 447, March 1990, pp. 43–9.

'Gespräch mit Stefan Heym' in *Neue Deutsche Literatur* 38, no. 449, March 1990, pp. 5–12.

Reinhard Zachau, *Stefan Heym*, Munich, 1982.

–6–

'Das lebendige Erzählen':
Johannes Bobrowski Poet of Recall and Readjustment

Brian Keith-Smith

1989 was perhaps a particularly appropriate year in which to reconsider Johannes Bobrowski's aims and achievements, not only as the 200th anniversary of the French Revolution, but also as the 50th anniversary of the invasion of Poland by German troops. He would have understood the need to remember both 1789 and 1939, even if he might have wished to see their forward-looking potential more emphasised. Indeed, we only have to look at chapter seven of his second novel *Litauische Claviere* to realise that for him the landscape of his childhood gained its particular resonance because of its links with the past and its visions into the future.

Bobrowski describes categories of time in terms of a wooden construction, a 'trigonometrischer Punkt' from which Potschka, the local collector of folksongs, can look out as if on a watchtower into the landscape:

> . . . Und von hier blickt man hinaus. Wo hinaus?
> In eine Landschaft. In eine Dunkelheit. In der es diese Helle gibt.
> In eine Zeit. Wenn man weiß: was das ist, Zeit.
> Das Gegenwärtige? Das schon immer, indem es bemerkt wurde, abgeschlossen ist, vergangen, Vergangenheit geworden.
> Das Zukünftige? Das immer herankommt, ganz nah heran, und nie eingetreten ist, immer draußen geblieben.
> Die Vergangenheit? Abgeschlossen, abgetan, nicht mehr zu rufen, weil ohne Gehör. Erkennbar vielleicht in leblosen Gegenständen, Gestorbenes, in einem Augenblick unkenntlich geworden.
> (III, p. 311–12)[1]

---

1. Page references are to Johannes Bobrowski, *Gesammelte Werke in sechs Bänden*, Berlin, 1987, of which four volumes edited by Eberhard Haufe have so far appeared. There is an excellent 79 page introduction in Volume 1.

Just two pages later, in his typically fragmentary, repetitive-fugue-like-prose style, the same phrases are picked up and given an extra dimension when words from the eighteenth-century Lithuanian poet, priest, lense-maker, constructor of barometers and of three pianos, Christian Donelaitis, are used to commemorate events that were repeated, for instance, in 1939. These events were merely repeat performances of similar acts of brutality going back to at least the times of the Teutonic Order of Knights. Each event, each piece of history, becomes an example:

> Aber ist das nicht alles abgeschlossen, abgetan, nicht mehr zu rufen, weil ohne Gehör? Erkennbar vielleicht, wie es hieß, an leblosen Gegenständen, Gestorbenes, unkenntlich geworden in nur einem Augenblick.
>
> Ja, es ist so. Das ist das Vergangene.
>
> Und die Zukunft? Wirklich nicht eingetreten? Immer noch draußen? Ja, es ist so. Und hier?
>
> Hier ist Dunkelheit, um diesen hölzernen Turm. Da sind Schritte, da stößt etwas gegen einen Stein.
>
> Die französischen Geister?
>
> Dann liegt also der vergrabene Schatz doch noch in der Erde? Unter dem Sand, nur noch tiefer vielleicht? Und ihr habt etwas zu bewachen, ihr napoleonischen Geister?
>
> (III, p. 315)

The landscape, *each* landscape, has its own points of reference back into time, specific enough for their lesson to be interpretable, nameable and hence usable as a reminder and as a warning for the future. Thus in that same chapter we find the essential call out into the darkness for which Bobrowski lived and which he practised: 'Rede, daß ich dich sehe, sagen wir. Rede, daß wir dich sehn' (III, p. 312). The *Du*-figure here is that Christian Donelaitis, the representative figure of *Humanitas* on whom an opera is to be written, a work to reconcile Germans and Lithuanians, an expression of Bobrowski's own central theme. His call to speak, we note, is first of all for his own sake 'daß ich dich sehe', but is extended immediately to the whole community 'daß wir dich sehn'.

This idea of *Humanitas* uniting the whole community is implicit at least in many of Bobrowski's short stories and underlies the correct use of celebration of anniversaries, as can be seen especially in *Litauische Claviere*. For here, the examples of the German celebration of the 'Luisenbund' and the 'Vaterländischer Verein' and of the Lithuanian celebration in the Festspiel *Vytautas Didysis* only serve to revive age-old nationalisms. The use of anniversaries to reestablish a sense of ethnic identity in such a border territory invites manipulation by apparently new, but in fact age-old forces, in this case by Dr Neumann and by the crypto-National Socialists. The novel itself and Bobrowski's works in general use specific reference to events in the past, focussing points by which he lays bare the ambivalent potential use of history particularly within a local community. It is against the sombre background of this theme of history and the manipulation of anniversaries that the special quality of Bobrowski's spirit stands out like a rainbow after the storm. And it is this, above all else, that makes his works so attractive to read. For they indeed render the human qualities summed up by the figure of Donelaitis visible.

Human qualities, age-old prejudices and the formative influence of cultural traditions were the major influences in Bobrowski's life. Born in 1917, his early years in Tilsit and in villages closer to the German-Lithuanian border made him aware of tensions in local communities with mixed faiths, languages and races. The border atmosphere and village-life as a world theatre in miniature inform his mainly landscape poetry and his prose works. When his family moved in 1928 to Königsberg – the town of Hamann and Kant – he came face to face with a rich literary and musical heritage and he here developed a taste for Baroque music, for Bach, Buxtehude and Mozart. He learnt also to appreciate the form and discipline of classical Greek and Latin writers. His war-service in the early 1940s, especially in the army invading Poland, made him realise just how fragile the common humanity in such cultural back-grounds can be. This influenced much of his early, often unpub-lished poetry and some of his short prose texts, where he came closer to the heart of human fears and motivations than many of the more cerebral anxiety-ridden expressions of his contemporaries. He struggled hard to achieve some modest recognition while working as a reader and editor and while he enjoyed a quiet family life, constructing for a few years his own cultural idyll in his collection and study of especially eighteenth-century and earlier texts and of music which he explored on his clavichord. His craftsmanship, with its haunting reminders of forms and measures from a pre-industrial age, and its constructivist application to situations that recalled the recent past, won for him increasing admiration in the last few years of his life (particularly after October 1962 when he was awarded the prize of the Gruppe 47). His death from peritonitis in 1965 was untimely and seen by many as a loss both to literature and to humanity in general.

When Bobrowski died, he seemed to have produced some of the most original and peaceful evocations of a lost world and landscape in his lyrics, some of the tersest and most challenging short prose texts in German since those by Heinrich von Kleist, and two remarkable regional studies in novel form. He was considered as a writer for connoisseurs, a name to be dropped in literary circles after say that of Paul Celan; he was commonly held to be a 'nature poet', to have written in a difficult style, to be a 'genuinely new voice', and to have been impersonal, strange and unpredictable. Now, thanks to the publication of four volumes of his *Gesammelte Werke*, of the *Bobrowski-Chronik* by Eberhard Haufe and Bernard Gajek and of the republished, lengthened volume *Selbstzeugnisse*, one can appreciate many of the finer points and subtleties that are so important in his work. Some excellent secondary literature has revealed major lines of development in his artistry and debts to writers such as Hamann, Herder and Klopstock and to the world of music, especially to Buxtehude and other eighteenth-century composers.[2] The complexity of reference and detail of these works, their concision and awareness of tradition, make them a happy hunting ground for philologist, musicologist, historian, art historian and literary historian alike. Yet they have for the average reader an almost soporific, nostalgic, rhythmic appeal that carries him over difficult passages and produces a sense of having read attractively written cameos of local importance. Twenty years on, it is not the singularity of Bobrowski's voice that encourages one to read his works, rather their spiritual 'Sinnlichkeit' (to borrow a phrase from one of his major mentors, Klopstock) demanding breadth and depth of reading, concentration and elasticity of attention.

One of the fascinations in reading Bobrowski's poetry is to follow lines of development in his poetic techniques. Bernd Leistner in particular has pointed out some general aspects in the chronological movement from the more 'naive' evocation of the past in the poems of the 1950s where, '. . . . mit Hilfe des eindruckstarken Wortes vorwiegend emotional wirksame Bilder gefügt wurden, in denen das Erinnerte oder Erfahrene in spezifischer Sicht durch den Autor poetische Gestalt erhielt',[3] and which

2. See Suggested Further Reading.
3. 'Aus der fliegenden Finsternis, tief . . .', *Weimarer Beiträge* 22, 1976, no. 9, p. 127. In a slightly altered version; Bernd Leistner, *Johannes Bobrowski. Studien und Interpretationen* Berlin, 1981, p. 37. Fritz Minde's article 'Das Zeichen-Gedicht' in *Lili*, 8, 1978, 30/31, pp. 122–39 examines ciphers, metaphors and symbols in Bobrowski's poetry.

contained a definitely epic quality, to those of the late 1950s where a tone of lament for the loss of a previous world became more evident, and in which the poetic image began to assume the qualities of a cipher. Also evident is Bobrowski's remarkable capacity for synthesising with delicate selectivity and accuracy details that recall whole worlds and series of events. He was a master in finding 'objective correlatives' and in setting them with great verbal economy and rich variety of poetic device. In short, the overall results of research so far prove that he was a writer ill-suited to an age more and more geared to what has been identified as a 'three-minute syndrome', an age in which concentration has been manipulated by the three-minute advertising slot on television, where immediate impact of message counts most. Most of Bobrowski's poems are short, but their statement and communication need far more than three minutes to unravel. Yet, as Alfred Behrmann has pointed out for the prose piece *D.B.H.* and the poem 'Nänie'- 'Man braucht die Biographie Buxtehudes, ein paar Partituren, ein Musiklexikon, den Atlas und einige Fakten aus dem Leben des Autors, um das kaum Verschlüsselte ohne besondere Mühe zu entschlüsseln. Wirklich verrätselt ist eigentlich nichts'.[4] Or as Renate von Heydebrand puts it: 'Bobrowski baut Hindernisse auf, gibt aber die Mittel an die Hand, sie zu überwinden'.[5]

The apparent similarity of Bobrowski's poems to one another vanishes the more one appreciates the, at times surprising, nuances of detailed application within them. For instance, Behrmann has shown convincingly how the poem 'Immer zu benennen' appears at first almost like prose yet is based on a subtle approximation to and application of many features from ancient ode verses.[6] Or one has only to study the various works in German on Thomas Chatterton to realise how much Bobrowski must have assimilated them and apparently applied them to the postcard he had seen of St Mary Redcliffe in Bristol to produce his 'Ode auf Thomas Chatterton' (I, pp. 103–4), a remarkable example, with its minor errors in detail, of a poet's empathy for a whole atmosphere so far removed from his own.[7] However, in a comment on his novel *Levins Mühle* we find perhaps one of the essential keys to interpreting his works, with all their variety:

4. Alfred Behrmann, *Facetten. Untersuchungen zum Werk Johannes Bobrowski*, Stuttgart, 1977, p. 45.
5. Renate von Heydebrand, 'Überlegungen zur Schreibart Johannes Bobrowskis' *Der Deutschunterricht*, 21, 1969, no. 5, p. 124.
6. Alfred Behrmann, *Facetten*, pp. 65–70.
7. See Sigrid Hoefert, *West-östliches in der Lyrik Johannes Bobrowskis* Munich, 1966,

Natürlich habe ich nicht im Sinn gehabt, einen historischen Roman zu schreiben. Ich habe im Buch mehrfach ausgeführt, daß diese Geschichte. . . . an sehr vielen verschiedenen Orten hätte geschehen können und zu sehr vielen verschiedenen Zeiten. Ich glaube nicht, daß die Handlung des Romans, so wie sie entwickelt wird, auf das Jahr 1874 notwendig festgelegt ist, sondern ich glaube, daß sie einen Modellfall für das Verhalten der Nationalitäten untereinander darstellt. (IV, p. 465)

Authenticity is not there for its own sake, but as a form of poetic reminder. The story of the grandfather deliberately damming up the river to cause an eventual flood and destroy his rival's mill – his rival being a Jew – and of the way in which the underdogs of the local community take their revenge on him, even though the Jew has to leave, has many attractive features; but it also shows in counterpoint to them the harshness of human rivalry and greed. Furthermore, although there are many examples of the theme of guilt towards Jews in Bobrowski's works, here at least the message is surely intended to be more than sectarian, more than symbolic of the post-second world war German need for atonement. The anniversary only wins its full significance, can only pretend to a full measure of 'Freude' once its lessons are accepted and applied to their full potential.[8]

In the at times diffuse lecture 'Benannte Schuld – gebannte Schuld?' (IV, pp. 443–8) Bobrowski declares more closely than elsewhere his views on literature in general, declaring it more than once to be powerless to change human behaviour. Using the specific example of anti-semitism, he points out the dangers of supposing that literature can correct or expunge guilt. For, as with all his works, the specific event or case is in the last resort meant as a 'Modellfall'. Consequently, his autobiographical sketches show that he dealt primarily with those events for which he felt most responsible, and he transfers these into literary form deliberately aiming to have an influence: 'Ich beziehe mich also möglichst auf das, was ich selber kenne, ich will möglichste Authentizität, weil ich denke, daß "wahre Geschichten" noch immer eher überzeugen: weil ich eine Wirkung wünsche' (IV, p. 447). His renaming of facts that many would rather forget is done 'nur auf Hoffnung' (IV, p.

pp. 44–51; also Brian Keith-Smith in: R. W. Last (ed.) *Affinities*, London, 1971, pp. 131–2.
8. See especially David Scrase, 'Point Counterpoint: variations on the "Fest" theme in Johannes Bobrowski's *Levins Mühle*' in *German Life and Letters* 32, 1979, No. 2, pp. 177–85.

448). His work, then, was not primarily that of an historian, rather that of a writer with a conscience towards the whole of humanity, he was a 'Gesamtdeutscher' whose educational aim to create dialogue between individuals and communities tried to refer inner German problems to a much wider historical and geographical perspective. That dialogue implies finding levels of language that are attuned to the other person, to the partner, not using formulae that exclude others. Hence in his final work, *Litauische Claviere*, the importance of the concept of 'Nebeneinander' is used thematically and structurally throughout and implied at least by the search for ways to write an opera on Donelaitis.[9]

Just as the poems of the 1950s were marked by a more 'naive' evocation of the past with their basically epic quality, and those of the late 1950s with a note of lament, the development of Bobrowski's prose works moved from evocation and assimilation of the past towards emphatic statements of a new sense of community and service – one thinks in particular of the story 'Betrachtung eines Bildes' (IV, pp. 151–4). However, this development can also be observed as much within individual prose works and poems as in the general maturing of his style. One can see this, for example, in the negative warning implied in the poem 'Das Wort Mensch' (I, p. 217) or in the poem 'Wiedererweckung' (I, pp. 203–4) where the past is first registered in totally negative terms, yet in the centre of the poem Bobrowski calls for a closer involvement with nature, and finally the act of naming – of finding the fitting poetic language – turns into an act of resuscitation.

In the poem 'Gestorbene Sprache' of 17 April 1960 the basic proofs of life – movement, utterance, growth, reproduction and decay – are set in a framework which makes use of connecting elements: 'Bogen' and 'Fluß'. Yet none of them reach meaningful existence in themselves. The active use is needed of a language whose implications and sense of human commitment to the landscape express the life of a reality that has died together with its mode of expression.

Der mit den Flügeln schlägt
draußen, der an die Tür streift,
das ist dein Bruder, du hörst ihn.
Laurio sagt er, Wasser,
ein Bogen, farbenlos, tief.

9. See as an interesting experiment the opera by Gerhard Wolf and Rainer Kunad, *Litauische Claviere*, libretto in *Theater in der Zeit* 30, 1975, no. 9, pp. 55–64.

Der kam herab mit dem Fluß,
um Muschel und Schnecke
treibend, ein Fächergewächs,
im Sand und war grün.

Warne sagt er und *wittan*,
die Krähe hat keinen Baum,
ich habe Macht, dich zu küssen,
ich wohne in deinem Ohr.

Sag ihm, du willst
ihn nicht hören –
er kommt, ein Otter, er kommt
hornissenschwärmig, er schreit,
eine Grille, er wächst mit dem Moor
unter dein Haus, in den Quellen
flüstert er, *smordis* vernimmst du,
dein Faulbaum wird welken,
morgen stirbt er am Zaun

(I, p. 26)

Two languages – German and Old Prussian – coexist in this poem and represent two different worlds. German here is the language of narration and half-realisation of the reality of the situation. Old Prussian is the voice of the challenge which nature's laws present, of myth, and of tragic consequences should man ignore them. The title, furthermore, does not specify which of the two is dead: is Old Prussian dead because it is not heeded, or German dead because it here no longer expresses 'brotherhood' of man and nature? Or can the title refer to the death of the poetic powers of evocation in both when they are separated? The Old Prussian has to be reinterpreted, its qualities spelt out in four German synonyms. The significance of '*Warne*' and '*wittan*' has to be translated and used as an explicit analogy to develop the present situation. The word '*smordis*' is no longer immediately charged with enough foreboding, is not at once comprehended ('verstanden'), but gathered ('vernommen'). But the German, too, by itself, needs the support of the world expressed by the Old Prussian for the narrated event to gain full poetic meaning – thus, for example, 'die Krähe hat keinen Baum' can only be understood in its full force when it is brought into connection with 'ich wohne in deinem Ohr'. One of the central features of the Old Prussian folk religion was the dependence of the family's fortunes on the health of the tree in which dwelt their protective spirit, which would often take the form of a bird and fly away when the tree was dying. The birds and their behaviour – to which Bobrowski frequently refers in his poetry – are an immediate and important pointer to the individual's fate, and their homes in trees signs of the family's fortune. Without Old Prussian's background of allusion, modern German is less directly poetic; without the explanation of modern German, the Old Prussian forgotten language is no longer comprehensible. In bringing the two together in this poem, Bobrowski has revitalised both and, at the same time, suggested the need for brotherhood.

One of the most attractive features about Bobrowski's work was his use of humour, whose special quality can be explained from words in an interview with Irma Reblitz that discuss his use of open form in narrative. This he preferred 'weil sie mir erlaubt, die Dinge so scharf nebeneinanderzustellen' (IV, p. 499), and implies a directed use of humour: 'Ich bring mit Vorliebe den Spaß herein in diese ernsthaften Geschichten und will damit so eine kleine Art Schocktherapie. Ich möchte den Hörer und den Leser zu einem Gelächter kriegen und möchte dann durch den Fakt, den ich dahintersetze, bewirken, daß ihm das Lachen im Hals steckenbleibt' (IV, p. 499). This can range from the punning use of a title e.g. the poem 'Chateau ohne Mäuse', i.e. Schloß Sanssouris (II, pp. 342–3), to the eighty or so 'Xenien' collected as *Literarisches Klima Ganz neue Xenien, doppelte Ausführung* (I, pp. 232–53). He matches such intellectual forms of humour with an earthier one in his prose texts, for instance in the description in *Levins Mühle* of grandfather going to the latrine at the bottom of the garden or the four episodes of *De homine publico tractatus* (IV, pp. 135–9), whether it be the means by which Petrat the post-office official can overcome Sunday closing and still sell Frau Krepsztakies a stamp without opening the post office, or how to get round the undignified action of licking stamps for every customer: 'Petrat führt daher ein: Brief hinlegen, Geld hinlegen, Zunge rausstrecken. An der herausgestreckten Zunge wird die Marke befeuchtet, Petrat braucht nur den Arm zu heben, die Marke liegt, gummierte Seite offen, auf Zeige- und Mittelfinger. Abstreifen, dann also Aufkleben, Stempeln, Aufwiedersehn' (IV, p. 137). Bringing the people what the state demands, while retaining the dignity of office, may demand some native cunning and sleight of hand, thus the introduction of radio to the village of Abschwangen:

Also läßt Petrat ausrufen: Heute abend Radio in der Post, Eintritt frei. Und steckt Briefträger Lemke mit seiner Ziehharmonika in den großen Schrank. Dann kommen die Leute, abends, und setzen sich hin, Petrat sagt: Radio fängt gleich an. Und Briefträger Lemke also spielt im Schrank, fein heimlich, es ist, als käme die Musik von weither, aus der Luft, von Berlin, auf diesen Wellen, wie Petrat gesagt hat (IV, pp. 137–8).

Examples of such applications of commonsense and practical wisdom show an understanding of human nature and a bringing down to earth of any false sense of superiority. They emphasise too Bobrowski's sympathy for some core of individuality in every person. The grandfather in *Levins Mühle* and the soldier in 'Mäusefest' (IV, pp. 47–9) are both sketched so that their harsher features are tempered by a humane streak, and the reader is bound to feel some sympathy for them. In every case humour is used to underline the unexpected, to insist on a form of freedom from stereotyping, to relieve the particular event or character from immediate restrictions and thus portray an extra dimension of common humanity.

Bobrowski highlights this streak of common humanity for instance in his depiction of the revolutionary artist figure in the short story 'Der Tänzer Malige' (IV, pp. 164–9) where Malige's independent dance totally defeats Leutnant Anflug's sadistic control over the local people, where the clown-figure in his individuality overcomes regimentation by military force. He uses it also to show the quiet confidence of Moise in 'Mäusefest', where at the centre of the story the mice return to find the breadcrust, and the narrator comments: 'Ein Mäusefest in kleinem Rahmen, versteht sich, nichts Besonderes, aber auch nicht ganz alltäglich' (IV, p. 48). The act of patient delaying holds up the Jew's fate, underscored by the final comment made by Moise to the moon (alias the narrator): 'Ich weiß . . ., da hast du ganz recht, ich werd Ärger kriegen mit meinem Gott' (IV, p. 49). We can smile at the ridiculous pettiness of the gesture, but the sense of peace created in this scene amidst the storm of the German advance into Eastern Europe reinstates the world of the little man, the world of intensity of living found on a private level.

Bobrowski's insistence on including the *comparatio tertius*, the perspective of the narrator, ensures that sentimentality is cut out, that the reader becomes aware of a directed form of detailed portrayal that serves to highlight the existence of different worlds of reality that co-exist. Perhaps the finest example of this comes in the longest of his shorter prose works, 'Boehlendorff' (IV, pp. 97–112), with its varied narrative techniques and sudden changes of perspective, never allowing the reader to feel he has found one underlying position on which to base a consistent interpretation. Furthermore, a glance at the so-called 'Doppelstücke' that Behrmann has listed where Bobrowski used parallel themes in prose and lyric form shows how this interpenetration of different levels in the same and in parallel works became a flexible instrument on which variants and counterpoints could be played out.[10] The 'Nebeneinander' is thus seen to be not only a social aim but also an essential part of Bobrowski's aesthetic practice. Furthermore, occasionally Bobrowski attempted to break free from his awareness of the closeness of earlier times and traditional forms, and the most obvious examples (three of the four pairs of Behrmann's 'Doppelstücke') show how the element of narrative seeks to overcome immersion into the past.

The undated poem 'Eichendorff' (II, p. 356), a work that Bobrowski did not publish, shows some of the techniques used in this sense of recall and readjustment in compressed form:

Eine Zeit der Brunnen
war und der Gärten – der Wald
ist wie ein Abend gekommen
vor ihm her ging der Efeu
die Erde in ihrer Tiefe
donnert von Strömen – ein Ruf
müßte aufstehen – das Horn
tönt und ich wend mich im Schlaf

Als ich erwachte ich fand
einen Weg um den Bergsturz ein Busch
war dort ich fing einen Vogel
er sang nicht so bin ich im Schlaf
so werd ich erwachen
zuletzt
so werd ich erwachen

The first part of the poem, typically, compresses a whole world of poetic images from an already highly structured work – Eichen-

10. These include on the theme 'Buxtehude': 'Nänie (I, 101)' and *D.B.H.* (IV, 68–72); 'Perun': *Die Taufe des Perun Kiew 988* (II, 327–8) and *Die Seligkeit der Heiden* (IV, 91–6); 'Zemaite': *Zemaite* (II, 292–3), *Gedenkblatt* (IV, 172–3) and Chapter 2 of *Litauische Claviere* (III, 244–58); 'Aufstand': *Der samländische Aufstand 1525* (II, 301–2), *Von nachgelassenen Poesien* (IV, 17–22) and Chapter 4 of *Litauische Claviere* (III, 275–289).

dorff's *Sehnsucht* – into eight lines that begin with Eichendorff's ending and work back as it were by association towards the beginning of Eichendorff's poem. This allows for a playful use of time-levels analogous to that of Eichendorff but leading to the all-important central word 'wend'. The past has been a dream whose sound-elements linger on in the bird's song of the second part, which however serve as a sort of reveille whose exact levels of reference to either the poetic self or as part of the reported song are deliberately vague. This produces an open form that suggests a potentially new situation emerging out of the memories of the past. In fact, this keynote of 'Wende' dominates as a structural element in many of Bobrowski's works. The central phrase or word in poetry and prose is often the key to interpretation, a point noted by many who have written on Bobrowski, but which has so far not been worked out in full and consequential detail. His intentions in general with such a device are at least implicit in words found in the interview 'Vom Hausrecht des Autors' (IV, pp. 474–7) of 17 November 1964 where he comes perhaps closest to defining his aims and methods as a writer:

> Ja, ich bin der Meinung, daß man zunächst einmal als zeitgenössischer Autor natürlich in jedem Sinne Gegenwartsliteratur schreibt, auch wenn man eine historische Erzählung macht. Natürlich gehört zur historischen Erzählung die Befassung mit dem Material. Nun, das Material – ich habe da einige Geschichten, bei denen das Material sehr spärlich fließt. Da ist man ohnehin angewiesen, sehr weit zu ergänzen und sehr frei damit zu verfahren. Ich glaube auch, daß es nicht Aufgabe des Schriftstellers ist, vergangene Zeit zu repräsentieren aus sich heraus, sondern immer von der Gegenwart her gesehen auf die Gegenwart hin wirkend, daß sich also diese Bereiche, der historische Bereich und die zeitgenossische Zeugenschaft, ständig durchdringen (IV, p. 475).

Narration, evocation of the past, bringing together past and present – such basic exercises make demands on the writer that require him to control the material through careful manipulation of the form: 'Es muß für den Erzähler Raum bleiben in diesen Dingen zwischen den Fakten, eine lückenlose Anordnung der Fakten tötet, glaube ich, das lebendige Erzählen (IV, p. 475).

'Das lebendige Erzählen' – that is the quality above all others to admire in Bobrowski's works, and this took several forms: whether in the potentially long lines of hexametric narrative in the poem 'Pruzzische Elegie', (I, p. 33) or in the trigonometric patterns of the novel *Litauische Claviere*, or in the idiosyncratic use of

'Das lebendige Erzählen': Johannes Bobrowski

thirty-four 'Sätze' in *Levins Mühle*, or in the shifting narrative perspectives of the story 'Boehlendorff' or in the rhythmic patterns of classical-type odes such as the 'Ode auf Thomas Chatterton', or in the fusion of Old Prussian and modern German in the poem 'Gestorbene Sprache' or in the controlled aperçus of the 'Xenien', or in the deliberately open form of the poem 'Eichendorff'. The freshness of Bobrowski's works depends on his success in keeping them free from nostalgia and sentimentality, his rare mastery of technical detail, knowledge of several historical atmospheres, a light touch and an eye for positive humanity. Because he was able to relate the individuality of neighbours and of neighbouring communities, of the past and of today's world to one another, he would no doubt have understood the anniversary year 1989 not as a reason for celebration but also as a challenge.

Secondary Material

Eberhard Haufe und Bernhard Gajek, *Johannes Bobrowski. Chronik – Einführung – Bibliographie*, Frankfurt am Main, 1977

Gerhard Rostin (ed.), *Johannes Bobrowski, Selbsterzeugnisse und neue Beiträge über sein Werk* Stuttgart, 1976, replacing the first version, Berlin, 1967.

For Bibliographies see:

Curt Grützmacher, *Das Werk von Johannes Bobrowski, Eine Bibliographie* Munich, 1974;

—— *Schattenfabel von den Verschuldungen. Johannes Bobrowski.Zur 20. Wiederkehr seines Todestages*, Berlin, 1985.

Among the monographs not otherwise mentioned in the notes see:

Dagmar Deskau, *Der aufgelöste Widerspruch. 'Engagement' und 'Dunkelheit' in der Lyrik Johannes Bobrowskis*, Stuttgart, 1975.

Brian Keith-Smith, *Johannes Bobrowski*, London, 1970.

Wolfram Mauser, *Beschwörung und Reflexion. Bobrowskis sarmatische Gedichte*, Frankfurt am Main, 1970.

Christoph Meckel, *Erinnerung an Johannes Bobrowski*, Düsseldorf, 1978.

Fritz Minde, *Johannes Bobrowski und die Tradition*, Frankfurt am Main, 1981.

J.P. Wieczorek, *Figures and Themes in the Work of Johannes Bobrowski* (Dissertation), Oxford, 1978.

Gerhard Wolf, *Beschreibung eines Zimmers. 15 Kapitel über Johannes Bobrowski*, Berlin, 1971.

Gerhard Wolf, *Johannes Bobrowski. Leben und Werk*, Berlin, 1982, first published 1967.

Also important is Peter Jokostra, *bobrowski and andere. Die Chronik des Peter Jokostra*, Munich, 1967.

−7−

Franz Fühmann:
A Neglected Legacy

Dennis Tate

In a volume intent on establishing the literary merits of the GDR's outstanding authors, the case of Franz Fühmann (1922–1984) is in some ways surprisingly difficult to argue. The impressive range of his creative output will be immediately evident to any reader who peruses the nine volumes of the Fühmann *Werkausgabe* published by the Hinstorff Verlag in Rostock. The selection of his work they represent covers the whole gamut of prose writing, from the traditional *Novelle* structures of his early war stories via unconventional autobiography to highly experimental 'dream stories'; a poetic *oeuvre* dominated by excellent translations of Czech and Hungarian modernists; reworkings of Greek myth, the *Nibelungenlied* and Shakespeare; a fascinating critical edition of the poetry of Georg Trakl; a volume of film scripts; and a collection of stimulating essays and interviews. A selection of his drama, including radio plays, ballet and opera, is promised, and there is much else of merit in his earlier published work which has slipped through the net of the *Werkausgabe*, notably *Die dampfenden Hälse der Pferde im Turm von Babel* (1978), a volume of language games ostensibly for children, which highlights his acute linguistic sensitivities as well as his congenial sense of humour.

Fühmann's role as a literary innovator is by now undisputed, even though his attempts as a young author in the Stalinist 1950s to revitalise socialist realist poetry with the help of techniques derived from the Expressionists, or to introduce passages of Freudian stream of consciousness into otherwise didactic portrayals of his war experience, may appear less than distinguished when viewed out of context.[1] They should, however, alert readers of Fühmann's

1. See my articles on Fühmann's early work, 'Franz Fühmann als Lyriker und

better known later work to the deep-rootedness of his sensitivity to the demands of authenticity and the criteria of modernism. The anguish caused to Fühmann by his inner conflict between political conformism and creative integrity drove him into alcoholism and almost killed him in the late 1960s, but when he finally resolved it around the beginning of the Honecker era in 1971, he emerged impressively into the forefront of cultural debate in the GDR. In the years between 1971 and his death from cancer in 1984 Fühmann articulated his now firm conviction that 'Literatur' had to take precedence over 'Ideologie'[2] with a courage and consistency matched only by Christa Wolf among the writers of his generation. In his essays and speeches he demonstrated the central importance to GDR culture of previously maligned German authors such as Georg Trakl, Ernst Barlach, Jean Paul Richter and E.T.A. Hoffmann, while seeking to transcend the national horizons of cultural heritage by urging a fresh critical engagement with the wider European legacy of Greek myth and the Bible. Not least because of his commitment to creative originality Fühmann also became a tireless advocate of the GDR's younger generation of authors – Uwe Kolbe, Wolfgang Hilbig, Wolfgang Hegewald and Christa Moog, amongst many others – who suffered acutely from the renewed conservatism of the SED's cultural politicians from the late 1970s onwards.

Fühmann's biography, when it is written, will provide an exemplary account of the corrosive impact of Stalinism on young converts to the cause who were motivated more by the horrors of Auschwitz than by the practice of Soviet communism, and of a lifelong struggle to make the GDR live up to its humanistic aspirations. Furthermore, his upbringing in the disputed 'Sudetenland' of Northern Czechoslovakia gives his turbulent life a Central European resonance of obvious current relevance, to which few other GDR authors – Johannes Bobrowski and Jurek Becker being amongst the obvious exceptions – can lay claim.

None of these factors alone could, however, justify close involvement with Fühmann's creative writing if, as is sometimes

---

Förderer der Lyrik in der DDR', in J.L. Flood (ed.), *Ein Moment des erfahrenen Lebens: Zur Lyrik der DDR*, Amsterdam, 1987, pp. 51–72, and '"Subjective authenticity" in Franz Fühmann's early prose writing', in M. Gerber et al. (eds), *Studies in GDR Culture and Society*, vol. 10, Lanham and New York, 1991, pp. 135–50.

2. See, for example, Fühmann's speech to the 1973 Writers' Congress, 'Literatur und Kritik', in his *Essays, Gespräche, Aufsätze 1964–1981*, Rostock, 1983, pp. 67–81.

hinted, he failed to produce work of enduring significance. Behind the almost universal respect expressed for Führmann as a personality and for his accessibility and perceptiveness as an essayist, there is a widespread reluctance to look seriously at an author who failed to write an undisputed masterpiece. Such reservations, to the extent that they emanate from the Federal Republic, may derive from at least partial ignorance, since the publication of Führmann's work there has been fragmented and incomplete, with no single publisher playing the co-ordinating role that Hinstorff has in the GDR since the early 1960s. English-speaking readers are, as usual, much worse off, having had nothing better so far than low-budget translations of Führmann's autobiographical volumes *Das Judenauto* (1962) and *Zweiundzwanzig Tage oder die Hälfte des Lebens* (1973) on which to judge his merits.[3] Great hopes were placed in the 'Bergwerkroman' at which Führmann was known to be working in the early 1980s, an ambitious meta-fictional project inspired by his regular visits to the Mansfeld copper mines in Thuringia. His narrative framework was to use the metaphorical associations of mining and writing as a point of departure, establishing a clear cultural link between Führmann's auto-biographical deliberations and German Romanticism's preoccu-pation with the theme of mining; the fictional core would then be provided by sequences of stories, in the Romantic tradition.[4] This massive undertaking was, however, thwarted by the onset of Führmann's cancer and had to be abandoned at a relatively early stage of its composition.

This failure at the eleventh hour to provide the major work which could have secured his reputation meant that Führmann never became, to use Wolfgang Hegewald's term, 'bestsellerverdächtig' in the West.[5] One response to this perceived deficiency has been to focus on the substantial sections of his prose writing and interviews which are broadly autobiographical and to define his achievement in terms of an unrelenting moral preoccupation with 'Vergangen-heitsbewältigung'.[6] The recent short monograph on Führmann by

---

3. Both appeared in the GDR's home-produced series of translations, Seven Seas Books, under the titles *The Car with the Yellow Star*, and *Twenty-Two Days or Half a Lifetime* respectively, but have been out of print for many years.
4. Ingrid Prignitz's afterword to the posthumous volume of Führmann's prose, *Das Ohr des Dionysios*, Rostock, 1985, provides a helpful reconstruction of his plan for the 'Bergwerkroman' (pp. 154–9). Hinstorff also has the manuscript fragment of Führmann's framework narrative (amounting to about 150 pages) which is likely to be published in due course.
5. 'Das Verhängnis der Poesie: Franz Führmann zum Gedächtnis', *Süddeutsche Zeitung*, 4 April 1987.
6. See, for example, Eberhard Mannack, '"Wie könnte ich je sagen, ich hätte

Uwe Wittstock devotes relatively little space to textual analysis, since Wittstock has an overriding psychological interest in Fühmann's inexhaustible efforts at self-analysis. In his conclusion Wittstock reserves his highest praise for Fühmann as an individual – 'Wie vielleicht kein anderer deutschsprachiger Autor seiner Generation hat er Trauerarbeit an der eigenen Vergangenheit und der seines Landes geleistet' – before referring briefly to the respect in which he is held as an 'Erzähler'.[7]

It is the latter assertion which still needs to be tested, and, in view of the uncertain status of Fühmann's longer autobiographical works as novels, it seems more fruitful to assess his creative achievement on the basis of the shorter prose which represents the main strand of continuity in his career. Many Western students of GDR literature will have made their initial acquaintance with Fühmann as the author of war stories such as 'Das Gottesgericht' (1958) and 'Die Schöpfung' (1966), included in the pioneering anthologies of the 1970s.[8] Far less attention has been paid to the body of Fühmann's shorter prose published after the decisive turning point of the late 1960s, after which the distinctive dramatic intensity of his narratives is no longer marred by the didactic finger-pointing of his earlier work. His later prose evolved in thematic cycles which, at first sight, bear little relation to one another: a first group, centrally concerned with the nature of Party authority in the contemporary GDR, were not published separately there in the aftermath of the infamous 'Biermann crisis' of 1976–7, in which Fühmann was prominently involved, although they did appear in the FRG under the title *Bagatelle, rundum positiv* in 1978;[9] the second collection, based on themes from Greek myth, appeared soon afterwards in both states as *Der Geliebte der Morgenröte*;[10] the third, and most surprising in the GDR context, involved reworkings of biblical stories and could only be identified as a related group after the publication of the posthumous collection *Das Ohr des Dionysios*

---

meine Vergangenheit bewältigt'': Beobachtungen zu Franz Fühmanns Dichtungen', in P.G. Klussmann and H. Mohr (eds), *Jahrbuch zur Literatur in der DDR*, vol. 3, Bonn, 1983, pp. 19–33.

7. Uwe Wittstock, *Franz Fühmann* (Autorenbücher), Munich, 1988, p. 85.

8. See H.-J. Schmitt (ed.), *19 Erzähler der DDR*, Frankfurt am Main, 1971, pp. 37–53, and L.-W. Wolff (ed.), *Fahrt mit der S-Bahn: Erzähler der DDR*, Munich, 1971, pp. 86–101.

9. The West German edition was published as a Suhrkamp paperback, Frankfurt am Main, 1978. See Author's Note at the end of this essay for key to all subsequent page references in the text.

10. First published by Hinstorff in 1978 and Hoffmann & Campe, Hamburg, in 1979.

in 1985.[11] Although it would be misleading to imply that these three cycles were chronologically discrete, or indeed that each represents the totality of Fühmann's work on that particular theme, their sequence does indicate a remarkable broadening of focus beyond the more parochial parameters of GDR *Kulturpolitik* – a development of growing significance as we begin to view the GDR in finite historical terms.

The qualitative turning-point in Fühmann's career as a writer of short prose is signalled by his abandonment of the subject matter on which his earlier reputation was based: his childhood as part of the German-speaking minority in Czechoslovakia and his wartime experiences in the German army. While the subjective honesty and the narrative force of his treatment of these themes should not be underestimated, the problem with most of the stories included in the volumes *Das Judenauto* (1962), *König Ödipus* (1966) and *Der Jongleur im Kino oder Die Insel der Träume* (1970) was the way they are predicated on the assumption that Fühmann's life had changed dramatically by the time the GDR was established in 1949. There are a few exceptions: *Barlach in Güstrow* and *Strelch* (both included in *König Ödipus*) provide darker hints that the power structures of the Third Reich have not yet become a thing of the past,[12] but it is only in the 1970s that the nature of Party authority in the GDR becomes a central concern of his shorter prose.

Characteristically, the first of these contemporary narratives, *Bagatelle, rundum positiv*, is also a profound self-criticism of his own earlier readiness to manufacture ideological propaganda from the flimsiest of evidence. It establishes a forthright first-person perspective and a clear commitment to depict everyday occurrences which reveal the failings of GDR socialism rather than the high-profile achievements glorified in the 'Bitterfelder Weg' literature of the period around 1960, when the events described actually took place. The narrative focus is on a ten-minute conversation with an industrial team leader ('Brigadier') whom the narrator had previously denounced in a newspaper article on the basis of hearsay and whom, as he now steadily realises, he has unjustifiably maligned. Despite acknowledging the irresponsibility of this 'Komplizenschaft mit der Betriebsleitung' (E, p. 485), the narrator ends up

11. Rostock, 1985. Much of the same material included in this edition was published in the FRG in the volume *Die Schatten*, Hamburg, 1986.
12. For a discussion of the ambiguous narrative structure of *Barlach in Güstrow*, see my article '"Subjective authenticity" in Franz Fühmann's early prose writing' (see note 1 above).

hiding behind the principle of Party collectivity and the fact that his article was 'rundum positiv' (E, p. 489). The original blame may lie with the unnamed manager, referred to throughout simply as 'der saloppe Kollege', who fed the narrator the incorrect story and is totally indifferent to the human consequences of his error; but the broader point about this 'beschämende Geschichte einer bewußten Selbsttäuschung'[13] is the length of time it has taken for the narrator to assume personal responsibility for his complicity.

Having exposed his own past irresponsibility in this way, Fühmann proceeded to focus his critical attentions on the continuing abuse of power by the SED élite and its isolation from the majority of the population. His 'Spiegelgeschichte' evidently arose directly from his visits to the Thuringian mines in the early 1970s. It is another densely composed 'kleine Geschichte' (E, p. 493), describing a sequence of events witnessed by chance at a reception for retired saltminers. The structure is again determined by precise references to the passing minutes, but with the focus now exclusively on the local Party secretary, observed through a mirror at the entrance to the clubhouse where the reception is taking place. His preparations for a piece of parochial power-play – deliberately arriving late to emphasise his importance – are minutely recorded with the full force of the narrator's irony, as are his reactions when this dramatic entrance is foiled by the absence of his subordinates, the trade union chairman and the firm's manager, as a result of a genuine emergency. Once the ritual has been disturbed, the mood turns nasty, with the Party secretary fulminating against his supposed inferiors when they do finally turn up: 'Ihr traut euch ja was! Die Partei warten zu lassen'. The narrator's devastatingly concise commentary speaks volumes: 'Wen? – Die Partei?? – Ihn???' (E, p. 503). The self-conscious awkwardness of the retired miners throughout the proceedings, the shy dignity with which they have endured their 'Leben im Salz' (E, p. 494), serves to highlight the political paralysis – 'Salzerstarrung' (E, p. 500) – which this obsession with hierarchy represents. The fact that the secretary is described as being 'sehr neu' (E, p. 507) is not an encouraging pointer to the potential for change in the Honecker era.

The most memorable of Fühmann's studies of the malaise of the one-party state is *Drei nackte Männer*, set in a Berlin sauna. Even in this supremely non-hierarchical environment, a trio of newcomers betray their status under the narrator's meticulous scrutiny of their

13. The phrase is Jürgen Engler's, from his review of *Erzählungen 1955–1975*, in *Sinn und Form*, vol. 30, no. 4, 1978, p. 889.

body language and their attitudes to those around them. There is no action, no dialogue, no ostensible link with the outside world, yet it rapidly becomes clear that one is a top-ranking Party functionary and the other two his bodyguards, shielding him from all possible contact with normal mortals who, even in the sauna, are viewed with suspicion. The ritual of this trio's progress through the various stages of the sauna evokes a similar sense of social paralysis in the narrator's mind as in the 'Spiegelgeschichte', expressed in this case in terms of his current aesthetic deliberations on the 'Unterschied zwischen lebendiger und erstarrter Form': he is convinced that such rituals reflect 'die Natur der Gesellschaft' (E, p. 513). Even after a succession of encounters between the three and the sauna's regular clientèle, the gulf is undiminished, and when the one attempt of their leader to crack a joke fails miserably, his basic arrogance becomes more pronounced: 'er sah uns alle in *einem* Blick an, gleichgültig, in lässiger Nichtbeachtung des einzelnen uns insgesamt abtuend' (E, p. 520). The only relief from an atmosphere which is in every sense 'gnadenlos' (E, p. 519) is the narrator's concluding fantasy of being waved to from their ministerial limousine on the street outside, then watching the car take flight and disappear into a multi-storey building. The likelihood of either of these events occurring is equally remote, on the evidence of what has gone before.

Fühmann blurred the distinctions between contemporary reality and futuristic fantasy even more in another collection of stories he began writing in 1974, the year when *Drei nackte Männer* was first published, and later entitled *Saiäns-Fiktschen*.[14] Despite the ostensible location of his narrative in the year 3456, in a world almost destroyed by two nuclear wars, there is a grim sense of continuity in the way the abuses of power depicted in the present-day context have now been taken to their logical conclusion in the Brave New World of Uniterr. Totalitarian control is now almost perfect, and the propaganda that this is 'die Wahrhaft Befreite Gesellschaft' where there is 'kein "Unten" und kein "Oben" mehr' (SF, p. 85) is reinforced by Orwellian mind-control, achieved by a panoply of 'Abhörgeräte', 'Gehirnprüfer' and 'Emotiographen'. The enemy in the unbridled capitalistic Libroterr is incessantly vilified in terms which only serve to expose the true nature of Uniterr, as the

14. First published in the GDR in 1981, but not so far in the FRG. For a discussion of these stories in the context of GDR science fiction, see J.H. Reid, 'En route to Utopia: Some visions of the future in East German literature', in *Renaissance and Modern Studies*, vol. 28, 1984, pp. 114–28.

Dennis Tate

narratorial irony underlines: Libroterr's population is floundering 'im drückenden Sklavenelend zügelloser Anarchie [. . .] ganz im Gegensatz zu Uniterr, wo, dank wohltuend unhohem Lebensniveau und ordnungserhaltendem Mangel an jener Unfriedensquelle, die man 'persönliche Rechte' nennt, das Volk in zufriedner Geborgenheit lebte' (SF, p. 113).

Saiäns-Fiktschen, however, seriously lacks focus in terms of characterisation, since Fühmann's authority-figures – 'der Anführer der Hauptstädtischen Kontrolltrupps', 'der Chefphilosoph', etc. – are highly abstract in comparison with the SED functionaries in his contemporary stories, while his trio of protagonists – Pavlo, Janno and Jirro – are largely interchangeable and, because of the repressive nature of Uniterr society, are only beginning to evolve their critical awareness. Fühmann's preface to *Saiäns-Fiktschen* is almost apologetic on this point, describing his protagonists as mere vehicles for the articulation of 'Bedrängnisse und Nöte' which he had not yet been able to represent in terms of coherent fictional characters (SF, p. 5), and making clear his determination not to continue writing in this vein.

A good illustration of the reasons for this self-criticism is provided in the final story of *Saiäns-Fiktschen*, 'Pavlos Papierbuch'. One of the few surviving books on Uniterr discovered by Pavlo is an anthology of 1998 which includes Franz Kafka's *In der Strafkolonie*. Pavlo's reading of this bewildering text by a totally unknown author is described in detail, with a mixture of textual quotation (a vital service to a GDR readership) and analysis of his reactions. It is a profoundly cathartic experience and supplies him with a key metaphor for the nature of Uniterr. Kafka's ambiguous ending, however, the flight of the panic-stricken traveller from the crisis he has helped to provoke, leaves Pavlo totally frustrated: 'Aber das war doch niemals ein Ende! Wo wurde denn erklärt, wer gut und wer schlecht war, wer recht und wer unrecht hatte, wem man nacheifern sollte und wen entlarven; wo war ein Fazit . . .? (SF, pp. 147–8) Ironically, part of the difficulty with *Saiäns-Fiktschen* lies precisely in the fact that it is rather too clear-cut, depending heavily on caricature and on the correlation between Uniterr and the worst features of the GDR: factors which make it less likely that the volume will exercise the spell over its readers which *In der Strafkolonie* exercises over Pavlo.

By the time he wrote 'Pavlos Papierbuch' Fühmann had, however, proved himself fully capable of conveying existential uncertainty through narrative structures as sophisticated as Kafka's. His involvement with the subject-matter of Greek myth since the 1960s gradually convinced him that there were limits to the creative potential of exposing corrupt authority structures. In a major essay of 1974, 'Das mythische Element in der Dichtung', he signalled his progression from 'Märchen' to 'Mythos', from all forms of writing seeking to impose a 'moralisches Koordinatensystem' on human experience to the expression of the 'tiefe Widerspruch der subjektiven Erfahrungen'.[15] The four mythical stories which followed the publication of 'Das mythische Element', collected under the title *Der Geliebte der Morgenröte*, show just how radical a progression this was.

On a first reading it might appear that Fühmann was simply continuing his onslaught on socialist authoritarianism using the subject matter of Greek myth as a convenient means of *Verfremdung*. The inner circle of the gods, collectively referred to in such all-embracing terms as 'die Oberen', 'die Hohen' and 'die Mächtigen', play the same kind of destructive role in the conflicts portrayed. Their laughter is a complacent defence mechanism against any threat to their sense of order (GM, pp. 377–8); Zeus prolongs the carnage of the Greek-Trojan war in order to cover up his change of mind as to who should be the victor (GM, pp. 351–2); the Immortals are incapable of sharing a loving relationship or admitting to self-doubts in the way that mere humans do (GM, p. 333), and so on. Yet Fühmann's focus is now far less on the disillusioning behaviour of the Olympian establishment than on the sufferings of those who come into contact with it. Two stories in particular, 'Marsyas' and 'Das Netz des Hephaistos', devoted to the dilemmas of mythical creative artists, provide the Kafkaesque intensity of self-analysis, unmitigated by any sense of moral or political certitude, which distinguishes the best of Fühmann's later fiction.

'Marsyas' is based on the myth of the unfortunate satyr who challenges Apollo to a musical contest and is flayed alive after he is adjudged to have lost.[16] Fühmann's account is narrated with the authority of a scholar who has closely examined all the earlier versions before arriving at his interpretation. The essential background details are sketched in with a clipped precision which allows maximum attention to be devoted to the protagonists and their confrontation. Marsyas is described sympathetically as an easy-going, sociable figure, a 'lustiger Saufkumpan' (GM, p. 356)

---

15. Included in Franz Fühmann, *Essays, Gespräche, Aufsätze 1964–1981*, pp. 82–140 (here pp. 93 and 115).
16. See Robert Graves, *The Greek Myths*, vol. 1, Harmondsworth, 1985, p. 77.

who, despite the physical deformities of a satyr (hooves, tail, donkey's ears and pot belly), has the creative talent to play the double flute with distinction. But the instrument has been cursed by its maker, the goddess Athene, and the guileless Marsyas ignores his dream-warnings to desist from competing with Apollo's lyre. It would be tempting to view Apollo, in view of the unspeakably cruel punishment he inflicts on Marsyas after the contest (a flaying recounted with unrelenting attention to its physical details), simply as a sadistic authority figure, and to assume a direct link between, say, the SED's handling of the 'Biermann Crisis' of 1976–7 and this shocking mistreatment of a non-conforming artist. But while Fühmann accepted that there was a contemporary political dimension to all of this,[17] his main interests lay elsewhere. Apollo is, after all, also the ultimate arbiter of artistic quality, and the protagonist of the story is quite clearly Marsyas.

It is at this point that the analogy with Kafka's narrative style can be shown to assist the process of interpretation: Fühmann is now transforming common metaphors into shocking literal truths in the manner Kafka pioneered in stories such as *In der Strafkolonie* or *Die Verwandlung*. The purpose of Apollo's punishment of Marsyas is to penetrate to the depths of his being – 'ihn ergründen' – in order to locate 'den Ort seiner Seele' and 'den Sitz seiner Überhebungskraft' (GM, p. 359). Is it hubris which impels this creature of the backwoods into creative endeavour which will be judged according to the highest aesthetic criteria? The narrator would have us believe this in his opening sentence – 'Marsyas war einer, der sich vermaß, mit Apollon in einen Wettkampf zu treten' (GM, p. 355) – yet even the most searching examination conceivable fails to locate Marsyas's soul and provide a clear verdict. The second fundamental question unforgettably posed by this story is whether Marsyas is capable of changing his nature: 'Könne [Marsyas] denn nicht aus seiner Haut?' (GM, p. 363). On the physical plane the answer to this conventionally unthreatening usage of metaphor is a resounding 'no': Marsyas's skin, like the rest of his immortal being, proves indestructible. Despite being scattered to the four corners of the earth, it never disappears, as a final comment of the narrator's disconcertingly suggests: 'und die Stücke am Weg, die wandern und wandern, vielleicht auch zur Sohle deiner Schuh' (GM, p. 368). For an author preoccupied as Fühmann was with the possibility of dramatic personality change ('Wandlung'), this image finally ac-

17. See 'Miteinander reden', Fühmann's interview of 1980 with Margarete Hannsmann, *Essays, Gespräche, Aufsätze*, pp. 429–57 (here pp. 449–50).

knowledges the deep-rootedness of identity and the impossibility of excising his earlier fascist or Stalinist 'selves'. In terms of his creative writing, however, 'Marsyas' provides incontrovertible proof of his success in shaking off the didactic urges which undermined so much of it before the 1970s.

Further confirmation that this cycle of mythical stories represents Fühmann's breakthrough into literary significance beyond the parameters of GDR cultural debate is supplied by 'Das Netz des Hephaistos', another relentless examination of the validity of creative endeavour and the motivation of the artist. Hephaestus, the crippled smith-god, is undisputedly a craftsman of the highest order, and Fühmann's interest in him, in the context of his planned 'Bergwerkroman', derives from Hephaestus's skill, when he descends into his underground workshop, in transforming rare metals into beautiful artefacts.[18] Yet the reason why Hephaestus is spurred on to create his invisible net from a uniquely pure metal is the desire to humiliate his wife Aphrodite and her lover Ares by trapping them *in flagrante delicto*. While the account of Hephaestus producing his net (GM, pp. 371–4) creates a powerful utopian vision of artistic labour as self-realisation,[19] its proposed use devalues his achievement, as the gods indicate by their derisive laughter. To them the net is only the invention of a cripple seeking to compensate for his disability. Furthermore, the price paid by Hephaestus for acceptance into the inner circle of the Immortals is now seen to have been catastrophically high. Having chosen to abandon the struggle led by his revolutionary friend Prometheus on the side of those who are 'das Andere zu den Oberen' (GM, p. 380), he has returned to a life of servitude on Mount Olympus. His final humiliation is being compelled to forge the indestructible manacles which will bind Prometheus to his rock in the Caucasus. This ironical narrative effectively highlights the contradictions inherent in all creative endeavour, while justifying its own existence in terms of the subtlety with which Fühmann has reworked his mythical source material.

While he continued to reinterpret mythic themes after the publication of *Der Geliebte der Morgenröte*, the final phase of Fühmann's career as a writer of short prose is marked by another pioneering departure, even more at odds with the conventional image of the

18. See Graves, *The Greek Myths*, vol. 1, pp. 86–8.
19. A good analysis of this story is included by Joseph Pischel in his review of the *Werkausgabe* volume of Fühmann's mythical texts, in *Neue Deutsche Literatur*, vol. 29, no. 7, 1981, pp. 147–154.

East German author. After completing his illuminating study of Georg Trakl, *Vor Feuerschlünden* (1982), he turned his attentions to the Bible, producing in a matter of months two important new stories, for what he envisaged as another 'Bändchen à la Morgenröte', and an equally remarkable essay 'Meine Bibel'.[20] Since the 1960s he had toyed with the idea of reworking a series of Old Testament stories for younger readers, as a complement to his versions of the *Iliad* and the *Odyssey*, and he had completed an account of the story of Abraham and Isaac, 'Erzvater und Satan', which remained unpublished. It was only in the early 1980s, in the face of the escalating threat of nuclear war between the superpowers, that he managed to overcome his reservations regarding the appropriateness of biblical subject-matter. At the 'Berliner Begegnung zur Friedensförderung' of December 1981, which brought together leading authors from both German states in protest against the renewed arms race, there were reminders of the religious basis of their convictions in, for example, Günter de Bruyn's reference to the Sermon on the Mount and the expressions of support for independent peace initiatives in the GDR, which were being co-ordinated around the slogan 'Schwerter zu Pflugscharen'.[21]

Fühmann's immediate response to this profound sense of crisis was to write 'Der Mund des Propheten', a text which shows him willing, under these extreme circumstances, to overcome the ambivalence regarding the validity of his creative writing articulated in 'Marsyas' and 'Das Netz des Hephaistos'. In his essay 'Meine Bibel' Fühmann was to justify his switch from mythical to biblical themes in terms of the ethical dimension of the latter – the assumption of individual responsibility for one's actions and the scope for changing one's ways – which he contrasted to the immutability of Fate in myth.[22] Thus we find the prophet, called Micha by the narrator as a tribute to his responsibility for the 'swords to ploughshares' vision included in a later part of the Old Testament story, prevailing courageously here against the ruthless power-politics of Ahab and Jezebel.[23] The narrative style is more direct than in the mythical stories, focussing on the essential conflict as rigorously as the latter, and now seeking to dramatise it through sustained dialogue without attempting to justify interpretative nuances. Fühmann sees

20. See Ingrid Prignitz's afterword to *Das Ohr des Dionysios*, pp. 151–4.
21. See *Berliner Begegnung zur Friedensförderung: Protokolle des Schriftstellertreffens am 13/14 Dezember 1981*, Darmstadt, 1982, esp. pp. 80–82 and 101–3.
22. *Das Ohr des Dionysios*, pp. 126–31.
23. The biblical story can be traced in *I Kings* xxi–xxii.

no reason to redefine the villainy of Ahab or Jezebel's image as a heartless schemer, and makes it clear that the rulers of the 'Südreich' which they are attempting to overwhelm are no better. He is more concerned here with the conflict between Micha, as the lonely voice of the truth, and the legions of corrupt court prophets, and with the resonance of Micha's condemnations of Ahab's regime. Even though the execution of this particular Micha on the orders of the king of the victorious southern state inevitably follows the latter's rejection of the utopian vision of a world without weapons, the narrator concludes on a note of reassurance that every generation produces its prophets of truth to continue the struggle.

To deduce from this expression of hope that Fühmann's move towards biblical themes heralds a sustained change of tone would, however, be mistaken. His other Old Testament story of 1982, 'Amnon und Tamar', which he referred to as 'dies Stückchen Ungeheuerlichkeit' (OD, p. 152), is centred on human suffering for which no relief is in sight. It also involves, in contrast to 'Der Mund des Propheten', a radical reinterpretation of the original text, in this case the story of King David's children Amnon, Absalom and Tamar.[24] In the original, Amnon's act of incest with his half-sister Tamar provokes her brother Absalom into murdering Amnon in revenge, while Absalom dies some years later in an insurrection against his father's kingdom. Fühmann complicates the brotherly relationship by portraying Amnon as the peace-loving heir to David's throne, who attracts Absalom's jealous hatred long before the incest occurs. He also suggests that Absalom is just as aroused by his sister as Amnon is, and he later reverses the outcome of the struggle between the two brothers, showing the victorious Amnon by now just as corrupted by the lust for power as Absalom has been throughout. However much the names of Israel's leaders may change in this brutal era, 'ein Wechsel der Herrschaft' (OD, p. 43) is nowhere in sight.

Fühmann's main interest lies in the figure of Tamar, whose fate after her violation by Amnon and subsequent rejection is entirely omitted from the Old Testament account. Tamar is portrayed here as a woman with powerful sexual needs, reciprocally attracted to both her brothers, although she alone is determined to resist the temptations of incest. Tamar's solution to her sexual dilemma regarding Absalom provides the story with a central poetic motif, deriving from a linguistic association in Fühmann's mind: she

24. See *II Samuel* xiii–xviii. Another interpretation of this story is provided by Stefan Heym in *Der König David Bericht*, Berlin, 1977, Ch. 20–23.

agrees to let their eyes embrace every morning as the first ray of the
sun strikes a nearby tamarisk tree. The delicate beauty and the
subtle changes of colour in the tamarisk leaves are juxtaposed
through the story with the catalogue of misery which befalls Tamar
after her moment of sexual fulfilment with Amnon: rejection,
humiliation, exploitation, the forlorn hope of rescue by Absalom,
and the hardship of a kitchen-maid's existence. She survives her
brothers, however, and she alone dies a dignified death, achieving a
special immortality through the tamarisk which, as the story's final
sentence assures us, 'grünt noch heute' (OD, p. 43).

Fühmann's hopes of completing a volume of biblical stories with
the emotional force and the poetic delicacy of 'Amnon und Tamar'
were dashed, like so many other of his plans, by his terminal
illness. He intended to incorporate these two biblical stories
together with an account of the relationship between Jonathan and
David, and the story of Rahab, within the narrative framework of
his 'Bergwerkroman', in thematic groupings involving similar
numbers of mythical and contemporary stories (OD, pp. 158–9). In
the absence of that ambitious multi-dimensional work, our assessment of Fühmann's achievement depends all the more on the extent
to which the stories in these three thematic categories which he
completed in the last decade of his life stand up to individual
scrutiny. The critical neglect up to now of stories of the quality of
'Drei nackte Männer', 'Marsyas' and 'Amnon und Tamar' may
derive from narrow thematic preconceptions of what represents
GDR literature. If that is the case, then there is every reason to
anticipate that one of the cultural consequences of the demise of the
GDR will be a new openness to the innovative richness of Franz
Fühmann's shorter prose.

Author's Note

The following editions and abbreviations are used for Fühmann's work:
E: *Erzählungen 1955–1975*, Rostock, 1977.
GM: *Irrfahrt und Heimkehr des Odysseus. Prometheus. Der Geliebte der
Morgenröte und andere Erzählungen*, Rostock, 1980.
OD: *Das Ohr des Dionysios. Nachgelassene Erzählungen*, Rostock, 1985.
SF: *Saiäns-Fiktschen*, Leipzig, 1985.

Secondary Material

Klaus Antes, '"Schreiben ist doch im Grunde die Erfahrung des Scheiterns". Im Gespräch mit Franz Fühmann', in *die horen*, 27, 1982, 4, pp. 73–8.

Hans Joachim Bernhard, 'Franz Fühmann', in Geerdts et al. (eds), *Literatur der Deutschen Demokratischen Republik in Einzeldarstellungen*, vol. 1, Berlin, 1974, pp. 279–96.

Stephan Brockmann, 'The possibility of possibility in Franz Fühmann's *Saiäns-Fiktschen*', in Gerber et al. (eds) *Studies in GDR Culture*, 8, pp. 191–203.

Günther Deicke et al., Weg der Wandlung. Franz Fühmann. 1922–1984', *Neue Deutsche Literatur*, 32, no. 11, 1984, pp. 122–133.

Malcolm Humble, 'Myth and ideology in Franz Fühmann's *König Ödipus*, in *Forum for Modern Language Studies*, 20, 1984, pp. 247–62.

Horst Lohr, 'Vom Märchen zum Mythos. Zum Werk von Franz Fühmann', in *Weimarer Beiträge*, 28, 1982, pp. 62–82.

Hans Richter, 'Vermächtnisse Fühmanns. Zum postum Erschienenen', in Rönisch (ed.), *DDR-Literatur im Gespräch*, Berlin, 1987, pp. 199–214.

Hans Richter, 'Das Beispiel Franz Fühmann. Zur DDR-Literatur des letzten Jahrzehnts', in Chiarloni, et al. (eds), *Literatur der DDR 1976–1986*, Akten Pisa, 1988, pp. 169–176.

Marianne Scharenberg, 'Franz Fühmanns *Der Geliebte der Morgenröte*. Zu Fühmanns Arbeit mit dem Mythos', in *Weimarer Beiträge*, 33, 1987, pp. 18–39.

Andreas Schrade, 'Veränderungen im Gegenstand – Veränderungen im Erzählen? Franz Fühmann's Erzählungen aus den 70er Jahren', in *Weimarer Beiträge*, 28, 1982, pp. 83–101.

Horst Simon (ed.), *Zwischen Erzählen und Schweigen. Franz Fühmann zum 65.*, Rostock, 1987.

Uwe Wittstock, *Franz Fühmann* (Autorenbücher), Munich, 1988.

Christa Wolf, 'Über Franz Fühmann. Gedenkrede', *Freibeuter*, no. 21, 1984, pp. 1–6.

Giusi Zanasi, 'Die Spirale der Wandlung. Bemerkungen zu Franz Fühmanns Erfahrung mit Dichtung', in *Literatur der DDR 1976–1986*, Akten Pisa, 1988, pp. 207–15.

Truth, Language and Reality in Christa Wolf

Ricarda Schmidt

Christa Wolf is the GDR writer who is best known and most widely translated in the West. Until the summer of 1990, when the publication of her story *Was bleibt* – an account of her surveillance by the East German secret police some ten years earlier[1] – provoked a public debate about Wolf's stance as a writer within GDR socialism, she had enjoyed a considerable reputation as a moral institution in both East and West Germany. Her fictional writing and essays are serious, moralistic, reflective, self-reflective, but were criticised repeatedly within the GDR for their difficulty and lack of a positive outlook. This criticism demonstrates that, though a loyal (yet critical) advocate of socialism, Christa Wolf has always broken official taboos. Indeed, in her later work, she adopts a more fundamental critique of socialism as practiced in the GDR. This not only tells us something about the development of the GDR, but emcompasses changes in the writer's relationship towards reality which provide insights of a much more fundamental nature about literature and society. I will here trace Wolf's increasingly radical questioning of social reality by examining a recurrent concern in her writing: the notion of truth embodied in the nexus between language and reality.

Wolf's first major work, *Der geteilte Himmel* (1963) tells the love story of an enthusiastic, warm-hearted young woman, Rita, and a disillusioned man, Manfred, in the reconstruction period. While Rita becomes drawn into a collective of workers and shares in the spirit of constructing a better world on socialist principles, Manfred is frustrated in his attempts to contribute to social

1. See, for instance, 'Was bleibt. Bleibt was? Pro und Contra: eine ZEIT-Kontroverse über Christa Wolf und ihre neue Erzählung' in *Die Zeit*, 1 June 1990, p.63.

development, and eventually decides to leave for West Germany. Faced with the decision between love, and life in a society that has a utopian vision, Rita leaves Manfred and returns to the GDR just before the Wall is built.

The novel combines a conventional rounded plot with experimentation with narrative techniques new in the GDR at the time, such as flashbacks and shifts in the point of view, which allow the portrayal of more subjective experiences. Yet, figural narration and inner monologue are, sometimes clumsily, interrupted by an omniscient narrator, who provides the 'right' perspective on things, and who has already, in the introduction, prepared the tone for the positive, though not happy, ending: deadly dangers are mentioned, but they are overcome, and trust in life has been regained, states the omniscient narrator, using an undefined first person plural pronoun that can include not only narrator, heroine and people in 'the city' the narrative is set in, but also the GDR readership: 'Wir gewöhnen uns wieder, ruhig zu schlafen. Wir leben aus dem vollen, als gäbe es übergenug von diesem seltsamen Stoff Leben, als könnte er nie zu Ende gehen' (G, p. 8).

The fact that the omniscient narrator's introduction precludes the heroine's evaluation of her decision indicates that 'the truth' as seen in this story exists independently of the individual. At the end of her recollecting, her mentor Schwarzenbach says that he came to hear from her, and, indirectly received, an answer to the question: 'Hat es Sinn, die Wahrheit, die man kennt, immer und unter allen Umständen zu sagen?' (G, p. 253). While the 'truth' he knows refers directly to the critique of party dogmatism in teaching, the context implies also the known 'truth' of socialism as the social order which one should acknowledge in its superiority over other social orders, even if, like Rita, one might find oneself in a situation where a denial of that 'truth' would make a difficult decision easier and favour personal inclinations.

Schwarzenbach (expressing Rita's thoughts and functioning as a mouthpiece for the omniscient narrator) tautologically defines the moral superiority of socialism as its capacity for confronting the truth for the first time in history: 'Zum erstenmal sind wir reif, der Wahrheit ins Gesicht zu sehen [. . .] Die reine nackte Wahrheit, und nur sie, ist auf die Dauer der Schlüssel zum Menschen. Warum sollen wir unseren entscheidenden Vorteil freiwillig aus der Hand legen?' (G, p. 254) Since socialism is thus doubly equated with truth, it comes as no surprise that the heroine, in looking back at her despair when she left her lover in the West, can only see her past state of mind as an illness and her present hope in a socialist future as calling things by their proper name (cf. G, p. 260). These proper names exist independently of her, are merely revealed in time. Heinz-Dieter Weber called this a 'vorkritische[r] Umgang mit der Vergangenheit'.[2] Truth is portrayed as preceding subjective insight, things and language form a unity. The claims of ideology are thus confirmed in this story, in spite of its criticisms of isolated aspects of real socialism and in spite of its not fulfilling all the requirements of the then dominant literary concept of socialist realism.

Ironically, moreover, the opposition 'krankhaft' vs. 'richtig'(= 'gesund') recalls Goethe's phrase of romanticism as illness and classicism as health, which Christa Wolf in her later writing strongly rejects for its blindness to the restrictive social conditions the Romantic writers were struggling against. In *Der geteilte Himmel*, Christa Wolf follows for the last time the classical example of integrating an individual into society.

In her subsequent work, *Nachdenken über Christa T.* (1968), Wolf leaves behind the authoritarian stance, the insistence on possessing the truth. Here we encounter for the first time the tone that is so uniquely Christa Wolf's: those characteristic elliptical sentences, those searching formulations which alternate with subjective insights expressed aphoristically. This text is about an outsider, Christa T., because Wolf has come to believe that society needs what this outsider has to offer, although her importance does not lie in her achievement, but in her being. Moreover, the subject of this narrative is not the life story of Christa T., but rather – as Wolf herself explained in 'Selbstinterview'[3] – the first-person narrator's recalling and reflecting on her dead friend. In this text Wolf introduces her unique contribution to contemporary literature, the category of subjective authenticity. Subjective authenticity means the inclusion of the author's experiences in fiction, though not on a superficial factual level, but rather in the sense of an inclusion of the insights gained by the author in reflecting on her experiences. In this process, the identities of the heroine, the first-person narrator and the author are not clearly separated. The borders between them are blurred, yet upheld in a fluid tension in which the construction of identity appears as an open process just like the search for truth. The text refuses narrative certainty, for 'Die Farbe der Erinnerung trügt' (N, p. 7).

2. Heinz-Dieter Weber, '"Phantastische Genauigkeit". Der historische Sinn der Schreibart Christa Wolfs', in Wolfram Mauser (ed.), *Erinnerte Zukunft. 11 Studien zum Werk Christa Wolfs*, Würzburg, 1985, p.89.
3. Christa Wolf, 'Selbstinterview', in Christa Wolf, *Die Dimension des Autors*, Darmstadt and Neuwied, 1987, p.32.

Christa T., while feeling a deep affinity with the aspirations of GDR socialism in the postwar years cannot experience the longed-for self-realisation promised by that society. Her alienation is expressed in an awareness of an incongruity between words and things, or, in more political terms, between ideological proclamations and reality: 'Sie zweifelte ja, inmitten unseres Rausches der Neubenennungen, sie zweifelte ja an der Wirklichkeit von Namen, mit denen sie doch umging; sie ahnte ja, daß die Benennung kaum je gelingt und daß sie dann nur für kurze Zeit mit dem Ding zusammenfällt, auf das sie gelegt wurde' (N, p. 37).

Yet, Christa T.'s mistrust of language is only partial. She needs words, more precisely written words, to work through her experiences. The narrator quotes from Christa T.'s diary: *'Daß ich nur schreibend über die Dinge komme!'* (N, p. 36). But Christa T. never realises her talents. The narrator speculates on the disillusionment about the gulf between words and reality which might have prevented Christa T. from trying to become a professional writer: 'Ich frage mich sogar, ob man zu früh davon erfahren und für immer entmutigt werden, ob man zu früh klarsichtig, zu früh der Selbsttäuschung beraubt sein kann. So daß man verzichtet und die Dinge ihrem Lauf überläßt (N, p. 35f.). The kind of linguistic and social naivety that was displayed in *Der geteilte Himmel* is here overcome and yet, as is indicated by the repetition of 'zu früh', preserved by being accredited a strengthening – though temporary – function. 'Einmal im Leben, zur rechten Zeit, sollte man an Unmögliches geglaubt haben' (N, p. 53), the narrator states apodictically in defence of this particular kind of blindness.

Beyond this youthful idealism, the narrator unfolds complex relations between language and knowledge, language and perception. Language is seen as a means of discovering reality: 'denn man weiß nicht wirklich, was noch nicht ausgesprochen ist' (N, p. 45). And yet language can never hope to convey the full complexity of reality, since its linearity inevitably simplifies the tangled web of reality (a problem Wolf will raise again in each of her subsequent books):

Wie man es erzählen kann, so ist es nicht gewesen. Wenn man es aber erzählen kann, wie es war, dann ist man nicht dabeigewesen, oder die Geschichte ist lange her, so daß einem Unbefangenheit leichtfällt. Allein daß man trennen muß und hintereinanderreihen, um es erzählbar zu machen, was in Wirklichkeit miteinander vermischt ist bis zur Unlösbarkeit . . . (N, p. 65)

Christa T., while insisting on the humanist utopian promise of socialism in the face of an increasingly technocratic society whose citizens have become opportunistic, has difficulties in expressing her sense of herself in language: 'Über die Schwierigkeit, ich zu sagen' (N, p. 165) is a key statement of Christa T.'s which the narrator mentions repeatedly. For 'ich' in this emphatic sense is not merely referential but utopian, it signifies the self as it could be, the fulfilled self. In search of self-realisation and afraid of not achieving it, Christa T. talks

> vorsichtshalber in der dritten Person, man selbst kann es sein oder irgendeine, die man zum Beispiel "sie" nennt. Von der kann man vielleicht eher wieder loskommen, muß sich nicht hineinziehen lassen in das *Unglück ihres falschen Lebens*, man kann sie neben sich stellen, sie gründlich betrachten, wie man sich angewöhnt hat, andere zu betrachten. (N, p. 113)

Pronouns as a means of distancing oneself – this is an insight that also applies to the narrator of *Christa T.*, and, in a slightly varied way, to Christa Wolf as the author of *Kindheitsmuster*, thus pointing to Christa Wolf's increasing refinement in working through certain basic recurrent topics.

The insistent questioning of social reality from the point of view of one who could not fully adapt to it is provided with a silver lining at the end, and, significantly, not through a change in the individual, but a change in society which gains in insight: 'Es beginnt, was sie so schmerzhaft vermißt hatte: daß wir uns selber sehen' (N, p. 177). Since the narrator had insisted on self-knowledge as the basis for a humanitarian society, this implies optimism about the potential of GDR society to realise its utopian aim. The narrator can finish her confrontation with the shortcomings of her society with an optimistic trust that time will provide the proper words: 'auch Worte haben ihre Zeit und lassen sich nicht aus der Zukunft hervorziehen nach Bedarf. Zu wissen, daß sie einmal dasein werden, ist viel' (N, p. 180).

In *Christa T.*, the openness of the process of remembering and reflecting is thus counteracted by a clinging to cherished convictions: Wolf's belief in the potential of GDR society to bring about a closing of the gap between words and things.

---

4. Cf. Jeanette Clausen, 'The Difficulty of Saying I as Theme and Narrative Technique in the Works of Christa Wolf', in *Amsterdamer Beiträge*, vol. 10, 1980, pp. 319–33.

Ricarda Schmidt

Kindheitsmuster (1976) continues to explore modes of subjective authenticity. It is a novel which examines Wolf's own childhood in the Nazi period, but the autobiographical element is distanced by narration in the third and second persons and by the intertwining of three time levels: a childhood from 1933–47, a journey in 1971 to the narrator's birthplace which now lies in Poland, and reflections on writing, memory, the past, and contemporary political events during the period of writing this novel between 1972 and 1975. The childhood level is narrated in the third person because the narrator experiences herself as so different from her childhood self that the pronoun 'I' could not encompass both. The narrator makes use of 'Form als Möglichkeit, Abstand zu gewinnen' (KM, p. 154) to support her in the painful exploration of a younger self deeply tainted by Nazi ideology. It is a memory that had long been suppressed. Moreover, it did not fit in with the official GDR view of having had succession to an anti-fascist tradition. But a temporary relaxation in the political atmosphere at the beginning of the Honecker era probably contributed to making it possible to work through a traumatic, repressed past (cf. KM, p. 90) in an authentic experimental manner: 'indem man sich mit ins Spiel bringt und den Einsatz nicht zu niedrig hält. . . . Ein Spiel in und mit der zweiten und dritten Person, zum Zwecke ihrer Vereinigung' (KM, p. 149).

What the narrator discovers about the past is not the secure knowledge of an ultimate truth but rather the subjectivity and relativity of our notion of truth: 'daß das Gedächtnis kein festgefügter Block ist, der in unserem Gehirn unveränderlich festsitzt; eher schon, falls große Worte erlaubt sind, ein wiederholter moralischer Akt' (KM, p. 135). The narrator recognises this moral act of remembering as essential for a utopian vision. Connecting the personal and the political, she reconstructs how her former self learned to modify her perception and her moral feeling in such a way that she could 'honestly' make Nazi reality coincide with Nazi propaganda. Yet the narrator avoids a black-and-white picture in which the lies of the past would set off the truth of the present. She recognises that truth is not pure, that even her present insights, so painfully gained, are not objective:

Da aber die Mitteilung zum Wesen der Wahrheit gehört, produziert er [der Schreiber], oft zweifelnd, eine vielfach gebundene Wahrheit: an sich selbst gebunden, den Mitteilenden, und den immer begrenzten Freiheitsraum, den er sich abgezwungen hat; gebunden an den, über den er aussagt, und nicht zuletzt an jene, denen die Mitteilung gilt und die man nur warnen kann: Nicht 'rein' – mehrfach getrübt ist die Wahrheit, die

sie erreicht, und sie selbst werden sie, durch Urteil und Vorurteil, noch
einmal verunreinigen. So mag sie brauchbar sein. (KM, p. 296)

Moreover, the present is still not a framework that would encourage the expression of everything one has experienced. The narrator
has won the freedom to be critical of some aspects of her society,
but at the time of writing there are still many taboos she can only
hint at or name rather than examine, for reasons of both external
and internal censorship.[5] Under the heading of autumn crises (KM,
p. 153), she mentions the years '56, '61, '68 without any comment.
Most European readers would be able to decipher them as referring
to the Russian suppression of the Hungarian uprising, the building
of the Wall, and the suppression of the Prague Spring, where GDR
tanks were also involved. More explicit is the reference to the
Moscow trials of 1937 as a taboo area the narrator has become
conscious of (cf. KM, pp. 138f., 228f.), yet is unable to confront.

Dealing with memories of an atrocious and strongly suppressed
past leads the narrator to reflect not only on political and philosophical problems of voicing the truth and the morality of writing
instead of acting (cf. KM, pp. 159f.) but above all to explore
psychological aspects. 'Überhören, übersehen, vernachlässigen,
verleugnen, verlernen, verschwitzen, vergessen' (KM, p. 141) are
now recognised as typical mechanisms (not only of the Nazi
period) that serve to shut out what one does not want to know.

The narrator realises that feelings, even in that zone where they
come into being, before language is mingled with them, are not
unmediated and pure, but, in her childhood at least, contained
calculation and repression. She also becomes aware of the socialis-
ing, conservative force of language: 'die Einsicht, daß die Sprache,
indem sie Benennungen erzwingt, auch aussondert, filtert: im
Sinne des Erwünschten. Im Sinne des Sagbaren. Im Sinne des
Verfestigten' (KM, p. 215) leads to a process of self-censorship
which further threatens the 'truth': 'Zu genau weißt du, was dir
schwerfallen darf, was nicht. Was du wissen darfst, was nicht.
Worüber zu reden ist und in welchem Ton. Und worüber auf
immer zu schweigen' (KM, p. 255).

Nevertheless, the narrator tries to push the boundaries of what
can be said out against the numbing of areas of feeling and memory
which results from the continuing struggle between two opposing
tendencies: 'Der Hang zur Übereinstimmung. Die Anstrengung,

---

5. Cf. the narrator's reflection on self-censorship as the most common and
general experience, pp. 211f.

dagegen anzuleben' (KM, p. 358). Since language in the Nazi period was so blatantly at odds with reality, the narrator has learnt to pay attention to subconscious levels of knowledge/feeling which convey a truth denied by words. She understands illness as a psychosomatic expression of our deeper repressed concerns and throughout her narrative has included dreams she had while working on this book in order to incorporate subconscious levels of feeling/knowledge/truth. Following the subverted quotation from Wittgenstein, 'Wovon man nicht sprechen kann, darüber muß man allmählich zu schweigen aufhören' (KM, p. 167), *Kindheitsmuster* extends the limits of what can be said without claiming to have overcome them. It ends with the sentence: 'Sicher, beim Erwachen die Welt der festen Körper wieder vorzufinden, werde ich mich der Traumerfahrung überlassen, mich nicht auflehnen gegen die Grenzen des Sagbaren' (KM, p. 378).

Between the writing of *Kindheitsmuster* and her next book, *Kein Ort. Nirgends* (1979), Wolf experienced a severe rupture in her relationship to the state, in her utopian vision and in her view of her role as a writer. The expulsion of the song-writer Wolf Biermann from the GDR in 1976 and the subsequent authoritarian stance of the Party shook Wolf's belief in socialism. It became clear to her and other writers that the state no longer needed them, and to work through this realisation she turned to historical figures.

The early nineteenth-century writers Heinrich von Kleist and Karoline von Günderrode, who both committed suicide, are portrayed as precursors of the (unsuccessful) struggle of later writers (Wolf herself) to defend humanitarian ideals against restrictive social conditions.

In a complex narrative with subtly shifting viewpoints,[6] which creates an early nineteenth-century tone by incorporating many extracts from the correspondences of the two main characters, Wolf imagines a meeting between Kleist and Günderrode. In these two figures she paradigmatically explores alienation at the beginning of the bourgeois era. It was a time that promised, but failed to realise, the ideals of 'Liberté, Egalité, Fraternité'. Kleist and Günderrode find a common bond in their refusal to adapt to conventional notions of propriety, behaviour and truth. Kleist criticises the state's utilitarian notion of truth (cf KON, p. 88). Günderrode, like Wolf herself, defines truth subjectively: 'alles,

6. Cf. Linda Dietrick, 'Appropriating Romantic Consciousness: Narrative Mode in Christa Wolf's *Kein Ort. Nirgends*', in Michael S. Batts et al. (eds), *Echoes and Influences of German Romanticism*, Frankfurt am Main, 1987, pp. 211–23.

was wir aussprechen, muß wahr sein, weil wir es empfinden: Da haben Sie mein poetisches Bekenntnis' (KON, p. 45).

Neither of them can achieve a harmonious relationship with society. This is the time of early industrialisation in Germany, of specialisation, fragmentation, absolutism, militarism, war; the time when women begin to become aware of themselves but have no role in public life. Inner monologues confront us with the (gender-specific) external difficulties of both protagonists. But even more shattering are the ambiguities and insoluble double-bind feelings the two writers discover in themselves. Kleist's unhappiness consists in the knowledge, 'von Bindungen abzuhängen, die mich ersticken, wenn ich sie dulde, und die mich zerreißen, wenn ich mich löse' (KON, p. 52). Günderrode names as her most difficult experience, 'daß zerstörbar in uns nur ist, was zerstört sein will, verführbar nur, was der Verführung entgegenkommt, frei nur, was zur Freiheit fähig ist' (KON, p. 112) And 'gräßlich wahr' (KON, p. 123) she calls the barbaric drives in us. The split ('Riß'), so often mentioned in Wolf's work, goes right through the individual.

Günderrode knows that we cannot know the entire truth about ourselves (cf. p. 148), but nevertheless she (like Christa T. and the narrator of *Kindheitsmuster*) insists on the importance of self-knowledge for gaining insight into utopian possibilities: 'Menschen, die sich nicht über sich selbst betrügen, werden aus der Gärung einer jeden Zeit Neues herausreißen, indem sie es aussprechen. Mir ist, als ginge die Welt nicht weiter, wenn das nicht getan wird' (KON, p. 105). The word is not just the vehicle for transporting these visions, but as the conjunction 'indem' indicates, it is the method of finding them.

Although words also have their inherent dangers, and Kleist and Günderrode have both experienced them ('Durch Benennung bannen, auch töten' (KON, p. 131), the narrative ends with a confirmation of literature – a kind of literature that grows from the experience of suffering and can therefore never show classical harmony and beauty: 'Gezeichnet zeichnend. Auf ein Werk verwiesen, das offen bleibt, offen wie eine Wunde' (KON, p. 150).

At this point of insight (that includes Günderrode and Kleist, and, in the undefined plural pronouns, by affinity also Christa Wolf) words are no longer based on their relation to things/material reality but rather on belief, hope, vision, which oppose factual reality: 'Unser unausrottbarer Glaube, der Mensch sei bestimmt, sich zu vervollkommen, der dem Geist aller Zeiten strikt zuwiderläuft' (KON, pp. 150f.).

Christa Wolf's own revitalising of the Romantic writers (cf also her essays on Günderrode, Bettina von Arnim and Kleist) contributes to making the knowledge of Kleist's and Günderrode's suffering and of their ultimate suicides less oppressive, for by her sensitive and sympathetic appreciation she has given these writers' concerns a place in our time.

If Wolf's utopian vision did not find understanding in the late 1970s, her words, too, by implication, might be taken up again at a later time. Thus, Wolf's own work has produced enough optimism to enable her to continue writing and to continue to believe in the power of the word to influence reality. Her optimism is so great that she can even fantasise a utopian moment in which Günderrode and Kleist recognise each other's personalities fully and communicate at such an intense level that the limitations of their personal identities are broken down and merge into a momentary 'wir'.

Christa Wolf's Cassandra project gives evidence of another major shift in her world view: her exploration of alienation is now undertaken from an explicitly feminist perspective rather than a traditionally marxist one. She attempts to convey insights about contemporary society by consciously examining it as a patriarchal society and by relating what she perceives as its final stages (which might lead to nuclear annihilation) to its assumed historical origin about 3000 years ago.

As with many of Wolf's fictional texts, the story *Kassandra* is also accompanied by essays of an explanatory nature. Here, Wolf examines words from a perspective that is informed by the *Dialectic of Enlightenment* and post-structuralist feminism. She perceives language as constituting subjectivity, even ruling, dominating the subject:[7] 'Aber ist es nicht gerade das Wort, das die Herrschaft über unser Inneres angetreten hat? Macht sein Fehlen nicht, daß ich mir verlorengehe? Wie schnell wird Sprach-losigkeit zu Ich-losigkeit? (V, p. 25). Wolf also recognises her own implication in logocentrism: 'Die Zentrierung um den Logos, das Wort als Fetisch – vielleicht der tiefste Aberglaube des Abendlands, jedenfalls der, dem ich inbrünstig anhänge' (V, p. 25).

While Wolf has previously emphasised the critical aspect of literature that points beyond the conditions it originated in towards a utopian vision, she now views literature, at least classical Greek literature, as having contributed to the establishment of the instrumental utilitarian rationality of patriarchy: 'Und die Literatur hat,

---

7. Cf. Irmgard Roebling, '"Hier spricht keiner meine Sprache, der nicht mit mir stirbt." Zum Ort der Sprachreflexion in Christa Wolfs *Kassandra*', in Wolfram Mauser (ed.), *Erinnerte Zukunft*, pp. 207–32.

indem sie sie beschrieb, die Doppelmoral mit strukturiert' (V, p.40). She doubts the ability of words to transcend reality: 'Weil das Setzen von Worten an Voraussetzungen gebunden ist, die außerhalb der Literatur zu liegen scheinen' (V. p. 85).

Literature from classical Greek times to the proletarian revolution could serve to structure the identity of the groups it grew out of, Wolf believes, but words seem to fail in face of the contemporary situation of imminent catastrophe. In spite of Wolf's awareness of the inadequacy of words she does not, of course, renounce them. On the contrary, in a situation that seems to leave no alternatives, that seems to preclude any effectiveness of insights which run counter to the great social institutions (cf. V, p. 98), Wolf writes a story that constitutes a model of female dissident subjectivity – in order to influence history. Wolf lends her voice to a precursor of the woman writer, the illiterate seer Cassandra about whom we only know because male writers have depicted her. Thus she aptly symbolises the fact that women have had no voice in this civilisation. Wolf has come to see objectification of women and instrumental rationality as integral to our male-dominated civilisation, which has brought the world to the brink of self-destruction (cf. V, p. 101). In the psychoanalytical inner monologue of her Cassandra, she not only paradigmatically and very subtly explores a woman's entanglement in patriarchal society (here depicted as a transitional period that still shows traces of older matrilinear structures), but she also portrays an exemplary process of gaining perfect insight into and detachment from patriarchal society, thus laying claim to an ultimate truth and closing the split Günderrode and Kleist had experienced in their personalities. *Kassandra* exemplifies the attainment of the imaginary aim of complete autonomy in a way that is reminiscent of classical eighteenth-century German literature: Cassandra is a heroic anti-heroine who chooses death rather than compromise her ideals.

Thus in her narrative, Wolf reproduces the aesthetic structure she had identified as patriarchal in her essays (cf. V, p. 117, p. 147).[8] Perhaps this shows the truth of Wolf's insight: 'Ästhetik [. . .] ist, wie Philosophie und Wissenschaft, mindestens im gleichen Maß, zu dem Zweck erfunden, sich die Wirklichkeit vom Leib zu halten, sich vor ihr zu schützen, wie zu dem Ziel, der Wirklichkeit näherzukommen' (V, p. 150).

---

8. Cf. Anna K. Kuhn's defence of the exemplary heroine and her relativisation of the closed form in her study *Christa Wolf's Utopian Vision. From Marxism to Feminism*, Cambridge, 1988, p. 190ff.

In *Kassandra*, she exposes the manipulative use of words by those in power in order to influence social behaviour. Pain/suffering is named, just as in the previous narrative *Kein Ort*. *Nirgends*, as the prerequisite to correcting corrupt language: 'Wer wird, und wann, die Sprache wiederfinden. Einer dem ein Schmerz den Schädel spaltet, wird es sein. Und bis dahin, bis zu ihm hin, nur das Gebrüll und der Befehl und das Gewinsel und das Jawohl der Gehorchenden' (K, p. 10). Within the fictional framework itself, Cassandra is portrayed as such a person who finds true words through pain. But judging the text from an aesthetic viewpoint, it seems that perhaps the experience of pain can also lead one to look for consolation and political effectiveness in the familiar patterns of a closed form.

Having separated the narrative from essayistic reflections in *Kein Ort. Nirgends* and *Kassandra*, Christa Wolf returns to a fusion of these genres in *Störfall* (1987), which continues to explore the mortal dangers instrumental rationality has produced. The subtitle 'Nachrichten eines Tages' is an allusion to the news of the nuclear accident at Chernobyl that reached the world in May 1986. *Störfall* records the first-person narrator's reactions to and reflections on this news during the course of one day, and, parallel to that, in the form of an imaginary conversation, the narrator's empathetic thoughts about her brother, a scientist, who undergoes dangerous, but ultimately successful surgery for a brain tumour on that same day. Wolf thus links both individual illness and the destruction the world has escaped by a hair's breadth to one-dimensional rationality, while maintaining the narrator's faith in the surgeon operating on her brother and thus making him into a symbol of the other, humanitarian, side of science.

The – rather too neat – parallelism between brain tumour and nuclear accident also serves to include scientific research on the development of the human species, and of the human brain in particular, in the narrator's exploration of the question where and why humanity went wrong and what would have to be changed to alter the destructive and self-destructive tendencies of our civilisation.

Her own implication as a writer and the role of language in this destructive process become more and more important subjects of examination in the course of the narrative. She comes to the conclusion that it is not artistic imagination, even if it is dystopian, that contributes to destructive tendencies. It is not what writers said that is cause for guilt, but rather what they left unsaid for banal and paradoxical reasons: 'Aus Unsicherheit. Aus Angst. Aus Mangel an Hoffnung. Und, so merkwürdig die Behauptung ist: auch aus Hoffnung. Trügerische Hoffnung, welche das gleiche Ergebnis zeitigt wie lähmende Verzweiflung' (S, p.68).

In pursuing the relation between the writer's words and reality further, even in her dreams, the question of her responsibility for the drive towards destruction remains, initially, a blind spot.[9] But she hovers around this taboo zone, and anthropological research leads her, the believer in language, to recognise its Janus face: 'Sprache, die Identität schafft, zugleich aber entscheidend dazu beiträgt, die Tötungshemmung gegen den anderssprechenden Artgenossen abzubauen. Die gleiche Sprache, die den Sprung in den "vollmenschlichen" Zustand markiert, Bewußtsein öffnend, dabei bisher Bewußtes ins Unbewußte drängend' (S, p.91). Consequently, as a writer, the narrator has to ask herself whether language itself might be her blind spot, preventing her seeing the crucial assumptions and faults of our civilisation since it is through language that she is programmed with its values. Since language represses the intuitive functions of our brain in favour of the rational ones, she now believes that it is so inseparable from our civilisation's instrumental rationality that personal attempts at truthfulness via self-knowledge cannot fully redeem it from its destructive context. The disgust she experiences at words, her own words, turns into disgust at herself for having objectified people in her writing (cf. S, pp. 108f.).

Having probed so far into the use of words the narrator then begins her work of regaining confidence in the word by turning to earlier writers who did manage to convey important insights into the blind spots of their time. That such writing is now more important than ever if we are to stop society's destructiveness is implied by the nightmare of destruction with which the book ends, and the narrator's comment to her brother: 'Wie schwer, Bruder, würde es sein, von dieser Erde Abschied zu nehmen' (S, p.119).

Wolf's penultimate book, *Sommerstück* (1989), was partly written in parallel with *Kein Ort. Nirgends*. It is a more personal, intimate, though far from unmediated, account of Wolf's experience of political disillusionment in the mid-1970s. Alternating between inner monologues, figural and first-person *plural* modes of narration, the narrative focusses on the communal yet differential experiences of a group of friends, largely avoiding the privileged

9. Wolf's concept of the blind spot seems to be a free adaptation of Virginia Woolf's 'spot the size of a shilling at the back of the head which one can never see for oneself' in *A Room of One's Own* (1929), London, Granada, 1981, p.86. In contradistinction to Virginia Woolf, Christa Wolf's optimism shows in her belief that it is possible for the writer to gain insight into her own blind spot and that of her time.

centralising viewpoint of a first-person narrator. These friends, pushed to the edges of society, create an island for themselves by enjoying the intense though momentary feeling of fulfilled life which a summer in the country with like-minded people offers them.

Published more than a decade after the narrated experience came to an end, *Sommerstück* evokes that past embedded in a complex web of references to previous and subsequent experiences, in order to uphold a glimpse of a utopian vision in the midst of the loss of hope. At a time which has abandoned political dreams and even the experiment of alternative living on a small scale, the narration of that short moment of fulfilled life with friends is given an exaggerated political importance: 'bezeugen, daß, wonach wir uns sehnen, als Möglichkeit in uns angelegt ist' (ST, p.160). Thus Wolf tries to preserve what she considers as literature's humanitarian function, to keep awake an 'Ahnung von einer Art Leben, von der die unzähligen normalen Leben abgedrängt worden waren' (ST, p.66).

As in Wolf's previous work, the text records periods of disgust at words (ST, p.37), at the gap between words and things (ST, p.41, p.214), at pressing people into stories (ST, p.213), at 'killing material into art' (ST, p.85). The destruction of her self-confidence leads to a writer's block in the figure of Ellen. Yet, ultimately Ellen, Wolf's alter ego, is able to overcome this inertia by gaining self-knowledge. In a process reminiscent of Cassandra's disentanglement from the values of her society, Ellen begins to change:

Daß sie sich nicht mehr wie ein von falschen Wörtern und Vorstellungen besetztes Land vorkam. Scham spricht nicht. Sonst müßte sie sagen: Ein mit eigener Zustimmung, aus eigenem freien Willen besetztes Land. Am allersichersten Ort hatte die fremde Macht, die Gewalt über sie gehabt hatte, sich vor ihr versteckt gehalten: in ihren Augen. So daß die fremde Macht mit meinen Augen sah, durch mich selbst, dachte Ellen. Und keiner des anderen, aber ich auch meiner selbst nicht gewahr werden konnte. Und daß ich denken mußte, den Fremdkörper von mir abzutrennen, würde mich zerreißen. (ST, p. 137)

Since this process of change is narrated with Ellen as a focaliser, the reader, in turn, sees it through Ellen's eyes. By comparing the self to a country, and the individual's words and conceptions, which are now perceived as wrong, to an occupying army, the assumption is made of an essential self that is separable from merely external influences. Once erroneously perceived as parts of the self, the latter are now called 'fremde Macht' and 'Fremdkörper', thus echoing the terminology of the Romantic period in which the other was first explored as a repressed aspect of the self.[10] However, the Romantic discovery is here reversed by a neat separation of the self from the foreign power, and thus the idea of a harmonious true self, modelled on classicism, is regained. I would argue that it is ultimately this mythic experience – however transitory – of finding an 'authentisches Selbst' (S, p. 92) beyond language which renews not only Ellen's, but also Wolf's, faith in the capacity of language to express truth and effect change.

Wolf's writing is characterised by, on the one hand, a striking continuity of certain motifs and concerns, documented by an intricate web of self-quotations, and, on the other, ruptures in attitudes, perspectives and ways of writing. Starting as a loyal socialist with issues specifically related to the period of reconstruction in the GDR, Wolf has grown more and more critical, first of her society, and eventually of the process of civilisation itself. In each of her books she has explored new and ever wider perspectives to probe the question of 'Wie sind wir so geworden, wie wir sind'. She has traced the roots of alienation increasingly far back in history, from contradictions within the GDR to Nazi Germany, to the beginnings of industrialisation, the beginnings of patriarchy, and even to the beginnings of human being's capacity for rational thought.

All Christa Wolf's books are about the regaining of a utopian faith. Her confrontation with reality leads her again and again to experience despair at the destruction of cherished hopes. But writing about the loss of ideals seems to regenerate her belief in the capacity of words to convey truths of an increasingly complex kind that will, one day, effect a change.

Her optimism, her need for harmony, her view of women's humanising potential (though argued historically, not biologically), as well as her universally acknowledged great role in contemporary literature, have, paradoxically, brought Wolf closer to the classical Goethe than to the Romantic writers whose insoluble conflicts she has portrayed so sympathetically.

10. Cf. E.T.A. Hoffmann, 'Der Sandmann' in E.T.A. Hoffmann, *Fantasie- und Nachtstücke*, Munich, 1976, pp. 331–64.

Ricarda Schmidt

Author's Note

The following editions and abbreviations are used for Wolf's works:

G: *Der geteilte Himmel. Erzählung* (1963), Berlin and Weimar, 1975.

N: *Nachdenken über Christa T.* (1968), Darmstadt and Neuwied, 12th edition, 1979.

KM: *Kindheitsmuster* (1976), Darmstadt and Neuwied, 3rd edition, 1979.

KON: *Kein Ort. Nirgends* (1979), Darmstadt and Neuwied, 4th edition, 1980.

K: *Kassandra. Erzählung*, Darmstadt and Neuwied, 1983.

V: *Voraussetzung einer Erzählung: Kassandra*, Frankfurter Poetik–Vorlesungen (1983), Darmstadt and Neuwied, 6th edition, 1986.

S: *Störfall. Nachrichten eines Tages*, Darmstadt and Neuwied, 1987.

ST: *Sommerstück*, Darmstadt and Neuwied, 1989.

Suggested Further Reading

Other works by Christa Wolf:

Moskauer Novelle, Halle, 1961.

Lesen und Schreiben. Aufsätze und Betrachtungen (1972), Darmstadt and Neuwied, 2nd, revised edition, 1980.

Unter den Linden. Drei Unwahrscheinliche Geschichten, Darmstadt and Neuwied, 1974.

'Der Schatten eines Traumes', in Christa Wolf (ed.), *Karoline von Günderrode. Der Schatten eines Traumes. Gedichte. Briefe. Zeugnisse von Zeitgenossen*, Darmstadt and Neuwied, 1979.

'Nun ja! Das nächste Leben geht aber heute an. Ein Brief über die Bettine', afterword to Bettina von Arnim, *Die Günderode*, Frankfurt am Main, 1982.

Fortgesetzter Versuch. Aufsätze, Gespräche, Essays, Leipzig, 1982.

Gesammelte Erzählungen, Darmstadt and Neuwied, 1982.

'Kleists "Penthesilea"', afterword in Heinrich von Kleist, *Penthesilea*, Berlin/GDR, 1983.

Die Dimension des Autors. Essays und Aufsätze. Reden und Gespräche 1959–1985, Darmstadt and Neuwied, 1987.

Was bleibt. Erzählung, Frankfurt am Main, 1990.

Secondary Material

Angela Drescher (ed.), *Christa Wolf: ein Arbeitsbuch. Studien, Dokumente, Bibliographie*, Berlin and Weimar, 1989.

Sonja Hilzinger, *Christa Wolf*, Stuttgart, 1986.

Therese Hörnigk, *Christa Wolf*, Göttingen, 1989.

Manfred Jurgensen (ed.), *Wolf. Darstellung, Deutung, Diskussion*, Bern and Munich, 1984.

Mechthild Quernheim, *Das moralische Ich: kritische Studien zur Subjektwerdung in der Erzählprosa Christa Wolfs*, Würzburg, 1990.

Klaus Sauer (ed.), *Christa Wolf. Materialienbuch*, Darmstadt, 1979, 3rd., rev. and exp. ed. 1985.

–9–

Marxist - Postmodernist - German:
History and Dramatic Form in the Work of Heiner Müller

Moray McGowan

Can there be such a thing as marxist post-modernism? Can marxism, with its faith in linear historical development, cohabit in a single intellectual construct with post-modernism, which declares that history is over, or which aims to subvert or deconstruct history? From the perspective of the early 1990s and the apparent collapse of communism in Eastern Europe, seen by commentators like the US State Department official Francis Fukuyama as the 'End of History', these questions are posed by an investigation of the work of the most productive and most controversial of GDR playwrights, Heiner Müller. Moreover, the return of the national question to the centre stage of German history invites a further reflection: That aspect of Müller's work typically characterised by Ernst Wendt in 1978 as his 'Anspruch, die wichtigsten Traditionen deutscher "Nationalliteratur" fortzusetzen', namely his persistent theatrical representation of 'die deutsche Zerrissenheit' and 'der ewige deutsche Bürgerkrieg' remind us that this marxist post-modernist is also a quintessentially German author.[1]

Though Müller's work enjoys three fairly distinct receptions – in the GDR, the German-speaking West, and the wider European and North American avant-garde – he has been writing in and for the GDR since the early 1950s. His plays thus accompany the development of the GDR as a continuous critical engagement with its problems and contradictions, offering alternative histories. Frequently, they have been subjected to censorship; some, like *Germania Tod in Berlin*, were completed in the 1970s but not published or

---

1. Ernst Wendt, 'Ewiger deutscher Bürgerkrieg', *Der Spiegel*, 16, 1978, pp. 263 & 260.

performed in the GDR till the late 1980s. As Müller's 60th birthday in 1989 approached, Western recognition – expressed in numerous Müller festivals and symposia as well as countless individual productions – impelled the GDR cultural bureaucracy, not for the first time, to acknowledge an author it would rather shun; it is rumoured the award of the *Nationalpreis 1.Klasse* to Müller in 1988, for an oeuvre then still partly unpublished in the GDR, was a grudging response to reports that he had been nominated for the Nobel Prize.[2] Once official sanction was given, however, theatres throughout East Germany clamoured to perform his work.

Müller's work has often been divided into three broad phases: first, the so-called 'Produktionsstücke' (a term Müller rejects) of the late 1950s and early 1960s, like *Der Lohndrücker, Die Korrektur* or *Der Bau*, which focus on the contradictions and conflicts of the GDR's 'Aufbauphase'; second, a phase of adaptations, in particular of classical drama, such as *Philoktet* or *Herakles 5*, but also of Brecht, Shakespeare and Soviet writers like Gladkow, plays in many of which – this is especially true of *Philoktet* – the icy dialectic of the means and the end is translated into dramatic tension by the severity of the form; finally the disorientating, often alienating extremism of his plays of the later 1970s and the 1980s, extravagant, fragmentary, violent, radically anti-Aristotelian montages which left audiences bemused and critics either ecstatic or enraged: this third phase runs roughly from *Germania Tod in Berlin* through *Leben Gundlings Friedrich von Preußen Lessings Schlaf Traum Schrei* and *Die Hamletmaschine* to *Verkommenes Ufer Medeamaterial Landschaft mit Argonauten*.

This division is problematic: sometimes but not always because of censorship problems, some of Müller's texts may only emerge ten, twenty or thirty years after they were written, and then not necessarily as independent plays, but as fragments in a montage of disparate elements: this is the case for example with *Germania Tod in Berlin* (dated 1956/71, published 1977, premiered 1978 in the West, not until 1989 in the GDR). Secondly, virtually all Müller's work is in a sense adaptation, not only of existing literary models, but also of his own past work. For example: in 1988 his adaptation of his play *Der Lohndrücker*, the first version of which had not been seen in the GDR since its brief first production in 1958, was staged in East Berlin. This new version bedded the original *Lohndrücker* in a mosaic of other material: two film sequences, his earlier play *Der*

2. Ellen Brandt, 'Trinken, rauchen, sterben', *Die deutsche Bühne*, 60, 1989, 1, p. 12.

Horatier – which was played through twice – and the satirical sketch *Kentauren* which is also the fourth part of Müller's play *Wolokolamsker Chaussee*.

One thread through what soon becomes a bewildering labyrinth of textual and chronological cross-references and borrowings is Müller's view, or perhaps views, of history and the consequences this has for the dramatic form of his plays. In the later 1980s, works like *Wolokolamsker Chaussee* and the new version of *Der Lohndrücker* confirm this precisely in the way in which they contradict the neat three-part categorisation of Müller's work.

Moreover, Müller's controversiality in the GDR was rooted in the fact that his view of history was more differentiated and more uncompromising than that of the state and the party, whose propagated view of history had quite different intentions. Müller's plays insist on the historically dynamic quality of conflict and contradiction. 'Ich glaube an Konflikt. Sonst glaube ich an nichts.'[3] Thus in their form as well as in their themes his plays deliberately juxtapose jarring elements: dramatic representations of dialectical materialism; humanist utopias; enlightenment and critique of enlightenment; extreme forms of sexuality; dionysiac celebrations of death and rebirth; fragments of reality, mythology and literature.

In Müller's earlier work it is relatively simple, if never unproblematic, to demonstrate his view of history and its effect on the form of his plays. The work of the 1970s and 1980s however, in its attack on historical representation, on the fact that history is always written by the victors, shifts ambiguously between several positions: sometimes it seems to declare history at an end, no longer capable of moving forward, and to seek, via radical negation, to set history in motion again; sometimes it seems to declare that the very representation of history as progress in a set direction is an oppressive force, a treadmill from which liberation must be sought; sometimes it seems to apply the doctrine of historical inevitability very rigorously: the doctrine of the unceasing generation of class contradictions, a process by which every once historically progressive class is eventually replaced in this role by another: the feudal by the capitalist, the bourgeois by the proletarian etc. Müller, one could argue, applies the marxist philosophy of history to take the narrative of history beyond the end point which has been set to it by the class interests of a particular and possibly now historically anachronistic epoch, that of the East European socialist

---

3. *Gesammelte Irrtümer*, Frankfurt, 1986, p. 86; future references identified in the text by GI and page number.

states. For in many of his plays of the 1970s and 1980s Müller declares the whole historical tradition of European patriarchy to be played out, and sees the potential for historical change only in those who are excluded from this tradition: in women and in the Third World (in itself, of course, neither a new, nor an unproblematic idea).

All these positions suggest that change is achievable but that it is likely to be found outside extant ideologies of 'progress'. It is integral to Müller's view of the world as a writhing serpent's nest of dialectically interwoven opposites that he links this implicit optimism with a vicious pessimism: 'Ich bin ein Optimist. Ich glaube an den 4. Weltkrieg.'[4] Humanity will survive, but continue to rend itself apart, but survive . . .

The implication that change is necessary and possible appears to sit uneasily with post-modernism. Yet post-modern forms and themes are everywhere in Müller's work. He differs from conventional marxist positions in suggesting, through the structure of his plays – their fragmentary, self-referential, circular form; their eschewal of the unities of plot, place, time, character – that the world is, de facto, post-modern. 'History', in the sense of linear progressions of self-determined individual or collective actions by rational subjects, will not explain contemporary experience. But it can be argued that Müller ultimately seeks to retain, or perhaps regain, an advocacy of the necessity of history. He will not deny the world's post-modern condition; but he will not accept it.

It is important to see this central aspect of Müller's work in the context of the role of history in marxism and in the GDR. Marxism, as a materialist refinement of the Enlightenment belief in progress, understands history as a rationally explicable, linear process, 'eine aufsteigende Linie ökonomischer Gesellschaftsformen' as a West German commentator on Marxist historiography puts it.[5] Again and again, says Marx in *Zur Kritik der politischen Ökonomie*, 'geraten die materiellen Produktivkräfte der Gesellschaft in Widerspruch mit den vorhandenen Produktionsverhältnissen [. . .] Aus Entwicklungsformen der Produktivkräfte schlagen diese Verhältnisse in Fesseln derselben um. Es tritt dann eine Epoche sozialer Revolution ein.'[6] As Joachim Streisand says in *Deutsche*

4. Quoted in *Die deutsche Bühne*, 60, 1989, 1, p. 10.
5. Johannes Küpper, 'Die Geschichtsschreibung der SED im Umbruch', *Deutschlandarchiv*, 1985, 3, p. 281. See also Andreas Dorpalen, *German History in Marxist Perspective*, London, 1985, for a definitive study of this aspect.
6. Karl Marx, 'Vorwort zur *Kritik der politischen Ökonomie*' in Boris Goldenberg (ed.), *Karl Marx Ausgewählte Schriften*, Munich, 1962, p. 426.

Geschichte von den Anfängen bis zur Gegenwart. Eine marxistische Einführung, a quasi-official standard work in the GDR, Marx demonstrates 'der Weg der Menschheit von der Urgesellschaft über Gesellschaften, deren Geschichte durch Klassengegensatz und Klassenkampf geprägt ist, wie die Sklaverei, den Feudalismus und den Kapitalismus, zur kommunistischen Gesellschaft'. Streisand admits that 'Stagnation' and 'Rückschritte' accompany this process, for 'solche Gesetze setzen sich nicht unabhängig vom Denken und Handeln der Menschen durch' (and indeed GDR historiography became increasingly sophisticated in its appropriation of ever more of German history to the role of prelude to socialism), but this does not fundamentally alter the principle of historical inevitability, or the view of history as a rising progression.[7]

For GDR historiography specifically there are two further principles: firstly the legitimacy of the GDR as the 'rechtmäßiger Erbe aller revolutionären, fortschrittlichen und humanistischen Traditionen der deutschen Geschichte und vor allem der deutschen Arbeiterbewegung', as the 1972 Central Research Plan for the Marxist-Leninist Social Sciences in the GDR puts it;[8] secondly the leadership role of the SED as the representative of this historical vanguard class, the working class. In the interests of legitimating the state, and its own domination, the SED clung fast to these principles. Streisand's work demonstrates this legitimation function of the marxist view of history in the GDR: 'Fortschritt in der Geschichte – das ist uns Bürgern der Deutschen Demokratischen Republik eine selbstverständliche Erfahrung, wird uns doch ein solcher Fortschritt im Alltag ständig sichtbar.'[9]

One would expect any critical artist to question such rose-tinted views. But perhaps no GDR author has devoted him- or herself more intensively and extensively to the problems of history than Heiner Müller in his four decades as a writer. Moreover, it is worth stressing that Müller's critical method is a marxist one insofar as he maintains a belief in dialectic contradiction as a critical tool and as the driving force of history. Müller's view differs from orthodox marxism in that where individual and collective history are at odds he does not declare individual interests to be subjective, i.e. secondary and irrelevant; also in that he sees history as constantly at risk of stasis, so that it is necessary, if one wishes to move history onwards, actively to subvert the dominant narratives of history which

7. Cologne, 1976, pp. 10–11
8. Quoted in Küpper, 'Die Geschichtsschreibung der SED in Umbruch', p. 283
9. Streisand, *Deutsche Geschichte*, p. 10.

in fact cement the existing situation: this includes active subversion
of a marxism which has ossified into a state religion. 'Marx hat ja
kein System entworfen, sondern er hat an der Negation des Be-
stehenden gearbeitet, und so war er prinzipiell offen für neue
Realitäten.'[10]

In the 1950s, GDR society displayed the contradictions generated
by the historical nearness of the fascist past and by the structural
problems of building a new socialist society. In this historical phase
Müller wrote the 'Geschichten aus der Produktion' (as the Western
'Rotbuch' edition calls them), like *Der Lohndrücker* and *Die Korrektur*, whose theme is the transitional phase 'zwischen Eiszeit und
Kommune', between fascism and socialism, the remains of old
attitudes still present in consciousness, the yet-to-be overcome
fallibility of the new, the compulsions and compromises of this
phase of 'Aufbau', what Müller in a symptomatically entitled essay
'Sieg des Realismus' of 1953 called the 'Kampf zwischen Altem und
Neuen im Innern des Einzelnen'.[11] An engineer remarks in *Die
Korrektur*: 'Die ersten Bauten stehn, Schornsteine, Kühltürme, das
Stahlgerüst für die Montagehallen, Fundamente, und [. . .] die
Wohnstadt für die Arbeiter [. . .] beim Menschen geht der Umbau
langsamer [. . .] Sie verdienen viel und trinken mehr, gehn heim
und schimpfen im Vorbeigehn auf die Transparente, auf denen
Sozialismus steht, und stehn früh an ihrem Platz und baun mit
schwerem Schädel am Sozialismus.'[12] Not every contradiction is
reduced in this way into a conflict between the wise and efficient
system and the foolish, recalcitrant individual. But there is a sense
in which these plays can be seen as contributions to the development of a socialist consciousness, their author as participating in
correct marxist manner in the social process of production. Hence
Müller spent time in factories and construction sites gathering
material for *Die Korrektur*, discussed the play with workers, and
responded to their criticisms by writing a new version.

However, these plays experienced incessant difficulties. In 1961,
for example, Müller was barred from the Schriftstellerverband and
Die Umsiedlerin banned; the suggestion that the GDR was in a
transition phase 'zwischen Eiszeit und Kommune', originally ut-
tered by a worker figure in *Der Bau*, led to attacks on play and

10. 'Da trink ich lieber Benzin zum Frühstück. Heiner Müller im Gespräch mit
    Frank Raddatz', *Transatlantik*, 1989, 2, p. 10.
11. Quoted by Theo Girshausen, *Realismus und Utopie. Die frühen Stücke Heiner
    Müllers*, Cologne, 1981, pp. 109–10; see also Wolfgang Schivelbusch, *Sozial-
    istisches Drama nach Brecht*, Darmstadt and Neuwied, 1974, p. 104.
12. *Geschichten aus der Produktion* (Texte 1), Berlin, 1974, p. 50

author at the 11th plenum of the SED central committee in 1965. Müller's problems in this respect stemmed largely from his critical view of socialist realism. By giving the writer an 'Auftrag', a defined task, socialist realism promises her or him participation in the social process of production, and so, in marxist terms, participation in history; but in fact it *debars* him or her from this participation. An art whose subject is a reality supposedly formed according to already-known laws and analysable with infallible scientific tools does *not* participate in history in the sense of instigating a productive process of change. Art of this kind remains static.[13]

Müller in contrast refused to banish antagonistic contradictions – the sort supposed no longer to exist in socialism – from his picture of the GDR present into that society's prehistory. The reasons for this were not only ones of content: like Brecht with his 'Verfremdungseffekt', Müller wished to use the dramatisation of irreconcilable contradictions as a tool of dislocation, of disruption of previously unquestioned assumptions, and thus of intellectual production, both in himself as author and in his audience. *Der Lohndrücker* for example negates its antecedents not only in content but also in form. Unlike his model, the activist Garbe (who repaired a cracked furnace while it was still blazing hot so as not to hamper production), Müller's Barka is a negative hero, an obsessive, egoistic worker, who in the Nazi period denounced his fellow workers for sabotage, and whose workaholic attitude is more resented and resisted than welcomed in the new society too. The montage structure of the play prevents any harmonious synthesis at the end. According to Müller, the new society will not grow out of the pathos of onstage declarations of socialist community, but from the negative energies of contradiction and conflict. His goal is not to resolve conflicts on stage in uplifting dénouements, but to carry them into the audience, and so into the society where these conflicts are actually fought out.

Certainly the difficulties Müller experienced in getting these 'Produktionsstücke' performed were one reason why in the 1960s he turned his attention to adaptations, especially of ancient Greek drama. But as the example of *Philoktet* shows, this movement in Müller's work is more than just a search for a 'Sklavensprache', a language of oblique reference to outwit the censor.

13. David Bathrick, 'Affirmative and Negative Culture: The Avantgarde under "Actually Existing Socialism" – The Case of the GDR', *Social Research*, 47, 1980, 1, pp. 177–8.

During the Trojan war, the crippled Philoktet lives on the island where Odysseus had marooned him ten years before. He burns with hatred of Odysseus. Odysseus needs him for the war effort. He deploys his companion Neoptolemos to bring Philoktet back to the cause with a series of lies, but Neoptolemos is driven to kill Philoktet to save Odysseus. Undismayed, the latter takes Philoktet's corpse back to Troy, where, by blaming his death on Trojan treachery, he will be able to fan anti-Trojan feeling in the Greek army to the benefit of the war effort.

Philoktet, though reflecting the experience of Stalinism, is not a parable about Stalin, except insofar as Stalinism typifies certain deep contradictions between humanistic ideals and their realisation, between ideals and the realities of a rule which represses and destroys these ideals in the present with the declared goal of realising them in the future. Müller's Odysseus is a pragmatist, who instrumentalises reason, deploys dialectics to cement his power, and justifies his present exercise of power with the promise of a better future. Thus Odysseus urges Neoptolemos to take no account of the suffering of Philoktet: 'Nur blind für seine Wunde heilst du die/Nur taub für seinen Jammer stillst du den.'[14] Müller's critique is not primarily moral; the formal severity of the play heightens the sense that the figures are acting under compulsion. Müller once said his strongest impulse was 'Dinge auf ihr Skelett zu reduzieren, ihr Fleisch und ihre Oberfläche herunterzureißen'. (GI, p.102) By stripping away all elements of milieu or secondary plot, Müller produces an intense, linear dramatic structure which forces our attention onto the complete instrumentalisation of the human beings of the Philoktet myth, of the history of the Graeco-Trojan conflict which Odysseus's narrative occupies and directs for his own purposes,[15] and of the principle of reason which, since the Enlightenment, European society has enthroned as humanity's hope for the future. The icy logic of the classical form emphasises the dialectic of end and means, as for example in Müller's use of *stichomythia* in an argument about lying:

NEOPTOLEMOS: Aus faulem Grund wächst wohl ein Gutes nicht
ODYSSEUS: Eins ist der Grund, ein anderes ist der Baum

---

14. *Mauser* (Texte 6), Berlin, 1978, p. 14; future references identified in the text by M and page number.
15. Just as GDR historiography can be seen as practising an 'ungeschminkte, geradezu brutale politische Instrumentalisierung', as Johannes Küpper says in his essay 'Das Geschichtsbewußtsein in der DDR', in W. Weidenfeld (ed.), *Geschichtsbewußtsein in Deutschland*, Cologne, 1987, p. 167.

NEOPTOLEMOS: Den Baum nach seiner Wurzel fragt der Sturm
ODYSSEUS: Den Wald nicht fragt er.

(M, p. 11)

This structure drives the drama compulsively, irresistibly, towards its conclusion. This formal structure has its exact parallel in the discursive logic of which Odysseus, whom Helen Fehervary calls the 'Patriarch der Aufklärung', intent on domination, is master.[16] This logic reintegrates all potentially centrifugal elements into the overall structure. Ambiguity, ambivalence and polymorphism have no place in this totalitarianism of reason.

Precisely the formal perfection of a play like *Philoktet* compels Müller to change in his later work: the radically heightened representation of conflict and of violence now takes place in open dramatic structures in which the various elements of conflict are clashingly juxtaposed. This, and the giving of parallel titles to scenes (as for example in *Germania Tod in Berlin*) creates the connections between them, and not conventional dramatic logic. The titles of these plays themselves are often telling: *Leben Gundlings Friedrich von Preußen Lessings Schlaf Traum Schrei* or *Verkommenes Ufer Medeamaterial Landschaft mit Argonauten*. These titles suggest the structural principles of his more recent drama: in keeping with the post-modern dissolution of unitary conceptions like historical progress or the integral individual subject, the unities of time, place, plot and character are exploded. In 1978 Müller said: 'Es besteht keine Substanz für einen Dialog mehr, weil es keine Geschichte mehr gibt.' (GI, p. 54) Stage images and fragments of text, mostly monologues, are piled up in a multi-medial assault on the consciousness of the audience. It is perhaps not surprising that for a time in the early 1980s Müller co-operated with Robert Wilson, the American director of supposedly post-modern theatre spectacles like *Death, Destruction and Detroit* or *CIVIL warS*.

However, Müller's purpose remains essentially a political one. Müller's audience is bombarded with myth-laden images, to break up the immobility of order, to create a confusion from which change can emerge. 'Es ist unmöglich geworden', says Müller in 1982, 'sich die Utopie innerhalb des historischen Prozesses vorzustellen. Die Utopie steht heute jenseits oder neben der Geschichte, jenseits oder neben der Politik' (GI, p. 84). Müller's dramatic

16. Helen Fehervary, 'Autorschaft, Geschlechtsbewußtsein und Öffentlichkeit. Versuch über Heiner Müllers *Die Hamletmaschine* und Christa Wolfs *Kein Ort. Nirgends*', in Irmela von der Lühe (ed.), *Entwürfe von Frauen in der Literatur des 20. Jahrhunderts*, Berlin, 1982, p. 133.

practice must aim, therefore, at new forms and practices of representing history. He wants to deconstruct the one-track, one-directional conception of a seamless reality in the consciousness of the audience: 'Die Fragmentarisierung eines Vorgangs betont seinen Prozeßcharakter, hindert das Verschwinden der Produktion im Produkt'.[17] Art's task is to disrupt the smooothness of this process which makes history invisible. 'Am Verschwinden des Menschen arbeiten viele der besten Gehirne und riesige Industrien. Der Konsum ist die Einübung der Massen in diesen Vorgang, jede Ware eine Waffe, jeder Supermarkt ein Trainingscamp. Das erhellt die Notwendigkeit der Kunst als Mittel, die Wirklichkeit unmöglich zu machen', by means of sabotage of a reality both intransigent and dominated by the powerful who control its narratives, a sabotage which will make a different, non-excluding history possible again.[18] Thus, positively or negatively, history plays an important role in Müller's intentions towards the audience. It is not just a matter of history in the play, but also the play in history, the play as part of the social process or more often as an act of sabotage of the social process. His goal (in this respect a very Brechtian one) is 'das Bewußtsein für Konflikte zu stärken, für Konfrontationen und Widersprüche'. (GI, p. 86)

Müller's conception of conflict as a liberating, productive force can also be illustrated by another remark: 'Nur wenn ein Text nicht zu machen ist, so wie das Theater beschaffen ist, ist es für das Theater produktiv.'[19] This is only apparently paradoxical; demonstrating the limits of the existing theatre by confronting it with what it cannot do forces it to widen its possibilities.

There is a second important consequence of the problem of closed dramatic form in plays like *Philoktet*, related to the development of Müller's conception of himself as an author and therefore as a contributor to the historical process. The criticism in *Philoktet* of the instrumentalisation of human beings and of human reason is actually also a critique of the instrumentalisation of the artist, an instrumentalisation which is involuntary and is often mistaken for its opposite, for subjective independence. For the apparently sovereign, even autocratic position of the artist towards the material at his disposal mirrors the Stalinist conception of the artist as a

17. *Theater-Arbeit*, Berlin, 1975, p. 125.
18. 'Gespräch über heutiges Theater', programme for *Die Umsiedlerin*, Dresden, 1985; quoted in Günther Heeg, 'Das Theater der Auferstehung', *Theater-ZeitSchrift*, 20, 1987, pp. 70–1.
19. 'Der Dramatiker und die Geschichte seiner Zeit', *Theater 1977. Jahressonderheft der Zeitschrift 'Theater heute'*, 1977, p. 120.

steersman of historical progress, an 'Engineer of the human soul'.[20] That is, the author's position towards his material is essentially that of Odysseus. The artist who insists on his own, individually determinable position in the process of production only apparently liberates himself from determination by larger forces; at a deeper level he remains tied to the existing order, since the autonomy of the artist towards the object world mirrors the domination of man over nature. The theory of history and the theory of artistic production coincide: man – nature; artist – material to be artistically formed.[21] Thus if the artist contributes to the historical process as an authorial subject, he participates in the process of history governed by its laws; he therefore remains unfree (the male pronoun has been consciously employed here; see the reflections on *Hamletmaschine* below).

Hence Müller's plays of the 1970s and 1980s work towards the 'Verschwinden des Autors', as he puts it.[22] They increasingly turn against conceptions of a socially critical, epic theatre as exemplified by Brecht. It is true that epic theatre rejected the simplistic imitations of existing reality both of naturalism and of socialist realism. But because it transforms the authorial subject into an 'epic', knowing super-ego, 'the collective subject of an ultimately rational historical process', epic theatre in fact sacrifices any possibility of a radical, unfettered subjectivity which could actually push history forward.[23]

In addition, for critical artists in the GDR an undialectic perpetuation of Brecht's aesthetics, conceived for a quite different historical context, increasingly came to seem self-satisfied, affirmative and irrelevant. In seeking a new aesthetics, Müller seeks to provoke change, movement, or, in other words, to contribute in a real sense to the historical process: an attitude Brecht would have welcomed. As Müller remarks: 'Brecht gebrauchen, ohne ihn zu kritisieren, ist Verrat.' (R, p.149)

Let us now look at the consequences of this in some aspects of Müller's later work: firstly his treatment of the theme of violence, secondly his deconstruction of the narrative or active subject, thirdly his explicit or implicit location of historical change, therefore of hope for the future.

20. See Bathrick, 'Affirmative and Negative Culture', p. 182.
21. See Bathrick, p. 181.
22. 'Der Schrecken ist die erste Erscheinung des neuen. Zu einer Diskussion über Postmodernismus in New York', in *Rotwelsch*, Berlin, 1982, p. 97; future references to *Rotwelsch* identified in the text by R and page number.
23. Bathrick, p. 183.

Müller rejects the orthodox marxist view of violence, in particular of fascism, as a wholly materialistically explicable phenomenon; he takes much more account of the imaginary, the irrational, the subconscious. Among Brecht's texts Müller has shown particular interest in *Fatzer*, a fragment, unpublished in Brecht's lifetime, where the view of fascism is considerably more complex than, for example, in *Die Rundköpfe und die Spitzköpfe* (e.g. GI, pp.31, 50ff.). With bloodstained images of violence, brutal sexuality or cannibalism Müller attempts in plays like *Germania Tod in Berlin* or *Die Schlacht* to articulate a hitherto silent, repressed and unacknowledged history, to be the historian of a collective amnesia. 'Um den Alptraum der Geschichte loszuwerden, muß man zuerst die Existenz der Geschichte anerkennen' (R, p.58). He excavates that German history which marxist historiography had long passed over in silence or safely pigeonholed in the negative section of a conveniently polarised view of historical responsibility.

Instead of resistance fighters and positive heroes Müller shows us cowards, traitors and opportunists, or more commonly, that these positive and negative behavioural characteristics can be found in one and the same person, are indeed, under existing social conditions, mutually determining. These plays remained controversial to the last in the GDR, but the 1980s did see their gradual breakthrough at the same time as GDR historiography painfully moved towards the recognition that the GDR's past is, as the GDR historian W. Schmidt put it, 'historisch nur als Resultat der ganzen deutschen Geschichte zu begreifen'.[24] Of course, Müller's view of 'die ganze deutsche Geschichte' was not that of the party, and collisions continued to occur: the positive view of the Prussian tradition as officially rediscovered in the GDR in the 1980s is not that of *Germania Tod in Berlin* or *Leben Gundlings Friedrich von Preußen Lessings Schlaf Traum Schrei*.

These plays also tend to ritualise death. In 1982 Müller, influenced by the ritual theatre of Antonin Artaud, declared that theatre should, through tragedy, celebrate death as change, metamorphosis, movement. The affirmation of death was a sign of the willingness to change, and theatre should become the ritual place for developing this willingness. 'Die Angst vor der Tragödie ist die Angst vor der Permanenz der Revolution.'[25] Clearly this distances

---

24. W. Schmidt, 'Nationalgeschichte der DDR und das territorialstaatliche historische Erbe', *Zeitschrift für Geschichtswissenschaft*, 1981, 5, p. 399ff.
25. Quoted by Horst Domdey, 'Mythos als Phrase oder Die Sinnausstattung des Opfers', *Merkur*, 40, 1986, 5, p. 404: I have drawn on this article for the

Müller from the Brechtian view of tragedy as at best unnecessary, at worst reactionary. Artaud argues that the fear of change is broken down by ritualised identification with the aggressor. This is highly problematic: death as meaningful ritual sacrifice is hard to square with the twentieth-century tradition of mass murder as an anonymous quasi-industrial process (the same is true of Lautréamont's image of death as an irrational beast of prey, invoked by Müller in *Leben Gundlings*); worse, it may provide a transcendental meaning and hence a legitimation to that process. This is not totally contradicted by the fact that ritual enactments of violence in a text, on a stage, do not – any more than ritual renunciations of violence – bear any necessary causal relationship to the same acts in the material world.

One could also argue that Müller's belief that the individual bourgeois subject must be destroyed as part of the process towards the 'NEUER MENSCH', his expressionistically coloured term for the collective individual, is not so very far from Nietzsche: tragedy is the punishment on individuals for setting themselves apart from 'das ewige Leben des Willens'. Individual destruction is an affirmation of a greater and more lasting life force. In the socialist myth of the collective, the irrational or pre-rational longing to be part of the universal life force and so to escape the agonies of individual experience is cloaked in a historical materialist garb which appeals to a Newtonian sensibility of the kind Müller himself, with his critique of Enlightenment arrogance and Eurocentrism, wishes to disrupt.[26] Such internal contradictions, which he seeks neither to repress nor to resolve in a doubtful harmony, give his work its power.

The final scene of *Leben Gundlings Friedrich von Preußen Lessings Schlaf Traum Schrei* evokes the myth of Dionysos, torn to pieces by the Titans and then awoken to new life by Rhea. Out of death, out of destruction new life emerges. That is an age-old mythic topos, perfectly compatible too with marxist views of history: the birth of the new via the destruction of the old is a central theme of revolution literature. But in Müller's play new life is not produced by rationally describable processes. On a back-projection we read: 'Hochzeit von Feuer und Wasser Menschen aus neuem Fleisch', which elevates the sexual intercourse and subsequent mutual mur-

section on the role of violence and death: see also Carlotta von Maltzan, *Zur Bedeutung von Geschichte, Sexualität und Tod im Werk Heiner Müllers*, Frankfur tam Main, 1988, pp. 118–66.
26. Domdey, 'Mythos als Phrase', p. 406.

der of Nathan and Emilie to a marriage of the gods of the sun and the sea. The 'Spartakus' references – references to the 1918/19 revolution, quotations from Lessing's dramatic fragment 'Spartacus' – seem peripheral, not central to the atavistic celebration of death.[27]

This needs to be qualified in two respects. Firstly, the subversive potential of invoking Artaud is much greater in the GDR context, dominated by a discourse of marxist rationality, than it is in the West. In 1976 Müller pointed out that left-wing theory had always neglected to take sufficient account of the irrational motivational forces in mass movements: 'Da ist Artaud eine sehr produktive Störung' (GI, p.46). Secondly, only a crude and one-dimensional view of history would insist that a process may not be both tragic and triumphant, necessary and wasteful. Moreover, Müller's stage figures in these plays are more often personified processes than people.

However, Müller is in any case not a full-blooded disciple of Artaud. This can be seen by looking at the at first seemingly atavistic motif of blood in *Germania Tod in Berlin*. The 'Hure Berlin' is washed with proletarian blood in 1918 and becomes the bride of the proletariat. At the end of the play 'Hure 1' is pregnant with the child of the young bricklayer. Though a very conventional symbol, echoing Expressionist apotheoses of womanhood, this is far from a crypto-fascistic myth of the purificatory, rejuvenating power of blood in a thin disguise of proletarian pathos. Instead, drawing on motifs from Brecht's *Trommeln in der Nacht*, it indicates that the foundation of the GDR with its promises of a glorious future were laid on very contradictory, inextricably interwoven inheritances, but that without the whole of this German history, or without this whole German history, all hopes for the future would be built on a false foundation.

In *Wolokolamsker Chaussee* too death has little to do with Artaudian rituals. The play is a sequence of independent short scenes, drawn partly from a past long politically taboo in the GDR. In the first part Müller treats a familiar theme: the tragedy of an unavoidable act of violence. It is Autumn 1941: the Germans are at the gates of Moscow. The Russians are badly equipped, their morale at an absolute low ebb. Terror of the seemingly unbeatable Wehrmacht is everywhere. In this situation a Soviet officer has a captain shot who tried to evade the forthcoming battle by shooting himself through the hand. This execution decisively stiffens resistance amongst the troops: 'So ging den ersten Schritt mein Bataillon/Auf unsern Weg von Moskau nach Berlin', but 'mein andres Ich/Wollte den Toten um Verzeihung bitten'.[28] This is not a ritual celebration of death, and it is not an ironic comment on the absurdity of an execution 'pour encourager les autres' as in Voltaire's *Candide*. It is the recall into social memory of a characteristic moment of terrible dilemma, whose emotive power results from the irreconcilable contradiction between compulsion and humane values, between collective and individual.

Müller aims in his work to articulate the excluded, silent history that has not been recorded in the official narratives, that which, applying the Freudian model of consciousness to the society as a whole, has been repressed from the officially sanctioned view of the past and reemerges as a psychosis: 'Bei uns wird die Vergangenheit so stark verdrängt, daß sie die Gegenwart beherrscht', he remarked in 1988.[29] To articulate this repressed history, he has to break with a dramatic structure founded implicitly on a sovereign and omniscient aesthetic subject – as for example in epic theatre, where the form may be open, but where the implicit interpretation of the experience represented follows the principles of marxist social analysis. Müller sees these principles as in a double sense a 'Fessel' – using Marx's term as quoted above – a shackle, a bond, which needs to be cast off.

One way to cast off this 'Fessel' is by the dissolution of the aesthetic subject, a process portrayed in *Die Hamletmaschine*. The title itself addresses the apparent polarity, which is in fact a parallel: between the aesthetic subject/artist Hamlet as moulder of his material and the machine as the symbol of dominance over nature. Moreover, a Hamlet machine, which produces Hamlets at will, calls the autonomous individual subject into question. Instead, the subject Hamlet dissolves into Hamlet and the 'Hamlet-Darsteller', who then also refuses this role too. 'Ich bin nicht Hamlet. Ich spiele keine Rolle mehr [. . .] Mein Drama findet nicht mehr statt [. . .] Ich spiele nicht mehr mit' (M, pp.93–4). The drama of the individual subject, whether bourgeois or proletarian, disintegrates. *Die Hamletmaschine* contains the stage direction 'Zerreißung der Fotographie des Autors' (M, p.96). Müller's view of the necessity literally to deconstruct the Enlightenment subject relates closely to the role of violence in his work in a kind of dionysian marxist

28. *Shakespeare Factory I*, Berlin, 1985, pp. 248–9.
29. Quoted in Frank Heibert, 'Ost-West-Passage', *Theater heute*, 29, 1988, 4, p. 27.

post-modernism: 'Der erste Schritt zur Aufhebung des Individuums in diesem Kollektiv ist seine Zerreißung, Tod oder Kaiserschnitt die Alternative des NEUEN MENSCHEN. Das Theater simuliert den Schritt, Lusthaus und Schreckenskammer der Verwandlung.'[30]

Die Hamletmaschine presents the male subject in all its patriarchal atrophy: 'Er war ein Mann nahm alles nur von allem' says Hamlet of his father. In this stunted state, the female is scorned as a distraction from male goals, as Hamlet bitterly recognises: 'Man sollte die Weiber zunähn, eine Welt ohne Mütter. Wir könnten einander in Ruhe abschlachten' (M, pp.89–90). Hamlet's declaration 'Ich will eine Frau sein' is not contradicted by the later declaration of the 'Hamlet-Darsteller', 'Ich will eine Maschine sein', but rather exposed for what it really is: both are escapist fantasies, desperate projections, colonisations (M, pp. 92 and 96). Hamlet steps into Ophelia's clothes, like the male author who seeks to cure himself of the sickness caused by the repressive processes of patriarchy by projecting himself into a fantasised female subjectivity, a process observable in Baudelaire, Flaubert, Herbert Marcuse, or recently in Stefan Schütz's *Medusa*.[31]

Müller, though, does not do this. Instead he shows in the figure of the 'Hamlet-Darsteller' the dialectic interdependence of perpetrator and victim which is intrinsic to patriarchy. 'Ich bin der Soldat im Panzerturm, mein Kopf ist leer unter dem Helm, der erstickte Schrei unter den Ketten. Ich bin die Schreibmaschine [i.e. both author/ruler and servant]. Ich knüpfe die Schlinge, wenn die Rädelsführer aufgehängt werden, ziehe den Schemel weg, breche mein Genick. Ich bin mein Gefangener' (M, p.94).

This shrivelling of human potential, even when and precisely when one participates in power as its self-alienated instrument, is satirically represented in *Kentauren*, part four of *Wolokolamsker Chaussee*, where law-enforcement bureaucrats are locked into the dialectics of cops and robbers and eventually fused with their desks in a grotesque coalescence of function and functionary.

Müller certainly does not believe the dynamics of historical contradictions have ceased with the establishment of communist

---

30. *Herzstück*, Berlin, second edition, 1983, p. 103; future references identified in the text by H and page number.
31. See Sigrid Weigel, 'Der schielende Blick: Thesen zur Geschichte weiblicher Schreibpraxis', in I. Stephan & S. Weigel (eds), *Die verborgene Frau*, Berlin, 1983, p. 109; Moray McGowan, '"Das Kapitel Mann ist beendet": Female Texts by Male Authors as Critiques of Patriarchy?', in A. Williams et al., *Literature on the Threshold*, Oxford, New York, Munich, 1990, pp. 277–8.

states in Europe on the basis of the patriarchal enlightenment. The process continues: the achievements of each epoch become, in the dialectic of historical development, shackles, which one must break if one wishes to move history onwards.

Initially Müller does not know where the new will be located. In the scene 'Nachtstück' in *Germania Tod in Berlin* we see a human being on stage who is also an outsized, mouthless doll covered with posters: an image of alienation, literally 'un-mündig' in Kant's sense. In a grisly pantomime it dismembers and blinds itself. Lice crawl from the empty eye-sockets. It screams, and the act of screaming causes a mouth to form in the hitherto mouthless face. Out of deepest despair and destruction there thus develops an impulse of protest, of growth, of change. As the location of language, the mouth is an image of the human. A universal dialectic process, the development of the positive from the negative, is dramatically realised, but without being socially or historically located.

Die Hamletmaschine begins to indicate where, at least in this phase, Müller perceives the potential for revolt and so for change. The play is set in the 'Ruinen von Europa'; a monologue by Ophelia is entitled 'Das Europa der Frau'. Her resistance against her socially-determined role generates revolutionary energy: 'Ich lege Feuer an mein Gefängnis [. . .] Ich grabe die Uhr aus meiner Brust die mein Herz war.' Tied in bandages by two men whose white coats proclaim authority, she screams her protest: 'Hier spricht Elektra. Im Herzen der Finsternis. Unter der Sonne der Folter. An die Metropolen der Welt. Im Namen der Opfer. Ich stoße allen Samen aus, den ich empfangen habe [. . .] Nieder mit dem Glück der Unterwerfung. Es lebe der Haß, die Verachtung, der Aufstand, der Tod. Wenn sie mit Fleischmessern durch eure Schlafzimmer geht, werdet ihr die Wahrheit wissen.' (M, pp.89, 92, 97)

This scene articulates the energy of revolutionary protest, the Artaudian celebration of violence as the axe to break out of the 'Versteinerung der Hoffnung [unter dem] Druck der Erfahrung' which Müller observed in the society around him, where, in the years leading up to the events of autumn 1989, the socialist revolution found itself 'in der Stagnation, im Patt'.[32] As a figure in Botho Strauß's novel *Rumor* (1980) declares: 'Es gibt Stunden des massiven Eisgeistes, wo Haß die einzige Wärme ist und nur

32. Quoted by Theo Buck on page 5 of his entry on Heiner Müller in Heinz Ludwig Arnold (ed.), *Kritisches Lexikon zur deutschsprachigen Gegenwartsliteratur*, Munich, 1978.

Sprengung Atem schafft.' But how far is it from this anarchistic impulse of liberation through aggression to fascist dreams of 'Verjüngung durch einen Schuß Barbarei'?[33] Müller's concept of liberation is not free of an ambiguous pleasure in aggression and violence; in 1987 he approvingly paraphrased Freud: 'Ein wenig mehr Krieg im Frieden und das Leben könnte ganz schön sein'.[34] But it is essentially more specific, more marxist in fact, insofar as it concentrates on those social forces which are currently oppressed and thus dialectically generating the revolutionary energy to resist their oppression. Müller demonstrates this both in the *Hamletmaschine* and in *Der Auftrag*, his play about an attempt, inspired by the revolutions in France and Haiti, to foment a slave uprising in Jamaica. As Arlene Teroaka says: 'Not the privileged intellectuals Hamlet and Debuisson are the true revolutionary figures, but Ophelia and the slave Sasportas, whose bodies have experienced oppression and abuse.'[35]

In 1983, looking back to *Philoktet*, Müller declared that his Odysseus was an 'Europäer': 'Mit ihm geht die Geschichte der Völker in der Politik der Macher auf, verliert das Schicksal sein Gesicht und wird die Maske der Manipulation' (H, p.104). In the 1980s Müller has repeatedly declared European culture to be dead, destroyed by instrumental reason, and has put his hope in the Third World (a term which for him appears to embrace anarchistic or subversive First World subcultures too). In *Verkommenes Ufer Medeamaterial Landschaft mit Argonauten* Jason is killed by his own ship: after the 'Limits to Growth', the limits of technocratic domination of nature, have been reached, the colonist is destroyed by his own technology of colonisation. In this context Müller remarked in 1982: 'Das europäische Geschichtsprinzip, das auf dem paternalen Prinzip fußt, ist erledigt. Ich sehe in Asien das Aufgehen des mütterlichen Prinzips' (GI, p.72). Or elsewhere: 'Die Änderungen oder Reformen, die in unseren Ländern nötig sind, hängen sehr von der Entwicklung der Dritten Welt ab. Das ist ein großer Wartesaal,

33. Botho Strauß, *Rumor*, Munich, 1980, p. 74; E.E. Dwinger, *Die letzten Reiter*, Jena, 1935, p. 175.
34. 'Geschichtspessimismus oder Geschichtsoptimismus, das sind nur zwei Begriffe für Geschichtsunkenntnis. Heiner Müller im Dialog', *Sprache im technischen Zeitalter*, 103, 1987, p. 197.
35. Arlene Teroaka, *The Silence of Entropy or Universal Discourse. The Postmodernist Poetics of Heiner Müller*, New York, Berne, Frankfurt am Main, 1985, p. 31. Sigrid Weigel, 'Das Theater der weißen Revolution', in I.Stephan, S. Weigel (eds), *Die Marseillaise der Weiber*, Berlin, 1989, pp. 154–74, stresses the way Müller's texts re-sexualise, and so re-embody the disembodied female allegories of revolution.

in dem alles auf Geschichte wartet. Und Geschichte ist jetzt die Geschichte der dritten Welt mit all den Problemen von Hunger und Übervölkerung' (R, pp.11, 25).

Characteristically, Müller's hopes for change are not rose-tinted fantasies of a paradisaical future.. The changes that the forces in the Third World which are now the motors of history will bring about, have grown out of suffering, contradiction and conflict and will be accompanied by, indeed will themselves generate, suffering, contradiction and conflict. *That* for Müller is the law of history. As early as 1958, Müller's short prose piece 'Der glücklose Engel', part of an unfinished libretto based on Brecht's fragment 'Reisen des Glücksgotts', alludes to Walter Benjamin's much cited interpretation of Paul Klee's painting 'Angelus Novus' and its image of progress as a storm of chaos driving history, her face a permanent mask of terror, onward.[36]

Müller shares Rosa Luxemburg's view that the alternative is 'Sozialismus oder Barbarei'; however, he has never considered the terms of the question to be static. Neither the foundation or continued existence of a socialist state, nor socialism's apparent demise in the 1990s render it redundant. Rather he considers it to be an ongoing, contemporary question, which must repeatedly be asked and answered. Whoever considers historical contradictions to have been solved or resolved, has more nearly given up on history than someone like Heiner Müller who on the one hand declared in 1985, 'Die Entwicklung der Menschen als Gegenstand der Anthropologie ist absolut minimal' (GI, p.149), and yet on the other hand addresses himself again and again to the demonstration and the advancing of contradiction and conflict as the paths to change.

This applies to the author him/herself, too, as Müller has always insisted. The author's privileged subjectivity must be combatted, by division into multiple voices and by pitiless self-criticism. In December 1989 Müller published the following poem:

Selbstkritik
Meine Herausgeber wühlen in alten Texten
Manchmal wenn ich sie lese überläuft es mich kalt
Das
Habe ich geschrieben IM BESITZ DER WAHRHEIT
Sechzig Jahre vor meinem mutmaßlichen Tod

36. See Walter Benjamin, *Zur Kritik der Gewalt und andere Aufsätze*, Frankfurt am Main 1971, p. 84ff.; Helen Fehervary, 'Enlightenment or Entanglement: History and Aesthetics in Bertolt Brecht and Heiner Müller', *New German Critique*, 8, 1976, pp. 93–5.

Auf em Bildschirm sehe ich meine Landsleute
Mit Händen und Füßen abstimmen gegen die Wahrheit
Die vor vierzig Jahren mein Besitz war
Welches Grab schützt mich vor meiner Jugend[37]

With characteristically bitter irony, Müller here articulates the helpless self-doubt of many GDR writers as in the autumn and winter of 1989/90 they watched their compatriots metaphorically and literally walk straight past them to embrace a very different utopia from their own. At the demonstrations on 4 November 1989 Müller's call for independent trade unions was met with indifference or hostility; the people's ever more apparent choice of consumer-orientated individualism was confirmed in the elections of the following March. Just as Müller began to be rewarded and recognised by the GDR cultural authorities, this state, with which he had lived in symbiotic conflict almost since its founding, and, perhaps more importantly, the principles from which it drew its legitimation and the idealism of its supporters, began to disintegrate before his eyes. Revolutionary change, much invoked in his texts as a dionysiac process of destruction and rebirth, showed a very different, bloodless but banal face. The end of history is the beginning of history: a Müllerean sentiment with which to break off – not, of course, to end – these reflections on Heiner Müller, for whom and in whose work marxism, postmodernism and an inescapable German historical identity are in continuous and artistically fruitful conflict.

37. *Die Zeit*, 15 December 1989, p. 62.

Suggested Further Reading

Bibliography of main works by Heiner Müller
(with date of first performance):

Zehn Tage, die die Welt erschütterten 1957
Der Lohndrücker 1958
Klettwitzer Bericht 1958
Die Korrektur 1958
Die Umsiedlerin 1961
Ödipus Tyrann 1967
Philoktet 1968
Prometheus 1969
Drachenoper (Libretto) 1969
Weiberkomödie 1970
Macbeth 1972
Zement 1973
Der Horatier 1973
Herakles 5 1974
Traktor 1975
Die Schlacht 1975
Mauser 1975
Die Bauern 1976 (revised version of *Die Umsiedlerin*)
Germania Tod in Berlin 1978
Leben Gundlings Friedrich von Preußen Lessings Schlaf Traum Schrei 1979
Hamletmaschine 1979
Der Bau 1980
Der Auftrag 1980
Herzstück 1981
Quartett 1982
Verkommenes Ufer Madeamaterial Landschaft mit Argonauten 1983
Anatomie Titus Fall of Rome Ein Shakespearekommentar 1985
Bildbeschreibung 1985
Wolokolamsker Chaussee I – V:
  I – Russische Eröffnung 1985
  II – Wald bei Moskau 1986
  III – Das Duell 1987
  IV – Kentauren 1988
  V – Der Findling 1988

Müller's work is published in several overlapping editions. The most comprehensive is the 'Heiner-Müller-Ausgabe' of the 'Rotbuch-Verlag', published as *Texte 1 – 9*, Berlin, from 1974.

Secondary Material

Heinz Ludwig Arnold (ed.), *Heiner Müller, Text und Kritik*, No. 73, 1982.

Norbert Eke, *Heiner Müller. Apokalypse und Utopie*, Paderborn, 1990.

Theo Girshausen (ed.), *Die Hamletmaschine, Heiner Müllers Endspiel*, Cologne, 1978.

Bettina Gruber, *Mythen in den Dramen Heiner Müllers*, Essen, 1989.

Frank Hörningk (ed.), *Heiner Müller. Material*, Göttingen, 1989.

J.H. Reid, 'Homburg-Machine – Heiner Müller in the shadow of nuclear war', in W.G. Sebald (ed.), *A Radical Stage. Theatre in Germany in the 1970s and 1980s*, pp.145–60.

Genia Schulz, *Heiner Müller*, Stuttgart, 1980.

Marc Silberman, *Heiner Müller*, Amsterdam, 1980.

Wolfgang Storch, *Explosion of a Memory Heiner Müller DDR*, Berlin, 1989.

Klaus Teichmann, *Der verwundete Körper. Zu Texten Heiner Müllers*, second edition, Freiburg 1989.

Arlene Teraoka, *The Silence of Entropy or Universal Discourse*, New York, Berne, Frankfurt am Main, 1985.

George Wieghaus, *Heiner Müller*, Munich, 1981.

-10-

'Be Realistic: Demand the Impossible'.

On Irmtraud Morgner's Salman Trilogy.

Agnès Cardinal

If, of a clement spring evening in the late 1980s in Paris, a casual stroller were to ascend the elegant Boulevard Saint-Michel to where it crosses the Boulevard Saint-Germain, she would see numerous brightly lit and crowded cafés, stroll past opulent bookshops and cinemas advertising films such as *Apocalypse Now* or *Good Morning, Vietnam*. Deafened by the roar of cars as they race to beat the amber lights, she would soon escape into the darker, quieter sidestreets, where, however, the pictures outside nightclubs would cause her to walk on quickly. But right around the corner, she would again be charmed by graceful and funny street performers, the fragrance of the pancake stalls and the hordes of carefree young people lounging on benches and tarmac. Little would remind her of the violent street battles which had raged on this selfsame spot only twenty years before. Gone are the cobblestone barricades, the burnt-out cars and the shrieking sirens. Gone too are the pools of blood spilt by warring youths, some wearing riot-police gear, others just jeans and sweaters. The poetic slogans chalked across the sober facades of this Parisian townscape too have faded, and only a faint memory remains of that electrifying atmosphere of a revolt which pitched itself against the old order, armed with words of poetry and the galvanising powers of the imagination, a notion so seductive that it was to become formative for a whole generation of European youth.

Our stroller might now turn up a side street and plunge into the silent chambers of the Abbaye de Cluny, an ancient place of retreat, now turned museum, where in the famous eleventh room, a circular hall, she would find exhibited six vast and magical tapestries. These tapestries, discovered in 1844 by George Sand in the small township of Boussac, display in a series of six tableaux a celebration of the female sensibility at its most poetic and tender. Against a scarlet background floats a blue island completely covered with an ornamentation that takes its inspiration from a multitude of plants. Thousands of blossoming bushes and fruit-laden trees are spread across not just the cobalt ground of the island at the centre, but also the scarlet sky which entirely surrounds the motif. Rabbits, dogs, wild cats and graceful birds take their place placidly amidst all kinds of paradisial vegetation and colourful banners, all around the central female figure which gives each work its focus. Of the six tapestries, the first five celebrate the human senses: sight, sound, touch, smell and hearing. The sixth portrays a medieval lady and her attendant emerging from a blue tent to inspect a casket of jewels. Lion and Unicorn hold the tent open for her and the inscription above it is 'A mon seul désir' or 'To my unique, my own, desire'. No one has been able to decipher the theme of this sixth tapestry.

Thus, within but twenty yards of the battlefields of May 1968, within earshot now of the deafening noise of the ever increasing traffic pushing through the oxygen-starved streets, behind walls three feet thick, and surrounded by a tiny, shrivelled and rubbish-strewn park, there hang, hermetically secluded, these fabulous carpets, silent and majestic.

This discursive beginning to my argument, besides being an attempt to ease gently into the complex artistic world of Irmtraud Morgner, is meant to establish a series of reference points against which the themes of her Salman Trilogy should be situated. After all, it is precisely in May 1968 on that street corner in Paris that the Trobadora Beatriz, the title figure of the first novel in the Trilogy, eventually begins to take control of her modern existence after a slow awakening from her 843-year-long 'Dornröschenschlaf'.

Irmtraud Morgner's *Beatriz* was published in 1974, and its sequel *Amanda* appeared in 1983. Her untimely death in May 1990 at the age of 57 has meant that the third volume *Die cherubinischen Wandersfrauen: ein apokrypher Salmanroman* will not, now, reach its final form. However, a short and anticipatory fragment from it was printed in a Zürich newspaper in 1988.[1] This extraordinary tale of a woman turned bird suggests that in her third novel Morgner has continued her exploration of reality in terms of the fantastic, in a way already established in the first two volumes. Given the vast-

---

1. *Neue Zürcher Zeitung*, 16/17 April 1988, pp. 67–8.

ness and complexity of these novels, my approach here is necessarily selective. It is nevertheless possible, albeit somewhat schematically, to identify a number of concerns which lie at the centre of Morgner's trilogy.

When asked in an interview about the principal motivation for her writing, Irmtraud Morgner stated without hesitation: 'Eintritt der Frau in die Historie'.[2] Women, she argues, have played virtually no active part in the creation of the history of mankind. If they appear at all in the narratives of our traditions, it is invariably only in an oblique way, in the position of an object perceived by a male subject. Morgner's Salman novels represent an initial, bold and experimental attempt to redress this imbalance. Her aim is the creation of what she sees as an historical, mythological and legendary space for womanhood as complement to man's own estate.

Because of such claims Morgner has often been described as an uncompromising feminist. While it is true that she is indeed passionately involved with feminist issues, her work reaches far beyond the narrow confines of political and social demands for female equality. What we are invited to contemplate in her work is the liberation and the celebration of the feminine principle in universal, non-gender-differentiated terms. In her novels, the concept of *homo humanus* or 'die Vermenschlichung des Menschen' is a recurring utopian ideal, which, as becomes clear as the novels unfold, will only be achieved through the harmonious fusion of the creative potential of both the feminine and the masculine principles. For the moment, what has to be aimed for is our systematic, step-by-step liberation from all constricting and stereotypical assumptions about the nature of men and women. Only when this is realised can a fruitful partnership between the two be envisaged. What will bring this *homo humanus* into being is without doubt the liberation of the individual's – any individual's – creativity through the activation of the imagination. Once this has happened, the world will change.

If her claim to alter the world by writing a poetic book strikes us as the dream of an unrealistic idealist, Morgner would counter our scepticism in the true spirit of May '68: 'Seid realistisch, verlangt das Unmögliche!' Since time is running out for humankind, only a truly desperate feat of the imagination is likely to change the course of events. She states: 'Mein Antrieb wäre nicht, Kunst zu machen, mein Antrieb wäre, Welt zu machen'.[3] Not content to work

2. Joachim Walther, 'Interview mit Irmtraud Morgner' in *Weltbühne*, no. 32, 1972, p. 1011.
3. Quoted in Patricia A. Herminghouse, 'Die Frau und das Phantastische in der

towards an as yet largely unrecognised feminine aesthetic, she sets out, through art, through poetry, to change the very nature of the world itself. She sees her first task as that of suspending the dividing line between the real and the imaginary, between fact and fiction. Only when these distinctions are no longer operative, she argues, will art and the imagination have an impact on the real world.

What prompts Morgner to make such apparently extravagant claims is, in part, the realisation, now widely acknowledged, that our awareness of our selves, of our origins, of our memories and our traditions, are in the last analysis always dependent on an interpretive narrative voice: that is, they are always fictional. What does history do other than tell us stories? What exactly is the nature of those facts which history relates to us? How do those facts differ from the truths embedded in myths, legends, fairy tales? All of them do but one thing, which is to link us in our collective and individual imagination to a shared past and a common origin, which crystallise in our minds into an awareness of our identity. In the images we have of ourselves, fact and fiction are thus not perceived as fundamentally different. Indeed, what makes us believe a fact, or a truth, is invariably that which is most convincingly, most satisfyingly narrated to us.

Thus, Morgner argues, it is always the nature of the narrative voice that determines what becomes accepted truth and which stories influence the cultural consensus. The more extravagant, the more memorable this voice, the greater its impact on the human mind, she contends. With her novels which literally revel in narrative exuberance, in evocative detail and the spellbinding intertwining of the fabulous and the real, she will thus attempt to woo the reader into developing a richer, more daring and more poetically versatile frame of mind.

Inevitably, Morgner was, as a woman, initially concerned with the liberation of the creative potential in women, an issue which shapes all her female protagonists and lies at the heart of both *Beatriz* and *Amanda*.

While in *Beatriz* the ideas and moods of May '68 galvanise the Trobadora Beatriz into action, the story of Laura Salman, her complementary 'Doppelgänger', unfolds meekly in the German Democratic Republic. The very first line of *Beatriz* reads as follows: 'Natürlich war das Land ein Ort des Wunderbaren'. Later the GDR

---

neueren DDR-Literatur – Der Fall Irmtraud Morgner' in Wolfgang Paulsen (ed.), *Die Frau als Heldin und Autorin: Neue kritische Ansätze zur deutschen Literatur*, Berne, 1979, p. 252.

is also referred to as 'das gelobte Land'. This is not so much an ironic comment, I feel; rather it expresses Morgner's belief that, if things can be made to change, the change will clearly be most likely in this new society, where Marxist-Leninist ideals and a socialist system have already effected miracles.

Morgner offers a perfectly practical suggestion for the bringing about of the liberation of female creativity. When asked how she would solve the eternal conflict between the sexes, she replied categorically: 'Den glaubwürdigen Lösungsvorschlag brauche ich nicht zu erfinden. Der ist längst gemacht. Er heißt: proletarische Solidarität auch im Privatleben'.[4] Morgner here builds on a vision of equality which reaches beyond even Marx's view of women fulfilling themselves as workers, in that it enters the intimate domain of the relationship between man and woman. The implication is that, even in a socialist state where women supposedly enjoy equal rights, and where it could be claimed that women are now truly emancipated in public terms, there remains the private or sexual sphere, where women have yet to achieve freedom on a par with men. 'Erotik verlangt Freundschaft, Kameradschaftlichkeit, Solidarität . . . Man kann seinen Unterdrücker nicht lieben, nicht wirklich lieben',[5] she contends, and suggests that it is the erotic power-play between the sexes that lies at the core of every social and political imbalance. Invariably, Morgner sees women as the principal victims of the abuse of such power.

Her novels abound in portrayals of the blighted lives of women typical of today. The almost universal downgrading of anything to do with giving birth, child-care, domestic responsibilities and the art of 'Hegen und Pflegen' in general, and the subordination of such tasks to all other activities in the public and private spheres, lead to the stunting of female creativity. Repeatedly, Laura Salman muses about the strange fact of this universal 'Unterschätzung leiblicher Schöpfungen gegenüber geistigen' (B, p.205). The merits of motherhood are still grotesquely overshadowed by the glamour of erotic encounters, of scientific and artistic pursuits and of abstract thought. It is this public neglect which saps women's creative energies, producing low self-esteem and causing them to fall into depression. Added to this comes the problem of the 'Doppelbelastung' whereby women, in an attempt to make up for the time they

4. Eva Kaufmann, 'Interview mit Irmtraud Morgner' in *Weimarer Beiträge*, 30, 1984, p. 1500.
5. Quoted in Christel Hildebrandt, *Zwölf schreibende Frauen in der DDR. Zu den Schreibbedingungen in der DDR in den 70er Jahren*, Frauenbuchbetrieb, Berlin, 1984, p. 95.

have apparently wasted in bringing up children and caring for others, try to keep pace with men in the public domain, so much so that they often come close to destroying their health and sanity. Laura Salman, the heroine of all three novels, makes her appearance in the very first chapter of *Beatriz*, looking the very picture of down-trodden misery. A woman in her mid-thirties, she stands weeping in the pouring rain. Shapeless and overweight, clad in a terrible coat and decked out with a perm like crinkled wool, she confronts her mirror-image Irmtraud Morgner as both make their way to the kindergarten. With one hand Laura holds on to her young son who is tugging impatiently; with the other she clutches a brown parcel containing the manuscript of her novel. This then is the Laura who will make such a powerful claim to a new and flamboyant creative identity as Morgner's trilogy unfolds.

While her novels speak out for women everywhere, Morgner was nevertheless a committed socialist, who lived and worked in East Berlin: her work is firmly rooted at home, in the GDR of her day. Laura Salman, the quasi-autobiographical heroine, might be the 'Sinnbild der durchschnittlichen berufstätigen Frau mit dem Tugendsortiment fleissig – genügsam – willig – unauffällig – verzichtgeneigt' (A, p.29), but she is clearly also the product of GDR history and culture. Like Morgner, she is the educated daughter of a 'Lokomotivführer' and is twelve years old when the war ends. Profiting from the GDR's policies which encourage young workers to take up higher education, Laura enters the Humboldt University to pursue scientific studies (unlike Morgner who went to Leipzig to read Germanistik). Laura becomes pregnant while still a student. Finding no help anywhere, she infllicts upon herself an abortion which nearly kills her. Later she marries the journalist Uwe Panitzke who is well-intentioned and disciplined but boring. Laura gives birth to Juliane but finds it difficult to look after the child while coping with her demanding job as a scientist. By now Uwe is often away on business trips. Pressed by urgent commitments at work, Laura brings Juliane to the crèche when the baby is slightly feverish. A week later the child dies of pneumonia, barely a year old. Laura gives up her prestigious job and becomes a tram-driver in Berlin. Uwe finds this unacceptable and the couple divorce.

The early story of Laura is told laconically and with total detachment in the page and a half of the seventeenth chapter of *Beatriz*. But from now on Laura's will be the story of a woman who is trying, against all odds, to evolve a new kind of existence, a utopian ideal of feminine fulfilment within the reality of the modern socialist state. Her quest, which will span all three novels, seems to focus in essence on three main goals: firstly, the achievement within socialism of an undivided, fully recognised and totally accepted, feminine identity; secondly, a new pluralistic, possibly androgynous, sexuality; and finally and most importantly a future for herself, her son, and indeed for humanity in general.

In her desperation Laura draws upon a powerful resource she discovers she has at her disposal: her imagination, which begins to express itself through the magic of words, first in spells and rhymes, then in longer texts which eventually develop into the very novels before us. Thus Laura writes her novel *Beatriz*, and in that first meeting in the rain tries to persuade Irmtraud Morgner to purchase and publish it, although Morgner points out that she herself is indeed busy trying to publish her own novel. Author and protagonist are thus locked in a competitive combat for public recognition.

Confusing and amusing, yet full of implications, is the role of Morgner herself in her own novel, where she appears as narrator but also as character, sometimes as the interviewer of her heroine and autobiographical double, manipulating and being manipulated by her characters. 'Die gute Fee Melusine', for example, takes the liberty of inserting into Laura's text in seven 'Intermezzi' an entire novel which Morgner had written earlier and had not succeeded in publishing. In *Amanda*, various characters in the novel discuss the merits and faults of Morgner's first novel, voicing criticisms which are sometimes outrageously biased but occasionally valid. In this capricious playfulness, the boundaries between author and novel, between fact and fiction, between 'Tatsache' and 'Text' become blurred and ultimately irrelevant.

Through another web of juxtapositions and contrasts we become familiar with the mundane details of Laura's everyday life, while at the same time being introduced to the fairy tale world of the marvellous. Against the realistic details of her work as a 'Triebwagenfahrerin' on night shift, her struggles with domestic duties and sleeping patterns which must accommodate her new son's waking hours, and against the fragmented bits of information about Laura's own childhood, there develops a breathtaking vision which takes the reader on a truly Faustian voyage far beyond the realities of contemporary East Germany. And it is through this medium that the troubadour Beatriz, herself half myth, half history, joins forces with Laura. Beatriz embodies that magical dimension of the imagination that Laura lacks so pitifully in her modern life. While Laura goes about her daily chores in Berlin, Beatriz cavorts around the world, turns up in Paris in May 1968, tries out various sexual relationships, and converses with mystical and legendary figures of Classical and Nordic origin. But it is Laura who, as Beatriz's 'Spielfrau', embarks on the serious game of writing this all-important novel.

And the experiment seems to be a success. *Beatriz* is a novel which ends on a distinctly hopeful note. The year is now 1973, and a change for the better is in the air. Laura, her new and delightful husband Benno, and Beatriz are staying up all night in their flat in Berlin to hear the election results in France. The socialists are winning, and Beatriz is so overcome with euphoria and wine that, at three o'clock in the morning, she begins to sing the Marseillaise. Paris, it seems, is about to become that utopian town of the future 'darin Menschen, Tiere und Pflanzen auf rotem Grund hausten' (B, p.618). The utopian vision of the Cluny tapestries is on the point of becoming real. On an impulse, Beatriz, who has begun to take over more and more of Laura's domestic duties, grabs a mop and bucket and begins to clean the windows: but she loses her balance and plunges to her death. Laura, inconsolable at first, is now on her own. However, it seems that she and Beatriz are no longer in need of separate identities, and indeed Beatriz had already become Laura in many respects. It is with Benno at her side, a man 'mit Gefühl für Kinder', that she can look confidently to the future. Having gone a good distance towards liberating her own creative forces, she can take Beatriz's place at the great mythical round table of King Arthur.

Morgner's first Salman novel ends with the story 'Geschlechter-tausch', in which another woman, the nutritionist Valeska, learns the trick of being man or woman at will and thus becomes the paradigm for a utopian sexuality deriving strength and pleasure from both genders. Indeed, at the end of *Beatriz* many of the divisive realities of our modern awareness seem on the point of disappearing. In the political sphere East and West are coming closer. In her private life Laura has been able to absorb into her own creativity Beatriz's flights of the imagination, while her husband seems to be able to develop the feminine side of his nature. Valeska even transcends the sexual boundaries.

The three aims of Laura's adventure – the liberation and full development of her creative energy, the evolution of a new, more fulfilling sexuality, and the securing of a safer future – seem to be nearing their fulfilment. It is true that they have not, as yet, been totally realised, but developments are pointing in the right direction.

It took Irmtraud Morgner nine years to write the sequel to *Beatriz*. And in *Amanda* the mood has changed. *Beatriz* reappears but has turned into a siren in the shape of an owl with a woman's face. She has lost her tongue and can no longer sing and spends her time in a cage in the Berlin Zoo laboriously scratching the words of her novel onto paper with her claw. Thus sadly diminished, Beatriz resents Morgner's earlier optimism: 'so ist aus dem Buch [. . .] ein unverantwortlicher Roman geworden' (A, p. 149), she grumbles. Indeed, the harmonious fusion of opposites envisaged in *Beatriz* has not worked out: in this second novel the motif of the disabling fragmentation of the individual assumes a new importance. We are told that Laura has been born with a 'hexische Hälfte', which under the name of Amanda soon assumes an existence of its own. Other women in the book also have troublesome doubles. 'Ich zum Beispiel hab meine störende Hälfte verschluckt' (A, p. 351), claims Vilma, the battered wife, who ends up in a mental hospital. Everyone's existence is truncated, maimed or only partially re-alised. Men keep their unacceptable doubles locked away in cup-boards. Human as well as mythical creatures all limp about, intent on redemption but incapable of realising it.

Despite all the hopes raised at the end of *Beatriz*, Laura's prob-lems intensify in *Amanda*. Her husband Benno is having difficulties coping with Laura's new confidence and her success as a writer. He admires her, but has lost that sense of fun, that 'Unbefangenheit' of their earlier relationship when Laura was a nobody. Moreover, whenever Laura cuddles her small son, Benno looks away in pain. He starts to drink too much and one day he crashes the car and dies.

In her new and grimmer life Laura, 'Triebwagenfahrerin' and mother of Wesselin, finds support in a zany kind of 'närrische Solidarität' with other women. Their recourse to laughter, to the feminine giggle, now shapes but also undercuts the tragedy of Laura's life. Everything becomes a kind of ironic romp – through life, literature and myth. Laura begins to summon up her own 'hexische Hälfte', Amanda, and as they dabble in experiments in magic and alchemy in Laura's kitchen, they discover that even the witches are dominated by 'Teufel' und 'Oberteufel'. Beatriz, the voiceless siren, Arke, the serpent who rushes through the skies on a broomstick like a virago concerned only with her need 'eine Wut spazieren zu führen' (A, p. 458), indeed all the ghostly inhabitants of the Hörselberg where the witches live, cannot make a stand against the powers of the Bocksberg and its devils. Laura and Amanda's search for a strategy, a ruse, which could be used in the struggle against the oppressive rule of such patriarchy becomes ever more desperate and extravagant.

Constantly dodging proposals of marriage from 'Oberteufel' Kolbuk and the subtle temptations of 'Oberengel' Zacharias, Laura is also hard put to counter the insistent challenges of the radical feminist witch Isebel who wants to wage a full-blown war against all males. Not surprisingly, Laura longs for a kind of holy retreat, a safe island where she might bring up Wesselin away from all intrusions. Amanda, alarmed at Laura's dangerous escapism, pleads with her to join forces to confront the 'Erpressertrinität' of Kolbuk, Zacharias and Isebel. But Laura, fearful of the consequences for herself and her son, is unable to listen to her. In a last bid Amanda threatens to lay claim to Wesselin's future, whereupon Laura, echoing the fate of Beatriz, loses her balance and jumps (or falls) out of the window of her highrise flat. Her body is never found: indeed, eye-witnesses swear they have seen a woman fly away on a stick. Whatever her new status, Laura now joins forces with Heinrich Fakal who sports long tresses as a sign of his latent femininity. Laura persuades him to try to steal the liberating potion from 'Oberteufel' Kolbuk. But Heinrich fails and is made prisoner. At the end of the book Laura collapses into a pathetic Gretchen figure who calls pitifully after her Heinrich, just as happens in *Faust Part I*. Sure enough, a disembodied voice informs her 'Er ist gerichtet' (A, p. 651).

In an interview following the publication of *Amanda* Morgner confesses: 'Als ich *Beatriz* beendet hatte, merkte ich, daß ich noch gar nicht richtig angefangen hatte mit dem Stoff'.[6] Indeed, *Amanda* is less a sequel to *Beatriz* than a reworking of it. But whereas in *Beatriz* an alternative reality is envisaged as a desirable possibility, in *Amanda* the realms both of reality and of the imaginary become ever more threatening to Laura herself. In *Amanda* we find the most vibrant and evocative stories about Laura's childhood, her parents, her crotchety grandmother and about her school days in the 1940s and 1950s. But these are gradually eclipsed by the turmoils of Laura's struggles with everyday life and by the carryings-on of 'Oberteufel', 'Sirenen' and 'Hexen'. The juxtaposition of and the tension between the chimerical and the realistic is essential to both novels, but gains, both in intensity and scope, in *Amanda*. Above all, through the tongue-in-cheek reworking of all manner of historical, literary and mythical motifs, the author succeeds here in conveying an artistic message far subtler and more complex than

6. In Doris Berger, 'Gespräch mit Irmtraud Morgner', in *GDR Monitor*, Winter 1984/85, no. 12, p. 29.

the 'Heilsbotschaft' of *Beatriz*. The novel *Amanda* impresses the reader not so much by its positivistic linear exposition of Laura's 'Bildungsgang' than by its desperately ironic play with the whole 'Spielfrau' material. On the very first page of *Amanda* we find a quotation from E.T.A. Hoffmann about laughter being no more than a 'Schmerzenslaut der Sehnsucht', and the novel ends with the image of the witch Girgana laughing herself to death, her laughter being a final response to universal annihilation. In more ways than one, then, *Amanda* reflects a much harsher vision of the future than its predecessor.

Morgner's narrative method of montage in which speeches, interviews, poems and intertextual references intermingle with fairly-tale stories and dialogues between real and mythological creatures is central to the effect of both novels. Each short chapter is a carefully planned, deliberately placed component in a complex structure. The continual interruption of the flow of the narrative and the introduction of all kinds of heterogeneous material achieve an alienating effect in which each new fragment comes as a surprise, looks out of place and cannot, at first, be assimilated. Both in form and content the novels embody that fragmentation and alienation which is Morgner's vision of modern womanhood. Indeed, she sees montage as the only possible, if not the inevitable, way for a woman to write. As novelist and mother in charge of children, she finds that her train of thought is forever being interrupted by the duties of nurturing. Only by working in short furious bursts in between her other commitments can she realise her creative potential. 'Die tägliche Zerstückelung'[7] has become tangible reality and we are at once reminded of that gruesomely graphic chapter 26 in *Amanda*, which describes how François Damien, the would-be assassin of Louis XV, was drawn and quartered in Paris in 1757.

Laura appears in multiply refracted images throughout the novels. To begin with, the author herself is a distinct mirror image of Laura (cf. B, p. 9), while both the Trobadora and Amanda act as further compensatory complements to Laura's diminished status. Indeed all the women who populate the novels assume in various guises aspects of the female condition in general. And Laura, the magical artist and 'Triebwagenfahrerin' on night shift, is clearly a traveller capable of crossing all kinds of borders, geographic, temporal and intellectual. At certain moments of crisis, of tension

7. Quoted in Ingeborg Nordmann, 'Die halbierte Geschichtsfähigkeit der Frau. Zu Irmtraud Morgners Roman *Leben und Abenteuer der Trobadora Beatriz*' in Jos Hoogeveen and Gerd Labroisse (eds), *DDR-Roman und Literaturgesellschaft*, Amsterdam, 1981, p. 454.

or rupture, she is apt to lose her sense of balance and through a symbolic 'Fenstersturz' tumbles into a new state of being, into a new refraction.

Within this fragmentation the reader must become sensitive to references metaphoric, poetic and literal in Morgner's portrait of modern existence. Only then will the mosaic of her prose begin to reverberate in all its allusive complexity. When Morgner was asked how a reader should approach her novels, she stressed the need for reading them extremely slowly. The art of 'langsam lesen',[8] the contemplative approach to a text, is the mode which will engage the imagination of the reader most effectively.

Morgner's readers were awaiting the publication of the third part of the Trilogy when the news of her death reached them. Her death coincides eerily with the spectacular collapse of the communist world in Eastern Europe. Just like her heroines Beatriz and Laura, the author herself has suffered her 'Fenstersturz' at a moment of crisis and traumatic change. In *Amanda* the chapter preceding Laura's fall ends in the line: 'Ostberlin hat Wind gesät. Es wird Sturm ernten. Frühlingssturm?' (A, p. 558). The end of a repressive brand of socialism might well seem to be the end of a dream, but it could equally herald a new era, a more peaceful and hopeful new beginning for the entire human community. Within such an interpretation the central concerns of Morgner's writings, which had gathered momentum as her Trilogy developed, have reached a new and crucial importance today. From the early impetus rooted in the May Events of 1968 Morgner evolved, in the 1970s, her ideas concerning the simultaneous liberation and harmonious fusion of the creative powers of opposites, and in particular, of man and woman. This might, at the time, have seemed like an idealistic dream, a gesture towards an almost fanciful utopian ideal. In the 1980s this notion, she felt, had become an issue on which the very survival of our planet depended. In a seminar which she held in Switzerland in 1984, she argued, furthermore, and with arresting passion, that since it is still largely the men in this world who hold the power to make the decisions on such crucial issues as ecology, armaments and profit, it is now the reactivation of the feminine aspects of *men*'s nature which must be brought back into play at all costs. If men do not soon learn to redevelop their own latent 'Fähigkeit zu hegen'[9] and if they do not learn to be tolerant, flexible

8. Kaufmann, 'Interview mit Irmtraud Morgner', p. 1506.
9. B.v.M. (Beatrice von Matt), 'Die Fähigkeit zu hegen', in *Neue Zürcher Zeitung*, 12 February 1985, p. 35.

and imaginative, there will be no future for humankind. Morgner's third Salman novel, it now seems clear, would have become her gesture towards this most urgent and yet most utopian of all concerns.

I would like, now, to come back to those streets in Paris where my argument began. The question surely must arise whether Morgner succeeded in realising that most ambitious of her aims, which was to bring her art, the triumph of her imagination, out onto the streets, so that it might become transitive and transform reality. By now it is clear that that cobalt-blue island of retreat, beautiful and seductive though it may have appeared to Laura, could never be the solution to the problems of the beleaguered feminine sensibility. As the motto 'A mon seul désir' on the Cluny tapestry indicates, its serenity is based on a radical turning away from the world, it suggests a self-seeking 'Verweigerung' which shelters from the world behind walls three feet thick.

Indeed, Laura Salman's failure at the end of *Amanda* must be seen as the result of her having sought redemption, precisely, in an individualistic and one-sided revolt tantamount to a retreat into an exclusive subjectivism. Looking at the idyllic Cluny tapestries, she may well be attracted by the poise and poetry of those images, but she must also be aware of the women's lives sacrificed to these fastidious works: of those who had to sit there every day knotting the silks until the picture took shape. Appreciation of artistic beauty must now encompass a much wider awareness in which boundaries are crossed. Our traditional differentiation between art and life, between the eternal and the temporary, the beautiful and the mundane, the feminine and the masculine, between the individual and the collective, and the bias in favour of one or the other are revealed in Morgner's novels as ultimately pernicious to our very existence.

But whether the dividing line between her text and the world can be effaced, whether Irmtraud Morgner's books can change the attitudes of a whole generation of readers, must remain an open question. At least in their gesture towards the impossible they steadfastly engage our hope.

Author's Note

The following editions and abbreviations are used for Morgner's works:
B: *Leben und Abenteuer der Trobadora Beatriz nach Zeugnissen ihrer Spielfrau Laura. Roman in dreizehn Büchern und sieben Intermezzos*, Buch Club 65, Berlin, 1976.
A: *Amanda. Ein Hexenroman*, Berlin and Weimar, 1983.

Suggested Further Reading

Other works by Irmtraud Morgner:
Das Signal steht auf Fahrt. Erzählung, Berlin, 1959.
Ein Haus am Rand der Stadt. Roman, Berlin, 1962.
'Notturno. Erzählung', in *Neue Texte. Almanach für deutsche Literatur*, Berlin and Weimar, 1964, pp. 7–36.
Hochzeit in Konstantinopel. Roman, Berlin and Weimar, 1968.
Die wundersamen Reisen Gustav des Weltfahrers. Lügenhafter Roman mit Kommentaren, Berlin and Weimar, 1972.

Secondary Material

'Irmtraud Morgner', in Joachim Walter (ed.), *Meinetwegen Schmetterlinge. Gespräche mit Schriftstellern*, Berlin, 1973, pp. 42–54.
Synnöve Clason, 'Auf den Zauberbergen der Zukunft. Die Sehnsüchte der Irmtraud Morgner', in *Text und Kontext*, 12, 1984, pp. 378–86.
Marlies Gerhardt (ed.), *Irmtraud Morgner. Texte, Daten, Bilder*, Frankfurt am Main, 1990.
Sheila K. Johnson, 'A new Irmtraud Morgner: humour, fantasy, structures, and ideas in *Amanda. Ein Hexenroman*', in *Studies in GDR Culture and Society*, 4, pp. 45–64.
Eva Kaufmann, 'Der Hölle die Zunge herausstrecken. Der Weg der Erzählerin Irmtraud Morgner', in *Weimarer Beiträge*, 30, 1984, pp. 1515–32.
Alison Lewis, 'Fantasy and Romance. A Feminist Poetics of Subversion and the Case of Irmtraud Morgner', in *Southern Review*, vol. 20, November 1989, pp. 244–57.

Ursula Püschel, 'Von dem Buch *Amanda* zu sprechen' in *kürbiskern*, 1981, 1, pp. 86–97.

Dorothee Schmitz, *Weibliche Selbstentwürfe und männliche Bilder. Zur Darstellung der Frau in DDR-Romanen der 70er Jahre*, Frankfurt, Berne, New York, 1983.

Lia Secci, 'Irmtraud Morgner: von der realen zur romantischen Utopie', in Gisela Brinker-Gabler (ed.), *Deutsche Literatur von Frauen*, vol. 2, pp. 428–32.

Siegfried Streller, 'Wiedereroberung des Phantastischen zur Wirklichkeitserhellung. Dargestellt an Irmtraud Morgners *Amanda. Ein Hexenroman*', in *Weimarer Beiträge*, 32, 1986, pp. 690–5.

–11–

Tales and the Telling:

The Novels of Jurek Becker

Martin Kane

'Kirschbaum hat nie einen Gedanken daran verschwendet, daß er Jude ist . . . was ist das schon, jüdische Herkunft, sie zwingen einen Jude zu sein, und man selbst hat gar keine Vorstellung, was das überhaupt ist' (JL, p. 80). The reflections of Kirschbaum, the Jewish doctor in Jurek Becker's *Jakob der Lügner*, who commits suicide rather than treat the ailing ghetto Gestapo chief, have a certain affinity with Becker's own tenuous relationship with his Jewishness. In a volume of essays entitled *Mein Judentum* he remarks how on being asked about his origins he always replied: '"Meine Eltern waren Juden"', and goes on to explain: 'Ich benutzte diesen Satz wie eine feststehende Formel, die in nicht zu überbietender Klarheit Auskunft gibt. Wenn der Frager mitunter dann konstatierte: "Sie sind also Jude", berichtigte ich ihn jedesmal, indem ich nochmal meine Formel sagte: "Meine Eltern waren Juden".'[1]

On the face of it, certain associations might be made here between Becker and Aron Blank, the hero of *Der Boxer* (1976). Blank, a survivor of Nazi concentration camps, creates a new and anonymous life for himself in postwar Germany by manufacturing an identity which has no point of contact with his Jewishness. He changes his first name from Aron to Arno, his place of birth from Riga to Leipzig. He retains his surname because it is 'neutral', but, in symbolic eradication of the period he had spent in the camps, he falsifies his age to make himself six years younger. But Jurek Becker is no Arno Blank. If, on one level, author and his creation have both distanced themselves from Jewish identity and origins, this is where the similarities end. Arno Blank's past leads him to a

---

1. In Hans Jürgen Schultz (ed.), *Mein Judentum*, Stuttgart and Berlin, 1979, p. 10.

Martin Kane

life of self-erasement and unproductive purposelessness: it induces a
paralysis of the will, 'eine Art von Müdigkeit . . ., die jede Aktion
unmöglich macht' (B, p. 251). Becker's past on the other hand has
led him to devote a considerable energy to the holocaust and its
repercussions. There is an element of inevitability here. Although
being Jewish now is a matter of some indifference to him, the fact
that he was born into a Jewish family has, as he notes, in *Mein
Judentum* 'für meinen bisherigen Lebenslauf nicht eben kleine Folgen gehabt'.

Becker spent the early years of his childhood in the Lodz ghetto
and the camps at Ravensbruck and Sachsenhausen, an experience to
which he has repeatedly been drawn: in his first novel *Jakob der
Lügner*, a huge commercial and aesthetic success, translated into
twelve languages and filmed; in *Der Boxer* and *Bronsteins Kinder*
(1986) as well as in a number of shorter prose works.[2] Nevertheless, it is necessary to be reminded that his reputation rests on much
more than a recurrent preoccupation with one of the monumental
themes of our century. He is also one of those East German writers
who have have eased GDR literature away from the notion of
'Auftrag' – of socially dutiful commission – to write about the
individual not as schematic exemplar and representative, but as a
private human being who has desires, aspirations and hopes which
are not always easily reconcilable with official expectations of him.
Precisely that dimension which is almost always missing in the
early 'Aufbauliteratur' of the GDR – where, for the sake of ideological purpose, all is played out at the place of work – is, in novels
such as *Irreführung der Behörden* (1973), *Schlaflose Tage* (1978) or
Aller Welt Freund (1983), shifted into the foreground and made the
object of wryly observant and reflective scrutiny. Here, centre
stage is occupied not by the individual as toiler on farm or in
factory where work, as Simrock in *Schlaflose Tage* ironically observes, is something which '. . . auf magische Weise vom Ar-
beitenden Besitz ergreif[t], seine Persönlichkeit bereicher[t] und ihn
beflügel[t]' (ST, p. 95), but by men and women as husbands, wives
or lovers. Authenticity of experience and feeling – reality if you like
– is plotted and traced in the bedroom or breakfast table exchange
and not at the milling machine.

This essay then will look at Becker's work from two points of
view. Firstly it will examine its contribution to our understanding

2. See particularly the stories 'Die beliebteste Familiengeschichte' and 'Die Mauer' in
   Nach der ersten Zukunft. Erzählungen, Frankfurt am Main (suhrkamp taschenbuch),
   1983, pp. 40–61 and 62–102.

of the holocaust and its repercussions. And secondly it will look at the ways it has dramatised the texture of day to day life in the GDR: the struggle to attain a modicum of happiness and self-fulfilment, to resist the temptation to be opportunistic, and to reconcile the attractions of what Günter Gaus has called the 'Nische' of the private sphere with public and professional demands.

In looking at the first of these concerns – the holocaust, the camps, ghettoes and their aftermath – one must emphasise at the outset Becker's unorthodox approach, how intent he is on avoiding the melodramatic. Unlike, for instance, Bruno Apitz and his novel *Nackt unter Wölfen* – or rather the novel rewritten by a team of sub-editors delegated to ensure that the book yield up, in its portrayal of the communist party activists in Buchenwald, a certain propagandistic value – Jurek Becker and his novels and stories dealing with this subject cannot easily be deployed to legitimise the present by reference to the horrors and gruesome injustices of the past. In approaching the past, his own past, and its long shadow, Becker never reaches for the readily available heroic cliché, always avoids making easy emotional capital. He is very clear in his own mind about this, wanting no part of falsifying myths and legends. In an essay for a symposium in Toronto in 1983 he commented that the role of resistance in literature had become inflated, thereby diminishing the feats of those who actually had put up resistance.[3] He went on to relate how he had initially dismissed an idea of his father for a novel about a man in a ghetto who, until he had been discovered and shot, had used a hidden radio to provide his fellow inhabitants with news. He didn't, he said, '. . . . have the slightest desire to write about him. Because I had often read about this man – thousands of books had already been written about him. Strictly speaking almost every book I had read about the fascist era was about this very man'.[4] When Becker did eventually come to write his novel *Jakob der Lügner*, initially in the form of a film script, it was rejected. We may surmise that in his desire to write a ghetto story which steered its way past the idealised view of the resistance hero, Becker had failed to meet the expectations of authority. A further interesting snippet here is that Becker's father was so incensed by the gulf between the novel and his original version of the story that he refused to speak to him for a year.[5]

3. Jurek Becker, 'Resistance in *Jakob der Lügner*', in *Seminar*, 1983, no. 4, p. 271.
4. Ibid., p. 272.
5. In Volker Hage, 'Wie ich ein Deutscher wurde. Eine Begegnung mit Jurek Becker in Berlin und Anmerkungen zu seinem Roman *Bronsteins Kinder*', in 'Zeit Literatur', *Die Zeit*, 3 October, 1986, p. 2.

In searching for the fresh perspective on the ghettoes, for the
reality beneath the myths, Becker has two incalculably valuable
assets at his disposal. Firstly, his endless inventiveness, a talent for
spinning an interesting yarn which make him one of the best story
tellers to emerge from the GDR. And secondly, something which
occasionally has made the novel a subject of controversy, his
humour, a wryly ironic treatment of baleful fates and incident.

As we begin to grapple with *Jakob der Lügner* the revelation of
both these gifts is not slow in coming. The point on which the
novel turns – Jakob's fictitious radio, the source of invented stories
about the advance of the liberating Soviet army which lifts the
ghetto inmates out of the depths of despair – is built out of a series
of turns of chance and accident in which humorous incident and
potential catastrophe are but a slender hair's breadth apart.

How seductive the chain of incident which is set in motion.
Firstly Jakob is played a cruel trick by a guard who sends him to the
ghetto 'Revier' for supposedly breaking the curfew. While awaiting
his 'gerechte Bestrafung' he overhears a fragmentary radio report
that Russian troops are barely four hundred kilometres away. At
the same moment, in the act of eavesdropping – comedy cheek by
jowl with disaster – he catches his sleeve in the door. A scene of
Cleesian panic ensues, set to the frantic logic of Jakob's racing
deliberations on how to escape. Cut the sleeve off? No knife. Leave
the jacket behind? Perhaps; the coming winter could be coped with.
But no, he would have to abandon the yellow star sewn to it, with
certain fateful consequences. Pulling desperately at the trapped
sleeve, the door opens. He falls into a tumbled heap.

What does this scene remind us of? Or the one two pages later
with the duty officer on the sofa who, with Jakob nervously
waiting for him to wake, turns over, sighs, snorts, a lighter
dropping from his pocket to the floor? Becker's narrator helps us to
a formulation of an answer in the crucial subsequent scene when
Jakob rescues Mischa from the consequences of his uncontrollable
greed, and the totally reckless thought that he might be able to steal
some potatoes from under the noses of the ghetto guards, by
spluttering out – as a last desperate resort – that he has a radio.
What characterises these scenes and the one later when Kowalski
diverts the attention of a diarrhoea-stricken guard away from the
latrine where Jakob has hidden himself to scour the newspapers are,
of course, the elements of knockabout Chaplinesque farce:

> Mischa[. . .] macht sich an den Kisten zu schaffen, will eine auf die
> Kante stellen, da gibt ihm der Anführer eine von der Seite. Mischa dreht

sich zu ihm um, der Anführer ist ein Kopf kleiner als er, und es bereitet ihm einige Mühe, bis zu Mischas Gesicht hinaufzuschlagen. Es sieht beinahe ein bißchen komisch aus, nichts für die deutsche Wochenschau, eher wie ein Spaß aus der Stummfilmzeit, wenn der kleine Polizist Charlie versuchte, den Riesen mit den buschigen Augenbrauen zur Strecke zu bringen, und er müht sich ab, und der Große merkt es gar nicht. (JL, p. 33)

How are we to react to elements such as this in *Jakob der Lügner* where brutality is tinged with humour? Does Becker's use of them lay him open to charges of trivialisation or 'Verharmlosung', bringing the novel into that area of discussion about concentration camp and holocaust literature for which Adorno's comment on the barbarity of writing poems about Auschwitz has so frequently served as a convenient shorthand? Certainly not. One is reminded firstly of Helene Weigel's crucial intervention in the 1959 debate about Brecht's *Schweyk im zweiten Weltkrieg* that '. . . jede Diskussion überflüssig sei, wenn man meine, daß man über Mörder nicht lachen könne'.[6] But comedy in *Jakob der Lügner* has a further vital function: to remind us of the humanity of the victims of a system which has set out, methodically and calculatingly, to dehumanise. One of the first things which we learn about the ghetto is not only that there are no radios, but that all trees, pets, plants, rings and watches, as well as music of every kind, have been banished. Everything which reminds man of his humanity – 'Alles was den Menschen rund macht und menschlich' (Brecht) – has been ruthlessly removed as the precondition for disqualifying the Jewish ghetto dwellers as human beings: 'Laut Verordnung bist du eine Laus, eine Wanze' (JL, p. 21). And this as the first step to wiping them out all together. The hideous logic is not difficult to follow. It is much easier to exterminate those who are no longer considered to be members of the human race.

One final point needs to be made about the humour of the novel. In our reaction to the Jewish victims of National Socialism there is the danger of seeing them as victims remote in place and time from ourselves. Rooted as they are in a paradoxical but immediately recognisable mixture of everyday frailty and fortitude, one highly salutory function of the comic elements in *Jakob der Lügner* is to bring the victims closer to us, to remind us of the common humanity we share with them.

A further question which arises from one's reflections on this

6. See Pavel Petr, *Haseks 'Schwejk' in Deutschland*, Berlin 1963, p. 160.

novel is that of Jakob's lies. What, one asks, in the face of the inevitable, have they achieved? One reply might be that they have reminded us of the unquenchability of the human spirit, of a version of the sentiments with which Anna Seghers concluded her novel *Das siebte Kreuz* (see my essay on Anna Seghers in this volume pp.29–40). But this quality of indestructibility which Jakob's fictions release does not assert itself as conventional heroics: *Jakob der Lügner* is not the stuff of the typical resistance novel. It is well documented that, with the singular exceptions of Warsaw and Buchenwald, there was no resistance on any grand scale in the ghettoes and concentration camps. This is the gloomy truth to which Becker's narrator adheres: 'Und der Widerstand, wird man fragen, wo bleibt der Widerstand? . . . Kein einziger gerechter Schuß hat sich gelöst, Ruhe und Ordnung sind streng gewahrt worden, nichts von Widerstand. . . . Es hat dort, wo ich war, keinen Widerstand gegeben' (JL, pp. 98–9).

In the very posing of this question the narrator seems to signal the potential precariousness of his position. He knows full well what he is taking on when, in the late 1960s, and choosing to tackle this particular subject matter, he does not seek to make the most obvious kind of capital out of it. Is there, in the way the point is phrased, an echoing expectation of the question 'Wo bleibt das Positive, Herr Kästner?' – of the cry of orthodoxy and authority attempting to whip the deviant into line?

Perhaps. Whatever the case may be, the adoption of this particular perspective is a rejection of opportunism, a refusal to take the easy, more glamourous option. In one of the two different endings which Becker gives the novel, he ironises, in a deliberately heavy laying-on of pathos and melodrama, a whole tradition of literature in which the Soviet army is presented as the glorious liberators:

Ich male mir die Rache für Jakob aus, denn dies ist nach meinem Willen die kühle und sternenklare Nacht, in der die Russen kommen. Soll es der Roten Armee gelungen sein, die Stadt in kürzester Frist zu umzingeln, der Himmel wird hell vom Feuer der schweren Geschütze, sofort nach der Salve, die Jakob gegolten hat, hebt ein ohrenbetäubendes Donnern an, als wäre es von dem unglücklichen Schützen auf dem Postenturm versehentlich ausgelöst worden. Die ersten gespentischen Panzer, Einschläge im Revier, die Postentürme brennen, verbissene Deutsche, die sich bis zum letzten Schuß verteidigen, oder flüchtende Deutsche, die kein Loch finden, um sich darin zu verkriechen, lieber Gott, wäre das eine Nacht gewesen. (JL, p. 270)

But there is more to it than merely the ironising of myths. In also avoiding all the readily available clichés about resistance, Becker moves us closer to the psychological as well as to the historical reality of the ghetto. In the releasing, through Jakob's fictions, of modest optimism the novel reminds us in a multiplicity of ways of what the human spirit, even in the direst of situations, is capable. The briefest nourishment of hope can release the impetus to take up the threads of normality once more, to plan, to dream, to live like a human being again – but all expressed with an overlay of ironic reserve which does not allow us to forget the ultimate tragedy: 'Alte Schulden beginnen eine Rolle zu spielen, verlegen werden sie angemahnt, Töchter verwandeln sich in Bräute, in der Woche vor dem Neujahrsfest soll Hochzeit gehalten werden, die Leute sind vollkommen verrückt, die Selbstmordziffern sinken auf Null' (JL, p. 83).

Despite this, there remain in Jakob's own mind nagging doubts about the web of invention into which he has been dragged. It is as if he can never forget the ludicrous circumstances which had given birth to the fiction: 'Er ist gezwungen worden, verantwortungslose Behauptungen in die Welt zu setzen, der ahnungslose Idiot da hat ihn gezwungen mit seinem lächerlichen Mißtrauen, bloß weil er plötzlich Appetit auf Kartoffeln bekommen hat' (JL, p. 32). These misgivings come home to roost when Jakob reflects on Kowalski's suicide, the result of his discovery that the radio had never existed. Despite the narrator's reassurance: 'Nicht du bist schuld an Kowalskis Tod, sondern er hat es dir zu verdanken, daß er bis zu diesem Tag gelebt hat', Jakob cannot be consoled: 'Ja, ja . . . aber das hilft alles nichts' (JL, p. 257).

In conclusion it should be noted that it is not only Jakob in this story who is the begetter of outrageous fictions. The narrator, clearly no friend of the facile certainties of socialist realism, seems to be allying himself at points, albeit in much more self-ironical vein, with the entirely speculative approach to the grasping of reality of an Uwe Johnson. With his self-confessedly incomplete knowledge of the events retailed, he is much given to conjecture and invention as a way, as he puts it, of filling holes and, as already indicated, even provides us with two quite different endings to the story: one, heroic and upbeat, and then the real one, '. . . das blaßwangige und verdrießliche, das wirkliche und einfallslose Ende, bei dem man leicht Lust bekommt zu der unsinnigen Frage: Wofür nur das alles?' (JL, p. 272)

Does Becker's undisguised preoccupation throughout the novel with the act of creating fiction constitute a venturing into the sphere of dubious taste? Does it detract from the moral seriousness of the novel? Is this perhaps what annoyed his father about the book? Did he see experimentation and exuberant invention as an insult to the memory of the dead? Whatever one's answers to these questions might be, *Jakob der Lügner* is an undisputed *tour de force*. Bursting at the seams with narrative invention, precise and vivid in the evocation of the atmosphere and living conditions of the ghetto, entirely free of false pathos and yet profoundly moving. By comparison, Becker's next attempt to deal with related themes is something of a disappointment.

Der Boxer is constructed out of what at times resembles a cat and mouse game between the main protagonist in the novel, Aron or Arno Blank who had been released in his mid-forties from six years in the concentration camps, and a narrator/investigator who, through a series of meetings and interviews stretching over a period of two years attempts to reconstruct Arno Blank's efforts to create a new life for himself in postwar Germany: 'Unsere Begegnungen dienten ausschließlich dem Zweck, Aron Blank zu erkunden, ein möglichst ergiebiges Stück von ihm . . .' (B, p. 6). What is significant about Becker's choice of protagonist is that he is neither an example of the spectacularly scarred nor is he a figure, a victim who can be exploited for didactic purpose. It is true that he is haunted by the memory of the camps:

Du mußt nicht denken, so ein Lager ist von einem Tag auf den andern zu Ende. Schön wär das. Wirst befreit, gehst raus, und alles ist vorbei. So ist es leider nicht, ihr stellt euch das viel zu einfach vor, das Lager läuft dir hinterher. Die Baracke verfolgt dich, der Gestank verfolgt dich, der Hunger verfolgt dich, die Schläge verfolgen dich, die Angst verfolgt dich. Die Würdelosigkeit verfolgt dich und die Kränkung. (B, p. 102)

We do not, however, have the impression of a life shattered beyond all repair. Arno Blank seems to be picking up the pieces. With the help of an American search organisation he discovers what is with virtual certainty his surviving son. He has relationships first with Paula from the search organisation and then with a nurse, Irma. He works successfully as a bookkeeper for a black marketeer and then as an interpreter for the Russians. The common factor in all these relationships and occupations is the total lack of any commitment, conviction or purpose to them. Blank is unable to establish any real relationship with his son who eventually moves to Hamburg and thence to Israel where he is presumed to have been killed in the six day war of 1967. His ten year relationship with Irma ends as abruptly as it had begun in a sense of total indifference. It is as if once the value of a life has been set at nothing as Aron's had been – we recall his comment: 'Die Würdelosigkeit verfolgt dich und die Kränkung' – that it can never again be restored to a state of dignified and meaningful purpose. Facades may be erected to cope with the world, a *modus vivendi* may be fabricated. But the centre must forever remain hollow, inert. This is how Aron lives out his life. Drinking too much, neglecting his appearance, oblivious to the social and political world in flux and change about him and also impervious to the charge of the interviewer narrator: 'Ist es auf die Dauer ein erträglicher Zustand, Opfer des Faschismus und nichts anderes zu sein?' (B, pp. 248–9).

Where does the disappointment of *Der Boxer* lie? Perhaps in its failure to totally sustain our interest in the deliberately low-key treatment of its subject matter. Becker has clearly striven to avoid a didactic commonplace in the creation of his central character – no rediscovery of purpose here, for instance, in the regenerating ambience of a new, socialist society. But, on the other hand, to what extent does he succeed in maintaining our interest in a figure whose main characteristic seems to be a perpetual, ruinous tiredness? Despite the attention generated by the novel's narrative strategy – clever intercutting of Aron's life with the tensions and frictions arising in the course of the interviews and, finally, Arno's dependence on those interviews to give his life the sense of structure and direction it otherwise lacks – cannot disguise the fact that Becker has not quite managed to sustain our curiosity about a life which manifests itself in passivity and a refusal to engage.

One has no such reservations about *Bronsteins Kinder* a novel which demonstrates that despite Jurek Becker's reluctance to regard himself as Jewish, the question of what it is to be a Jew in a post-holocaust world still looms large in what preoccupies him as a writer.

Friction between the generations has been a subject for GDR literature since at least the early 1970s. Generally, it has been observed and registered in the inability of parents who are model socialists to pass on their convictions to disaffected offspring. Jurek Becker's *Bronsteins Kinder* does more than give this clash between fathers and sons a fresh twist. It stands it on its head. Here it is the father – Arno Bronstein, a Jew who has survived persecution by the Nazis – who feels himself an outcast, who has failed to find an easy relationship with the Germans of the new socialist society in the GDR, while his son is apparently fully integrated and assimilated. Too integrated and assimilated perhaps. At one point he notes: '. . .

ich bin ein fügsamer Kerl' (BK, p. 254), at another; 'Kein Mensch hatte mich gelehrt, Widerstand zu leisten, niemand hatte mir gezeigt, wie man das macht, was man für richtig hält. In der Schule war ich immer nur ein aufmerksamer Stiller: schon in der ersten Klasse fand ich heraus, wie wunderbar leicht man vorankommt, wenn man den Ansichten des Lehrers folgt' (BK, p. 85). A teenage forerunner – after the fact, perhaps – of the troubled conformists Gregor Bienek in *Irreführung der Behörden* or the teacher Simrock in *Schlaflose Tage*?

The other of Bronstein's children is Elle. In her late thirties, and in the benign confinement of a psychiatric hospital, she is prey to violent and unpredictable fits, the aftermath of a childhood spent in hiding during the Third Reich and of the callous treatment at the hands of her supposed benefactors – an unusual variation on the theme of the victim of fascism. Elle serves as a foil for the tensions between her father and a brother who is half her age, belongs to another world and refuses to see himself – not always successfully – as a prisoner of the past. Hans Bronstein rejects the notion of being 'der Sohn eines Opfers des Faschismus' (BK, p. 52) and declines to exploit the material advantages this would bring him. His sister makes her presence felt in the novel principally through letters which are a syntactically eccentric mixture of insight and whimsical delusion and provide oblique and eerie comment on the central events of the novel.

In an act of retribution which reverses the roles of persecutor and persecuted, Arno Bronstein and two fellow survivors of the holocaust are holding a former concentration camp overseer captive in a woodland hut. The scenes in which they attempt to extract from the wretched creature a confession of his crimes catch the reader by surprise in their brutality: chained to the bed in unsanitary conditions, he is periodically beaten up by Bronstein and his cronies. Hans, who has been using the hut for meetings with his girlfriend Martha, accidentally stumbles on the scene and is appalled. Why, he asks, not hand the man over to due process of law? Why exact a purely personal revenge? How can it be morally permissible for a man who was beaten up at thirty to reply in kind at sixty: 'Darf einer, der mit dreißig Jahren geschlagen wird, mit sechzig zurückschlagen?' (BK, p. 33).

The father's answers to these questions, his justification for taking the law into his own hands are quite unexpected and have a shattering effect on the son. Tainted beyond redemption not only by their collusion with Hitler, but also by what Bronstein construes as a historical supineness before power in any guise (it is only their

Soviet masters, he argues, who have forced the East Germans to pursue former Nazis with a much greater rigour than has been the case in West Germany), all Germans have forfeited the right to sit in judgement on those accused of crimes against the Jews. Justice is a prerogative which only the victim may exercise.

One might speculate that a possible awkwardness for Becker, as an exile in West Berlin who wished his work to be published in the GDR, of Bronstein's refusal to distinguish between East and West Germany as regards the prosecution of Nazi war criminals, is counterbalanced somewhat by the response of his son. Hans frees the prisoner who promptly seeks an unharassed retirement in the Federal Republic.

The interest of *Bronsteins Kinder* is not restricted to the bizarre nature of its central episode. The novel explores, in the relationship between Arno Bronstein and his fellow ex-camp inmates, the notion also found in both *Jakob der Lügner* and *Der Boxer* that the scarring effect of the camps manifests itself in feeling at ease only with those who have shared the experience. Hans's involvement on various emotional levels with other Jews opens his eyes to the fact that, despite different times and ideologies, assimilation and acceptance can have a certain fragility. It seems that even in a country such as the GDR which claims to take enormous pains to eradicate racist attitudes, all the old stereotypes are still intact. Hans's girl-friend Martha is cast in a film as a Jewess because of her semitic looks. Much to his chagrin, he himself is treated to a certain forbearance, his oversensitivity is excused, because he is Jewish. And finally – and at this point we return to Kirschbaum, the opening quotation and to Becker's reflections in the volume *Mein Judentum* on having Jewishness forced on him – Hans's attempt to liberate himself from his father's view that the family is set apart and doomed to be scarred in perpetuity by their past sufferings is, despite Arno Bronstein's death, left uneasily incomplete at the end of the novel. In this respect, *Bronsteins Kinder* may be said to offer a curious working, from a totally unexpected angle, of a theme which has recently preoccupied several German writers – one thinks particularly of Peter Sichrovsky's *Schuldig geboren. Kinder aus Nazifamilien* (1987), Klaus Schlesinger's somewhat less recent *Michael* (1971) and Peter Schneider's *Vati* (1987) – namely the tantalising German theme of fathers, sons and the past in the present.

In his second novel *Irreführung der Behörden*, which is located firmly in the GDR of the 1960s and deals with the private and professional life of a congenial and moderately successful writer

Gregor Bienek, Becker has broken away from the past and the concerns of *Jakob der Lügner*. Nonetheless, there are – in the ruminations on the nature of fiction which are built into these thematically so dissimilar novels – certain links. Becker's first novel avoided a stereotype view of a particular slab of history by creating an unexpected mode of telling. His second too brings fresh perspective to a not unfamiliar, and potentially troublesome theme – the East German writer and insistent official expectations – by a handling of the surface narrative which, as Philip Manger has so brilliantly demonstrated, challenges us to a hard, second look.[7] In the context of the author's own, not exactly unproblematic relations with authority – resignation from the *Schriftstellerverband* over the Wolf Biermann affair, expulsion from the party, barred from public readings – how is one to understand the title of Jurek Becker's second novel? It derives, of course, from Bienek's professor of law who advises him to complete his studies, but to deceive the university authorities about his long-term intentions by following his natural bent as a writer: '. . . gegen alle Erfahrung und wider besseres Wissen gebe ich ihnen jetzt einen Rat. Führen Sie die Behörden weiterhin in die Irre . . .' (IB, p. 60). Does this strategy of deception have relevance for the design of the novel as a whole? Might it be a broad hint that Becker intends his novel as an act of subterfuge directed at the smug prescriptiveness of cultural officialdom? Gregor Bienek, who, as his career progresses, is increasingly obliging in what he writes, is clearly no overt symbol of artistic integrity in an intellectually oppressive society. He is a writer of modest talents, one who suspects he may be a prisoner 'im Käfig seiner eigenen Mittelmäßigkeit' (IB, p. 173) and who is increasingly concerned to bring his ship into port as expeditiously as possible. For all his ability occasionally to break out into a world of bizarre fantasy, producing outlandish stories and scenarios which throw into pale insignificance the anodyne simplicities officially required of him, Gregor is no more the valiant intellectual dissident than is Jakob Heym the standard ghetto or KZ hero. The subversiveness of the novel must then lie elsewhere. This might not occur immediately to the ingenuous reader who could be tempted to ask himself if there was anything he might have missed, having been left with the sense of a book which although able to take wing on Gregor's highly entertaining and in part embryonic writing projects, as well as Becker's wry humour and a perky way with the

7. See Philip Manger, 'Jurek Becker's *Irreführung der Behörden*' in *Seminar*, 1981, no. 2, pp. 147–63.

everyday, is only intermittently conspicuous by the arresting nature of its characters and passage of events. Philip Manger's elegant analysis shows that he most certainly has. Drawing attention to the disparately uneven treatment of narrated and narrative time, the metaphorical possibilities of Bienek's love-hate relationship with his wife Lola (is she the voice of official cultural policy?), the playing with 'a whole gamut of reality-fiction relations', he concludes that the reader is being invited to view the novel's rather conventional structure and plot as 'a kind of smokescreen, an elaborate piece of camouflage from which to attack, in relative safety from counter-attack'.[8]

In singular contrast to *Irreführung der Behörden* and its oblique subtleties, *Schlaflose Tage* makes no bones about what is under attack: the sense of a novelist attempting to engage in dialogue with the forces controlling the society in which he lives is here completely out in the open; perhaps even too much so on occasion, as, for instance, the frequency with which dialogue and interior monologue are required to carry political critique or debate, while characters are made the voice for smoothly polished political and philosophical observations: 'Er wünschte zum Kommunismus eine innigere Beziehung, als sich immer nur akkurat an landesüblichen Regeln zu halten, die . . . verbesserungswürdig waren' (ST, p. 66). The novel's central character, Karl Simrock, is also a new departure as far as Becker's heroes go; neither a bone-weary Arno Blank nor an ultimately complaisant Gregor Bienek, he is, albeit on a modest scale and despite the fear that 'seine Resignation könnte in Wirklichkeit Faulheit sein' (ST, p. 121), something of a battler. If the conformist Gregor Bienek has reconciled himself to the 'Millionen Widrigkeiten, die man mit der Zeit als gegeben hinnimmt' (IB, p. 172), Karl Simrock is, as part of his search for authenticity, in open revolt at them.

His fundamental reappraisal of how to conduct his life is triggered off by a mild heart attack shortly after his thirty-sixth birthday. It plunges him into a kind of existential stock take of his career: 'Ich denke darüber nach, wie ich mein Leben von Grund auf ändern könnte' (ST, p. 26), he replies in answer to an innocent enquiry. Above all, however, he feels a desire for quintessential and authentic experience; he is prepared to overthrow all the certainties of a stable existence in order '. . . endlich nach dem neuesten Stand seiner Erkenntnisse zu leben' (ST, p. 29), and to be able '. . . endlich seinen eigenen Vorstellungen nachzugehen und nicht immer

8. Ibid., p. 152.

nur Vollstrecker der Absichten anderer zu sein' (ST, p. 134). This strategy, of course, represents a radical challenge, within limited, personal boundaries, to almost all of what the GDR has always stood for: which explains why the novel could only be published in the West. And, speculating ahead for a moment, it also explains the important role it will undoubtedly have when the question comes to be explored of the role East Germany's writers have played in plotting, in their fictions, the state of mind and social and psychological malaise which culminated in the events of November 1989.

Simrock pursues his quest, with equally fraught results, in both the domestic and the professional sphere. He announces to his wife Ruth that she will have no part to play in his search for enlightenment and self-discovery, and takes up with an apparent kindred spirit, Antonia ('. . . sie habe sich ein Leben in der ihr größtmöglichen Unabhängigkeit einzurichten versucht' (ST, p. 74)). In the classroom he attempts to dismantle some of the taboos and ingrained dishonesties and hypocrisy of the education system, reminding his pupils that attendance at the annual May Day parade is not strictly speaking obligatory and instigating a controversial discussion about Brecht's poem 'Lob des Zweifels'. The response to these sacrileges is not especially gratifying. His pupils clearly prefer their easy, spoon-fed certainties to the intellectual freedoms being tossed their way, the school authorities think the heart attack has affected Simrock's sanity as well as his health. They readily accede to his request for a brief sabbatical which will allow him to continue his search for truth, somewhat romantically as it transpires, as a bread delivery man. The crisis which is precipitated in his personal life when Antonia attempts to escape to the West while on holiday in Hungary, is compounded in his career when he is asked to resign after regaling a *Volksarmee* officer in the presence of his pupils with questions which are deemed impertinent. Despite these setbacks he remains sufficiently vitalised by his insights into a system that blocks all attempts at individual initiative to stick to his guns. He resists the act of ritualised self-criticism which would have given him his job back and, at the end of the novel, seems, in the heightened awareness he has gained of himself, to have taken a step in the direction of realising his goal: 'Den größten Ekel hat mir wahrscheinlich gemacht, daß ich mich nie gewehrt habe. Ich habe getan, dachte er, als sei es nicht meine Sache, mich gegen Bevormundung und Ungerechtigkeiten aufzulehnen. Und das bedeutet: ich habe mich nicht zuständig gefühlt für mich selbst' (ST, p. 157).

Like *Bronsteins Kinder* and Becker's penultimate novel *Aller Welt Freund*, which is located in a city resembling Berlin but given the imprecise contours of a political and social no man's land and deals, in humorous, satirically-edged fashion with the professional and personal repercussions of a news editor's failed attempt at suicide, *Schlaflose Tage* ends on a characteristically low-key and inconclusive note.

This leads us perhaps to what is most authentic and realistic about Becker's unforced examination of GDR society. His novels offer us a delicate tracing of the terms of the argument; they set forth the way in which the shortcomings of a political system may take their toll in the private sphere, but, like life itself, they have few consoling conclusions or answers with which to reassure us.

Author's Note

The following abbreviations and editions are used for Becker's works:

JL : *Jakob der Lügner. Roman*, Frankfurt am Main, 1979.
B : *Der Boxer*, 4th edition, Rostock, 1981.
IB : *Irreführung der Behörden. Roman*, 4th edition (suhrkamp taschenbuch), Frankfurt am Main, 1979.
ST : *Schlaflose Tage. Roman*, 2nd edition (suhrkamp taschenbuch), Frankfurt am Main, 1981.
BK : *Bronsteins Kinder. Roman*, Frankfurt am Main, 1986.
AF : *Aller Welt Freund*, 2nd edition, Rostock, 1986.

Secondary Material

Gregory Baum et al., 'Moral Issues in Jurek Becker's *Jakob der Lügner*: Contributions to a Symposium', in *Seminar*, 1983, no. 4, pp. 265–92.
Helmut Mörchen, 'Zur Darstellung zweier Lehrerschicksale in Romanen aus der DDR: Jurek Becker *Schlaflose Tage* and Günter Görlich *Eine Anzeige in der Zeitung*', in *Diskussion Deutsch*, 1985, no. 83, pp. 264–74.
Heidy M. Müller, 'Wertsetzung als Implikation der Erzählhaltung. Bemerkungen zur Judendarstellung in Jurek Beckers Romanen', in *Philosophica*, 1986, no. 2, pp. 61–75.
Chaim Shohaim, 'Jurek Becker ringt mit seinem Judentum. *Der Boxer* und Assimilation nach Auschwitz', in Albrecht Schöne (ed.), *Kontroversen, alte und neue*, vol. 5, Tübingen, 1986.

Leonardo Tofi, 'Der Kampf gegen die Müdigkeit: Jurek Beckers Romane von *Irreführung der Behörden* bis *Aller Welt Freund*', in Chiarloni et al. (eds), *Die Literatur der DDR 1976–1986*, Pisa, 1988, pp. 151–7.

Heinz Wetzel, '"Unvergleichlich gelungener" – aber "einfach zu schön"? Zur ethischen und ästhetischen Motivation des Erzählens in Jurek Beckers Roman *Jakob der Lügner*', in Albrecht Schöne (ed.), *Kontroversen, alte und neue*, vol. 8, Tübingen, 1986.

Heinz Wetzel, 'Fiktive und authentische Nachrichten in Jurek Becker's Romanen *Jakob der Lügner* und *Aller Welt Freund*', in Roland Jost and Hansgeorg Schmidt-Bergmann (eds), *Im Dialog mit der Moderne*, Frankfurt am Main, 1986, pp. 439–51.

Richard A. Zipser, 'Jurek Becker: A Writer with a Cause', in *Dimension*, 1978, no. 3, pp. 402–16.

–12–

Impertinence, Productive Fear and Hope:

The Writings of Helga Königsdorf

Margy Gerber

Unlike her colleagues Christa Wolf and Irmtraud Morgner, Helga Königsdorf did not become a writer at an early age, nor did she study *Germanistik* and work as a literary editor. Instead she is part of a frequently noted phenomenon of GDR literature in the second half of the 1970s: one of several women writers who, having pursued careers in other, often technical, fields – encouraged perhaps by the work of established women authors such as Wolf and Morgner – turned to writing in mid-life, publishing their first literary works in the late 1970s when they were around the age of forty.[1]

Trained as a physicist and mathematician, Helga Königsdorf (born 1938) was professor of mathematics at the Akademie der Wissenschaften der DDR when she made her literary debut in 1978 with a collection of stories entitled *Meine ungehörigen Träume*.[2] Since then she has published two additional collections, *Der Lauf der Dinge* (1982) and *Lichtverhältnisse* (1988), a longer prose work, *Respektloser Umgang* (1986)[3] and an epistolary tale *Ungelegener*

1. Other women writers in this group include Brigitte Martin, Helga Schubert, Rosemarie Zeplin, Monika Helmecke, Christa Müller and Christine Wolter. For more information, see Christiane Zehl Romero, 'Vertreibung aus dem Paradies: Zur neuen Frauenliteratur in der DDR', in Margy Gerber et al. (eds), *Studies in GDR Culture and Society* 3, Lanham/New York/London, 1983, pp. 71–85.
2. *Meine ungehörigen Träume. Geschichten*, Berlin/ Weimar, 1978. In the following I will be quoting from the second edition, which appeared in 1980. Subsequent page references will appear parenthetically in the text.
3. In the following I will be quoting from the West German edition of *Respektloser Umgang*.

Margy Gerber

Befund (1989) which have made her one of the leading contemporary writers in the GDR. She has received various literary prizes and other signs of official recognition, including the *Heinrich-Mann-Preis* (1985) and the *Nationalpreis, II.Klasse* (1989). Although she is not as well known in the West as in the GDR, three volumes of stories along with *Respektloser Umgang* and *Ungelegener Befund* have appeared in the Federal Republic.[4] Her interest in writing and her poor health – she suffers from Parkinson's disease – have caused her to reduce her commitment to mathematics and academia, but in 1989 she was still officially a *wissenschaftliche Mitarbeiterin* at the Academy of Sciences.

Frequently asked why she turned to writing, Königsdorf speaks of the 'Einengung' that she increasingly perceived as a mathematician, the constriction of personality and expressivity which resulted from her professional preoccupation with the purely rational.[5] She found science, to which she had dedicated herself 'mit Haut und Haaren'[6] for half a lifetime, to be ultimately dissatisfying because, as a consequence of the necessary exclusion of the subject and the subjective from scientific work, 'man [. . .] ganze Bereiche seiner emotionalen Persönlichkeitsstruktur mehr oder weniger ausschließen muß'.[7] The constant use of the language of mathematics had led to a sense of loss of 'normale Kommunikationsfähigkeit'[8] and this, coupled with the need she felt to confront human concerns which are not expressible with rational thought structures, had produced a crisis: 'Irgendwann begann sich mein Körper zu wehren. Meine Hand versagte beim Schreiben ihren Dienst [. . .] In dieser Situation brachen die ersten Geschichten [. . .] ungerufen aus mir heraus. . . .'[9]

The mathematician Königsdorf takes delight in the communicative possibilities of literature and literary language, which does not require that thoughts or feelings be ordered in a rational system, or indeed even be present in one's rational consciousness. 'Schreiben

4. *Mit Klitschmann im Regen. Geschichten*, Darmstadt/Neuwied, 1983, an abbreviated edition of *Meine ungehörigen Träume*; *Die geschlossenen Türen am Abend. Erzählungen*, Frankfurt on Main, 1989, includes stories from *Lichtverhältnisse* and the older collections.
5. 'Fiktiver Dialog. Helga Königsdorf und ihr neues Buch', *Sonntag*, 34, 1986, p. 4.
6. 'Gedankentäterin. "Wochenpost"-Gespräch mit Helga Königsdorf', *Wochenpost*, 30 December 1988, p. 14.
7. 'Schreib-Auskunft: Helga Königsdorf', *Neue Deutsche Literatur*, vol. 27, no. 4, 1979, p. 10.
8. 'Gedankentäterin', p. 14.
9. Ibid. See also 'Nachsatz' in *Meine ungehörigen Träume*, p. 145.

ist maximale Kommunikation', one of her characters maintains.[10] And despite the subjectivity of literary expression and the writer's depiction of individual thoughts and actions, literature shares the 'Verallgemeinerungsfähigkeit' of science since the images serve as metaphors.[11]

And what were the human concerns that she had long neglected and that 'one must speak about'? The ten stories collected in Helga Königsdorf's first book, *Meine ungehörigen Träume* (1978), have two basic themes: on the one hand, gender relations and the difficulties of women's self-realisation – this is a common topic of the group of women writers that began publishing at this time; and academia, the ambience and politics of the *Wissenschaftsbetrieb*, on the other. In both groups of stories there are common denominators, themes that, in a larger sense, lie at the base of all of Königsdorf's work, no matter how varied its subject and style: the criticism of vacuousness, of mindless ritual and routine that stifle both individual and societal development; and the necessity of freeing oneself from the shackles of arrogated authority and social convention in order to find one's own identity and self-fulfilment.

In the case of the stories set in academia, the criticism takes the form of satirical attacks on institutional bureaucracy, on the unwillingness to assume personal responsibility, and on the ineptness and inertia resulting from the academic machinery, including the central planning of research goals, which discourages creativity. In 'Eine Idee und ich', for example, the first-person narrator, a scientist at a large research centre, tells how he manages to implement his idea of establishing a consultation centre for applied 'Kübernautik' at his institute by outwitting his department head, who is determined to squash initiatives from below, and all others who resist change, including the trade union representative. On the other hand, once approved, the idea assumes a momentum of its own, receiving ever increasing attention in the media and being copied by other institutions – even though the consultation centre has since proven to be superfluous. As a result the department head is promoted and the narrator given his job. As an administrator, the narrator in turn immediately assumes the negative, braking attitudes of his predecessor. Thus the cycle is perpetuated.

10. 'Hochzeitstag in Pizunda', in *Meine ungehörigen Träume*, p. 130. See also 'Diskussion nach der Lesung von Helga Königsdorf', in Anna Chiarloni et al. (eds), *Die Literatur der DDR 1976–1986*, Pisa, 1988, p. 453.
11. 'Gedankentäterin', p. 14.

Margy Gerber

In the stories which deal with *Frauenproblematik*, and this is the larger of the two thematic groups, criticism is directed toward the personal 'Einengung' – the limitation of self – that occurs in a marriage or other relationship that has become routine and meaningless. In all the stories of this type, the starting position is one of 'Einengung', with the story then building on the woman's attempt to find a more meaningful existence, either by breaking out of the old relationship or revitalising it; in both cases the woman seeks new possibilities for self-fulfilment and self-realisation. As Eva Kaufmann concluded in her review of *Meine ungehörigen Träume*: 'Das Schwergewicht liegt in diesem Buch nicht auf der Auseinandersetzung mit dem, was ist, sondern auf der geistig-psychischen Anstrengung, über es hinauszukommen'.[12]

Königsdorf's female protagonists – both in this collection and in the rest of her writing – frequently have similar characteristics: they are professional women in their forties and fifties, women whose children are already grown and who, although usually not single or living alone, are lonely and unsatisfied in their relationships – in contrast to their male partners, who tend to be complacent and unquestioning. Looking back on their lives, the women realise the price they, but not only they – their men, as well – have paid for their successful careers; their concentration on work has led to one-sidedness, emotional impoverishment, and neglect of self.

In 'Bolero', the best-known story in *Meine ungehörigen Träume*, the highly educated protagonist and first-person narrator describes her long affair with a married man she met at a conference, a man she noticed during a tedious lecture only because he was taking notes so conscientiously. 'Eigentlich war überhaupt nichts Besonderes an ihm', she tells us. Still, out of sheer boredom, she lets herself be invited to dinner: 'Ich hätte aus Langeweile dem Teufel Gefolgschaft geleistet. Warum sollte ich also nicht mit einem angegrauten, lüsternen, dicken Mann ein kleines abgelegenes Restaurant aufsuchen' (T, p. 8).

The affair that ensues is determined entirely by the man. They meet in her apartment – he decides when – and she, coquettishly dressed, prepares exotic, gourmet dishes for him while Ravel's 'Bolero' provides mood music in the background. For the woman the relationship is unsatisfying; the man fills neither her emotional nor her sexual needs. On the other hand, she doesn't break it off, acquiesces in the secret affair, feigns cheerfulness when he is there,

12. Eva Kaufmann, 'Helga Königsdorfs Band "Meine ungehörigen Träume"', *Weimarer Beiträge*, vol. 25, no. 7, 1979, p. 112.

and otherwise immerses herself in her work. Until one evening, after the usual ritual, she plunges her lover over the balcony of her apartment – she lives on the twelfth floor – throwing his shoes and coat after him, as she calmly tells us.

With this surprising act – her laconic, matter-of-fact manner of narration in no way prepares us for it – the woman frees herself from the empty affair and, at the same time, overcomes her inconsistent behaviour. By outward appearances an emancipated, financially independent career woman; thus fulfilling the conditions which, according to Marx and Engels (and Bebel), should result in equality of the genders and true partnership between men and women, she has until now completely subordinated herself in the private realm. There is evidence that she has 'grown' as a result of her liberating act. As she ruminates: 'Nein, wie ich es auch wende, da war kein Grund, es zu tun [. . .] ich hätte nur "nein" zu sagen brauchen' (T, p. 13).

'Breaking out', having the courage to leave the old which has lost its meaning and risking the dangers of the new and uncertain, is the subject of the autobiographical 'Hochzeitstag in Pizunda'. Here Königsdorf uses the diary form to express the inner thoughts and struggles of her protagonist, a woman who has recently turned to writing. In this regard, the woman has already broken out. After many years of accepting patterns of behaviour stipulated by others and showing talent for doing what was expected of her, she has come to the realisation that she no longer knows who she is. Writing is to be a means of finding her identity, 'Ich wage jetzt das große Abenteuer. Ich begebe mich auf die Suche nach mir selbst' (T, p. 129).

The search for herself includes the possibility of leaving her husband of twenty years to join her lover, and the diary she writes while vacationing with her husband on the Black Sea centres on this decision; she ruminates on marriage, questioning whether marriage is 'eigentlich zeitgemäß' (T, p. 125), since it seems bound to end in boredom and routine. 'Wie hält man eine Liebe ohne Probleme von außen am Leben?' (T, p. 126), she asks. In spite of her fears and misgivings about entering into a new partnership, she decides in the end to risk it, driven by 'die irre Sehnsucht in meinem Leben [. . .] die zur unaufhörlichen Wandlung zwingt. Geliebte verhaßte Sehnsucht' (T, p. 125).

Overcoming mindsets and stereotypical behaviour presupposes an awareness of their shallowness, a questioning of the authority of societal convention, *Ungehörigkeit*. For the characters in Königsdorf's stories, a first step to this realisation is often accomplished by dreams.[13] In the title story of the collection, for example, the first-person narrator relates a series of five dreams in which one can trace the gradual change in her relationship to authority, here represented by the 'Direktor'. As Antonia Grunenberg has pointed out, the self-assurance of the narrator grows in direct proportion to her loss of awe for the director.[14] One may also assume that the *Fenstersturz* in 'Bolero', which differs so strikingly from the rest of the narrative, represents a liberating dream of the protagonist.

Königsdorf uses dreams as an anticipation of rational thought, as a trial run for possible future reality, the means of realising which need not yet be clear. What cannot yet be expressed in words, concepts or deeds can be dreamed. This is seen of course from the standpoint of the literary figure. As Königsdorf writes, the effect of dreams on the reader is intended to be similarly consciousness-raising: 'das ist gerade das Schöne am Traum als literarisches Mittel, man kann mit Dingen spielen, verblüffende Vorgänge, verblüffende Schlüsse benutzen, die eine Situation in grelles Licht tauchen und damit ein Problem erhellen, wie es durch einfache Beschreibung realer Vorgänge vielleicht nicht immer gelingt'.[15]

Königsdorf's use of irony, including self-irony, and parody, and of grotesque and fantastic elements, such as the surrealistic exaggeration of everyday situations, serves the same mind-expanding purpose. It sets her apart from the women writers with whom she made her debut in the mid-1970s. In this regard, Königsdorf is reminiscent of Irmtraud Morgner, to whom she pays homage in 'Meine ungehörigen Träume' (pp. 60–1).

Several of the stories in Königsdorf's second book, *Der Lauf der Dinge* (1982), continue the general themes introduced in the first volume: gender relations and the *Wissenschaftsbetrieb*. In this collection, however, there are conspicuously few positive examples of breaking away, or of *Ungehörigkeit*. And here dreams are more like nightmares: 'Meine zentnerschweren Träume' forms the pendant to 'Meine ungehörigen Träume'. Only one of the woman figures, the first-person narrator in 'Unverhoffter Besuch', has burned her bridges behind her, setting out with the goal 'in mir selbst heimisch zu werden' (L, p. 185). And she is still on shaky ground: 'Die Art

13. Cf. Eva Kaufmann's review of *Meine ungehörigen Träume*, p. 112. See also Antonia Grunenberg, 'Träumen und Fliegen. Neue Identitätsbilder in der Frauenliteratur der DDR', Paul Gerhard Klussmann and Heinrich Mohr (eds), *Jahrbuch zur Literatur in der DDR*, vol. 3, Probleme deutscher Identität, Bonn, 1983, pp. 159–67.
14. Antonia Grunenberg, 'Träumen und Fliegen', p. 161.
15. 'Schreib-Auskunft', pp. 11–12.

und Weise, wie ich meine Souveränität zur Schau stelle, ist verdächtig. Noch traue ich mir nicht. Zu gegenwärtig: Meine Angst. Meine Einsamkeit. Meine Sehnsucht nach Schutz [. . .] Selbstmitleid. Immer noch. Obwohl ich mich längst durchschaut habe' (L, p. 181).

Other women characters contain the spark that could lead to change – they are restless and dissatisfied – but the spark doesn't ignite. In 'Die Wahrheit über Schorsch' the first-person narrator, after three disappointing relationships, reverts back to her imagined lover Schorsch – a metaphor for self-gratification – who fulfils her every sensual desire. She retains her husband, however – in spite of '[d]as alte Gefühl der Unabhängigkeit und Stärke' (L, p. 49) that now returns to her – 'wegen der Leute': 'Eine Frau in meinem Alter, die keinen Mann vorzeigen kann, wird als wandelnder Mißerfolg eingestuft' (L, p. 49). The female protagonist in 'Der Zweite' is unhappy with her second husband, who has turned out to be no better than the first, as well as with herself for having tried to find a new identity through remarriage: 'Ich wechsle den Namen wie das Kleid. Ich liebe meine Identität nicht. Erhoffe eine neue [. . .] Ist der neue Name alt, bin auch ich die alte' (L, p. 152). But in spite of this insight, she doesn't attempt to find a new identity within herself, even though she thinks she could write poetry or invent something – 'Ich bin sicher, das steckt alles in mir' (L, p. 157). Instead, she brightens up at the thought that a third man has appeared on the horizon.

In this collection, the present generation of women are contrasted with the generation of their mothers and the new generation of women, their daughters. Comparing herself with her teenage daughter, the narrator of 'Unverhoffter Besuch' observes: 'Offensichtlich leidet sie nicht an jenem Unterlegenheitsgefühl Männern gegenüber, das mir bereits mit der Muttermilch eingeflößt wurde. Sie braucht später ihre Unabhängigkeit nicht hinauszuschreien' (L, p. 186). The instilling of this 'Unterlegenheitsgefühl' is illustrated in the story 'Wenn ich groß bin, werde ich Bergsteiger', which is told from the perspective of a little girl growing up during World War II. 'Vater ist viel klüger als Mutter. Männer sind viel klüger als Frauen', she says, repeating what she has heard (L, p. 93). The gender roles are already well-established: 'Mein Bruder ist der Hoferbe. Ich bin ein Mädchen. Ein "gutes Mädchen"' (L, p. 104). The girl's mother attempts to hobble her rebellious instincts, chastising her with the usual 'Girls don't do that'.

Negative characterisations of mothers in the older generation recur in Königsdorf's writing starting with this collection: women who are unhappy with their lot, but who raise their daughters in such a way that their situation is reproduced in the next generation; domineering mothers who tyrannise their families with the weapons at their command: maternal care and emotional extortion. In 'Das Krokodil im Haussee', for example, Mama moves 'wie ein Dompteur' (L, p. 25) in the family, leading her husband, children, and grandchild around by her apron strings, stifling individual development and eliminating all centrifugal forces that might cause a family member to leave the nest.

While the female protagonists tend not to break out of their behavioural patterns, some of the academics in the stories dealing with the *Wissenschaftsbetrieb* at least have attained a higher degree of awareness, even if they, too, seldom succeed in breaking away. While the satire in the earlier stories derives from the narrator, who derides both the institutional practices and the mentality of the bureaucrats and academics, in one of these stories, the third-person narrative 'Der unangemessene Aufstand des Zahlographen Karl Egon Kuller', it is the protagonist who criticises the academic ambience. Kuller, an internationally known scientist who has advanced to the top by a combination of clever planning and chutzpah, decides one day that he has had enough – 'Er wollte [. . .] die verlogene Kontruktion seines Lebens niederreißen' (L, p. 64) – and gives a formal lecture in which he develops an outrageous mathematical theory, expecting to be rebuked by his colleagues. To his dismay, his colleagues react as always, nodding approval, assiduously taking notes, or sleeping. Kuller's escape from the situation is to die of a heart attack.

This tragi-comic ending points to an important new theme in Königsdorf's writing, namely that of death and dying, a topic presumably bound up with her own fatal illness and physical decline. Marxist thought has failed to confront this basic human problem, offering no counsel to its adherents on how to cope with the fear and grief associated with death. In 'Hochzeitstag in Pizunda' the narrator notes in her diary: 'Wir weigern uns, nachzudenken. Über unsere Endlichkeit, über das Altern, über den Tod. Unsere Ideologie läßt uns im Stich [. . .] Gestorben wird allein. Aseptisch. Anonym' (T, p. 123).[16]

---

16. Irmtraud Morgner's heroine Laura Salman writes a letter with similar content to the editors of a philosophical journal (*Amanda. Ein Hexenroman*, Darmstadt/Neuwied, 1983, pp. 152–3). See also Magdalene Mueller, 'Alltagserfahrung? Bemerkungen zur Darstellung des Todes in der neueren DDR-Literatur', in Margy Gerber et al. (eds), *Studies in GDR Culture and Society* 8, Lanham/New York/London, 1988, pp. 127–40.

In the story 'Liriodendron tulipifera' the main figure, a woman doctor, attempts to come to grips with her impending death. Experienced in seeing others die, she had thought herself immune to the fear which she now struggles to control. With a few months to live, she clings to 'dieses verfluchte bißchen Leben' (L, p. 129), finding solace in the easy-going, uncomplicated man who has entered her life at the twelfth hour, a man with a different sense of time, enamoured of trees and unperturbed by their slow growth. The woman, Ruth, remembers once having seen an exotic water bird in flight:

> Die Zeit hing an ihm wie eine Kette. Hinter der Zeit die Vorzeit. Und die Vorzeit der Vorzeit. Und so fort. Ohne Ende.
> An ihr, Ruth, hing nichts. Jedenfalls spürte sie nichts. Da war nie etwas gewesen. Sie selbst war Anfang und Ende. Irgendwo hineingeworfen. Eingeschlossen in eine Schale, die sich unaufhörlich zusammenzog. (L, p. 122)

Königsdorf suggests that it is the feeling of solitariness, of being oneself the beginning and end, encapsulated in oneself, that makes dying so difficult. In her major work, *Respektloser Umgang*, she pursues this thought, causing her heroine to move beyond herself, to see herself in a larger perspective.

On one level, *Respektloser Umgang* (1986) is similar to the short stories. The protagonist of the first-person narrative is a woman physicist who, like other female figures in Königsdorf's work, has led a one-sided life, devoting herself to her career to the detriment of her family life and her own personal identity. She is suffering from an incurable disease which already has curtailed her ability to work and which will lead to ever greater physical decline and early death. In this existential situation she too looks back over her life, attempting to come to terms with the turn it has taken. In contrast to the short stories, however, the structure and content of this work are much more complex.

Respektloser Umgang has the form of an interior monologue, a process of reflection that involves both logical and intuitive thought as the first-person narrator seeks the source of her illness, thinks about herself, and contemplates her future. The result is a seemingly spontaneous mental montage of remembrances, day dreams and dream visions, factual information, scientific exposition, narration of daily events, and, above all, imagined dialogue.[17]

17. For a discussion of the form of *Respektloser Umgang*, see Klaus Hammer,

Her most important conversation partner is the renowned physicist Lisa Meitner, who worked with Hahn and Straßmann on the research that led to the splitting of the atom. Her appearing one day in the apartment of the narrator is at first attributed to the hallucinatory side effects of the strong medicine the narrator must take to stabilise her physical condition. It is not accidental of course that it is Lisa Meitner who 'appears' and becomes her sparring partner. There are many parallels between them: they share the same, traditionally male occupation; Meitner's career was likewise cut short when she was forced to flee Nazi Germany; the Jewess Meitner was of the same generation as the narrator's grandmother, who was also a Jew and who perished in a Nazi euthanasia clinic.

Meitner serves as a foil against which the narrator measures herself and her fate; comparison with Meitner brings problems into her consciousness and at the same time provides distance from them. Meitner's feisty nature, her resolute independence, and her apparent satisfaction at being the 'exception' to Max Planck's view that nature intends women to be wives and mothers rather than physicists are a provocation for the narrator to rethink and reevaluate her own identity as a woman.

The conversations with Meitner also cause her to look back into her past, to come to terms with her family's and her own experiences during fascism, and to consider the responsibility of resistance. Not only the political past, also the scientific past, the crucial period of the splitting of the atom, is recalled.[18] Looking back into history, the narrator gains a sense of continuity between the political and scientific past and the present, and, on the human level, between the responsibility of citizens and scientists then and now to resist harmful developments in society.

The emotional convalescence of the protagonist lies in perceiving herself in a larger perspective, in seeing beyond the borders of her own self: 'Nur durch die Relativierung des Ichs ist die eigene Existenz noch ertragbar', she ruminates (R, p. 27). The turning point in this development takes place in the *Spiegelkabinett*, at an imagined trial where her forebears – spiritual as well as physical –

'Mobilisierung der Humanität. Helga Königsdorf: "Respektloser Umgang" Aufbau-Verlag Berlin und Weimar', *Neue Deutsche Literatur*, vol. 35, no. 8, 1987, pp. 139–42; and Joseph Pischel's contribution to the 'Für und Wider' discussion '"Respektloser Umgang" von Helga Königsdorf', *Weimarer Beiträge*, vol. 33, no. 8, 1987, pp. 1353–7.

18. Werner Jehser speaks of the work's 'weltgeschichtliche Dimension' ('"Respektloser Umgang" von Helga Königsdorf', *Weimarer Beiträge*, vol. 33, no. 8, 1987, p. 1342).

are the judges. Staring in the mirrors, which reflect all the various shortcomings of her personality, she asks herself: 'Ging es mir wirklich jemals um den Zustand der Welt, oder immer nur um mich?' (R, p. 90).

Despite her poor physical condition, the narrator accepts the 'Auftrag' that 'Lisa Meitner' assigns her; she abandons self-centred introspection for active engagement in combating the negative effects of modern science; she masters her fear of dying by placing herself in a continuum of time, seeing herself as part of the chain of humanity. As she says: 'Der Sinn des Lebens ist das Leben [. . .] Unsterblich sind wir, solange diesem Leben Kontinuität beschieden ist' (R, p. 116).[19]

How does one protect the planet from the negative consequences of scientific and technological development? Königsdorf – the scientist – does not condemn modern science and technology as such. Neither she nor her narrator want to curb scientific experimentation or abandon nuclear technology, this modern Prometheus that has once again brought fire to the human race.[20] Imagining what she should say about the role of science to her son, who is an ardent student of physics, she rejects as 'dumme Maschinenstürmerei' (R, p. 92) the idea that physics has become a forbidden subject since the bombing of Hiroshima and Nagasaki: 'Gefährlich ist der Mythos, wir könnten mit ihrer Hilfe getrost jede Suppe auslöffeln, die wir uns einbrocken. Das Warten auf Wunder. Aber gefährlicher ist der Glaube, wir kämen ohne neue Erkenntnis aus' (R, p. 93). Science is essential, but the scientist must assume responsibility for scientific developments, 'weil es zwischen Verantwortung und Mitschuld in Zukunft nichts mehr gibt' (R, p. 94).

The basic principle and criterion of scientific development must be human dignity, the 'Würde des Menschen' (R, p. 94). Königsdorf further develops this concept in an essay entitled 'Das Prinzip Menschenwürde' (1989), where she defines a new ethics pertaining to the non-human as well as the human world and formulates a categorical imperative: 'Handle so und trage Sorge, daß so gehandelt wird, daß die Wirkungen dieser Handlungen für

19. Cf. Nancy A. Lauckner, 'The Treatment of the Past and Future in Helga Königsdorf's *Respektloser Umgang*: " . . für die Zukunft antreten? Mit der Vergangenheit im Bunde"', paper read at the 15th New Hampshire Symposium on the GDR, Conway, N.H., June 1989.
20. Cf. Christa Wolf's *Störfall* (1987), in which Wolf discusses the dangers of scientific development in the aftermath of the Chernobyl and which has many structural similarities with Königsdorf's narrative, including the juxtaposing of illness and modern technology.

Margy Gerber

gegenwärtiges und künftiges menschliches Leben, beträfen sie dich selbst, mit deiner Würde vereinbar wären'.[21] Only those scientific and technological developments that meet this ethical standard would be considered progress.

The hope for saving civilisation from ecological and nuclear devastation lies, as the narrator tells her son, in the mobilisation of humanity. Drawing a parallel between individual illness and the threat to the planet, including the unwillingness of people to think about them, she insists that the public must be told of the dangers, must be made to overcome its reluctance to become cognisant of them, since withholding the truth from the patient denies him the chance to mobilise his resources to fight the disease.

'Angst aus Wissen' is 'eine produktive Angst' (R, p. 70), for it can inspire resistance and turn into courage ('Mut aus Wissen').[22] It can transform the victim into an actor, a combatant who influences his destiny. One of the strongest messages in *Respektloser Umgang* is that man, instead of being the object, must become the subject of history and of his future.[23] The broad motif of resistance (*Widerstand*) links the various strands and levels of the work: resistance to illness, to fascism, to the misuse of modern technology and to the violation of human dignity.[24]

In a frequently noted passage, the narrator of *Respektloser Umgang* takes issue with Christa Wolf's assertion that women down through history have been objects, even objects of objects, since they have been dependent on men who themselves are ruled.[25] Königsdorf's narrator, whose pride as a woman is slighted at this thought, refuses to accept this condition as inevitable, responding

21. Helga Königsdorf, 'Das Prinzip Menschenwürde', *Neue Deutsche Literatur*, vol. 37, no. 10, 1989, p. 7. A shorter version of the essay appeared in *Die Weltbühne*, 13 June 1989, pp. 747–9.
22. Königsdorf: 'Es ist notwendig, von der Angst aus Wissen zum Mut aus Wissen oder trotz Wissens überzugehen[. . .] Und daß ich aus Angst Wachsamkeit mache, sie umsetze in Ermutigung und Verantwortung'. Quoted from Liane Pfelling, 'Nachdenken über Gefährdungen', *Wochenpost*, 31 July 1987, p. 14.
23. Cf. Klaus Hammer, 'Mobilisierung der Humanität', pp. 141–2.
24. See Eva Kaufmann's discussion of 'Widerstand' in her article 'Respektloser Umgang', Siegfried Rönisch (ed.) *DDR-Literatur '86 im Gespräch*, Berlin, 1987, p. 283.
25. Christa Wolf is addressing the question, to what extent there is such a thing as 'weibliches Schreiben'. She answers: 'Insoweit Frauen nicht zu den Herrschenden, sondern zu den Beherrschten gehören,[. . .] zu den Objekten der Objekte. Objekte zweiten Grades, oft genug Objekte von Männern, die selbst Objekte sind' (p. 54). Wolf's quotation is from her third lecture in *Voraussetzungen einer Erzählung: Kassandra* (1983).

that there are two sides to this suppression, that of the suppressors and that of the subjects who preserve their autonomy, that is, refuse to be objects (R, p. 54). In the larger context of the narrative, the idea applies not only to women but to human beings in general.

In her address at the Tenth Writers' Congress in 1987 Königsdorf spoke of a new Cassandra function of literature, perhaps here too alluding to Christa Wolf. Literature should not be a Cassandra that predicts disaster and is not believed, but rather a voice that, without beautifying the situation, encourages the reader to assert himself in face of disaster, that is, to resist.[26] The highest task of the writer is to encourage; in Königsdorf's use of the word, this means to mobilise, to move humanity to help itself. The writer like the scientist has a responsibility; it involves 'Angst aus Wissen' and 'Mut aus Angst' – the furthering of critical thinking and the awakening of human potential.[27]

The tone of Königsdorf's next work, the short stories collected in *Lichtverhältnisse* (1988), is darker. Women characters again predominate: women in crises ordinarily evoked by family problems; lonely, unfulfilled women, overachievers who look back on professionally successful, but otherwise empty lives; workaholics and alcoholics, women who yearn for love and tenderness. Seldom do the women find a solution to their problems: the stories tend to end as they begin; after the crisis has caused them to reflect on their lives, the women resume their old patterns.

The positive characters in this collection are often people who are not accepted by the 'system', or who become outcasts because they persevere against the bureaucratic societal order: for example, the limping woman in 'Sachschaden', who attends to a boy who has run into a car with his moped, while the other passers-by are interested only in the damage done to the car and in ensuring that the boy be held responsible for it; or the autodidactic inventor 'Kugelblitz', who continues to work on his centrifuge in his kitchen, at his own expense, after his unconventional methods cause him to be fired from his job and even arouse the suspicion of the secret police. Or the alcoholic science journalist Stiller (in 'Polymax'), who honestly evaluates the technical inventions he writes about and thus clashes with the 'societal' interests of his editors.

These latter figures can be considered examples of the new

26. 'Helga Königsdorf', in *X. Schriftstellerkongress der DDR. Plenum*, Berlin/ Weimar, 1988, p. 96. Speech first printed in *Neue Deutsche Literatur*, vol. 36, no. 3, 1988, pp. 57–9.
27. See also 'Das Prinzip Menschenwürde', p. 10.

emphasis on human dignity in Königsdorf's writings. Human dignity is at stake as well in her most recent treatment of the theme of death and dying, 'Der Rummelplatz', whose first-person narrator is in the final stages of an unnamed disease. The dying woman is so physically weak that she can no longer verbally communicate with the outside world; the reader learns her thoughts and fears from the inner perspective of her still active mind. Equally painful to her as her fear of dying is the humiliation she suffers at the hands of the people around her – doctors, nurses, her family and friends – who react to this shell of a person with disgust, indifference, and anger, since they have not learned to cope with death. The woman is horrified at the thought that she will be moved from her multiple-bed hospital room to a linen closet or a bathroom to die, as she has seen happen with other patients. She is determined to fight against this inhumane practice which disregards the dignity of the dying: 'Denn es ist eine Lüge, daß der Tod das Ende ist. Der Tod hat nichts mehr mit mir zu tun [. . .] am Ende steht das Leben. Dieses letzte bißchen Leben, dem der Tod seinen besonderen Wert verleiht und das wie ein Tropfen verrinnt' (LV, p. 171).

In summary, one can recognise a common thread in Königsdorf's work. It is the resolve to overcome the mechanisms, no matter what these might be – personal weakness, societal expectations, individual or societal mindsets – that prevent the individual from realising his/her potential, that lead to the loss of human dignity, or, on a larger scale, threaten society or the planet. All of her works argue against tutelage of the individual and of society, urge that both the individual and society assume responsibility for their own enlightenment and humanisation, and for that of the world around them. While her earlier works concentrated on the individual's emancipation and growth, the more recent works, especially *Respektloser Umgang*, have broadened the focus to include the individual's responsibility within society, and for the future as well as the present.

Author's Note

The following editions and abbreviations are used in discussing Königsdorf's work:

T : *Meine ungehörigen Träume. Geschichten*, second edition, Berlin and Weimar, 1980.

L : *Der Lauf der Dinge. Geschichten,* Berlin and Weimar, 1982.
R : *Respektloser Umgang. Erzählung,* Berlin and Weimar, 1986; (West German edition, Darmstadt, 1986).
LV : *Lichtverhältnisse. Geschichten,* Berlin and Weimar, 1988.
Ungelegener Befund. Erzählung, Berlin and Weimar, 1989; (West German edition, Frankfurt am Main, 1990).

Other editions:

Mit Klitschmann im Regen. Geschichten, Darmstadt, 1983 (abbreviated) edition of *Meine ungehörigen Träume,* containing only the stories dealing with 'Frauenproblematik'.
Die geschlossenen Türen am Abend. Erzählungen, Frankfurt am Main, 1989. (Contains many of the stories in *Lichtverhältnisse,* plus 'Heimkehr einer Prinzessin' from *Meine ungehörigen Träume* and 'Wenn ich groß bin, werde ich Bergsteiger' from *Der Lauf der Dinge.*

Suggested Further Reading

'Fiktiver Dialog. Helga Königsdorf und ihr neues Buch', interview with Klaus Hammer, *Sonntag,* no. 34, 1986, p. 4.
'Gedankentäterin. "Wochenpost"-Gespräch mit Helga Königsdorf', *Wochenpost,* 30 Dezember 1988, pp. 14–15.

Secondary Material

Sven-Gunnar Anderson, 'Jugendsprache und sprachliche Normen der Erwachsenenwelt', *Germanistische Linguistik,* no. 82/83, 1986, pp. 261–74.
Annemarie Auer et al., '"Respektloser Umgang" von Helga Königsdorf. Für und Wider', *Weimarer Beiträge,* vol. 30, no. 8, 1987, pp. 1338–57.
Sabine Brandt, 'Die Flucht in den Traum', review of *Respektloser Umgang, Frankfurter Allgemeine Zeitung,* Literaturbeilage, 30 September 1986.
Anna Chiarloni et al. (eds), 'Diskussion nach der Lesung von Helga Königsdorf', *Die Literatur der DDR 1976–1986,* Pisa, 1988, pp. 449–55.
Heinz Czechowski, 'Laudatio. Heinrich-Mann-Preis 1985', *Neue Deutsche Literatur,* vol. 33, no. 7, 1985, pp. 156–62.

Hans Carl Finsen, 'Das zentnerschwere Träumen der Helga Königs-dorf', *Text und Kontext*. *Zeitschrift für germanistische Literaturforschung in Skandinavien*, vol. 14, no. 1, 1986, pp. 133–9.

Wolfgang Gabler, 'Moralintensität und Geschlechterbeziehungen. Zur Prosa-Literatur junger DDR-Autoren in der zweiten Hälfte der siebziger Jahre', *Weimarer Beiträge*, vol. 30, no. 5, 1987, pp. 727–48.

Karin Hirdina, 'Frauen in der Literatur der DDR', *Formen der Individualität*, Mitteilungen aus der kulturwissenschaftlichen Forschung, 11, Berlin, 1982, pp. 87–108.

Gabriele Lindner, 'Weibliches Schreiben. Annäherung an ein Problem', in Siegfried Rönisch (ed.) *DDR-Literatur '87 im Gespräch*, Berlin, 1988, pp. 58–75.

Ilse Nagelschmidt, 'Sozialistische Frauenliteratur. Überlegungen zu einem Phänomen der DDR-Literatur in den siebziger und achtziger Jahren', *Weimarer Beiträge*, vol. 32, no. 3, 1989, pp. 450–71.

Lia Secci, 'Helga Königsdorf: eine "ungehörige" Schriftstellerin', in Anna Chiarloni et al. (eds), *Literatur der DDR 1976–1986*, Pisa, 1988, pp. 199–206.

Dietrich Segebrecht, 'Der Sinn des Lebens: das Leben', review of *Respekt-loser Umgang*, *Die Zeit*, Literaturbeilage, 7 November 1986, p. 6.

−13−

Volker Braun:

Literary Metaphors and the Travails of Socialism

Arrigo Subiotto

The political and social upheavals witnessed in the GDR in the autumn of 1989, in concert with the rest of Eastern Europe, will engender irreversible changes in its public organisations, power structures and economic methods. The effects will reverberate far beyond the front pages of newspapers, into the self-awareness of GDR citizens, the perception of that society from outside its frontiers, and the practice of cultural policies within. The world of art and letters has been released at one stroke from the inhibiting restrictions imposed by a narrow-minded, fearful cohort of administrative gurus whose cultural formation was shaped by a dogmatic concept of socialist realism. Its rigid tenets were forged in the early, Stalinist phase of the Soviet Union and proved too inflexible to accommodate the artistic realities of the GDR, whose writers shared a language − and all the weight of its heritage − with their West German colleagues and were also receptive to the pervasive cultural traditions of Western Europe.

Through four decades cultural policy in the GDR was directed, in the literary sphere, to subjecting writers to strict limitations in theme and expression aimed at suppressing any criticism of established assumptions and practices in the GDR. On coming to power in 1971 Erich Honecker enunciated his famous and apparently liberal doctrine: 'Wenn man von der festen Position des Sozialismus ausgeht, kann es meines Erachtens auf dem Gebiet von Kunst und Literatur keine Tabus geben. Das betrifft sowohl die Fragen der inhaltlichen Gestaltung als auch des Stils − kurz gesagt: die Fragen dessen, was man die künstlerische Meisterschaft nennt'.[1] This was

1. At the fourth Plenum of the Central Committee of the SED, December 1971.

greeted as offering a glorious opportunity to writers to voice their constructive criticisms of life in their society. Unfortunately, few realised that Honecker was emphasising the 'fixed position', not the 'socialism'. The result, a few years later, was the much-publicised expulsion of Wolf Biermann from the GDR and the ensuing haemorrhage westwards of artists and intellectuals who could no longer stomach the continued gagging of their talents, despite their good faith in seeking to improve socialism in their country.

Volker Braun was one who suffered most from the bigoted petty-mindedness of officialdom, because his impetuous temperament, coupled with his fervent commitment to socialism, impelled him to speak his mind in unambiguous terms. Yet it was this very commitment that kept him locked in loyalty to his country, racked by the paradox of his position, and prevented him from leaving as so many friends had, to his sad regret – 'Aber aus dem Kahn / Kippen sie' (G, p. 120).[2] His constant tussle with the restrictive powers throttling all initiatives in the GDR is well documented since the 1960s in both essay and imaginative work; the nadir was reached in the 1980s, when Braun's loyalty to a system that choked his questioning spirit reduced him to the status of an intellectual prisoner in his own country. Notes written during a trip to Hungary in August 1984 indicate the tormented nature of his ambivalent relationship to this society; Dante, in his classic persona of unwilling exile, is the inspiration: 'Gedanke zu einem Gedicht: im Inferno besucht mich Dante, in der komfortablen Hölle, die ich loben muß (dazu bin ich verdammt)[. . .] Aber wie ist der Ort beschaffen, mein Elbflorenz [i.e. Dresden]? In dem ich zerrissen schwebe, von welchen Hunden. Es ist DER ERSTE KREIS' (VF, p. 143). Dante's fourth canto inspired the thought: 'Zerreißender Schwebezustand, in dem wir uns nach dem Anderen sehnen, das sein wird / das wir werden, in unserem Vorhof zur Zukunft? Das alte Leben noch mächtig, das neue noch schmächtig. Das neue, in das wir unermüdlich vorwärtshasten in der alten / neuen Gangart . . .' (VF, p. 147). But despite his open dissatisfaction with a society that officially discredited the legitimate and honest criticisms of its intellectuals, Braun, like Dante, could not accept being thrust out of a community he felt he belonged to, for good or ill: 'Dante hat sich nie abgefunden mit der Vertreibung aus der kommunalen Gemeinschaft[. . .] So würde es uns im Ausland gehn, der Sozialismus die Heimat, die uns nicht erträgt; die ich verlassen kann, die mich nicht verläßt; die Herkunft und die Zukunft' (VF, p. 153).

2. See Author's Note at the end of this essay for key.

This tensely dialectical relationship continued unresolved over many years, and Braun remained recalcitrant: 'Mich wandeln – von wem zu wem? Ich war ja kein "Werkzeug mit ausgelöschtem Willen" wie der junge Dichter Fühmann, ich war im Gegenteil ungehorsam;[. . .] ich habe immer als Ungläubiger geschrieben' (VF, p. 150). Unlike many friends who deserted the GDR, Braun was prepared to ride out the pressures and seek new resources in literature: 'Wie gelähmt seit Monaten. Kunert fiel nichts mehr ein zu dem besseren Land; ich kann mir noch immer ein besseres denken. Aber die Suche nach dem *Stoff zum Leben* im literarischen Sperrgebiet' (VF, p. 149). In practical terms Braun's persistent integrity in pursuing the realities of socialist society in the 'no-go area of literature' led to interminable hindrances to permission to publish his work: the poetry of the early 1970s finally appeared in the volume *Training des aufrechten Gangs* (1979), while *Hinze-Kunze-Roman* (1985) and the poems of *Langsamer knirschender Morgen* (1987) also suffered long delays. The dichotomy of being an SED party member (a significant element in the cultural establishment) and yet retaining an individual voice, was becoming schizophrenic:

> Nicht nur die satirische Prosa: auch die Gedichte, nichts scheint mehr druckbar. Da jetzt "alles darauf ankommt, den Sozialismus zu stärken", ist nur sein Lob gelitten. Byzantinische Ästhetik. Aber wenn das, was ich schreibe, "im Widerspruch zur Partei" steht, wie kann ich dann . . . wie kann ich dann Mitglied sein? Niemand fragt mich das, aber es ist unerträglich, diesen Widerspruch zu leben: eine bedeutende Kulturpolitik mitzutragen und ihr ein Ärgernis zu sein. (VF, p. 146)

Braun's dilemma stemmed from the collision between his unwavering commitment to socialism and the growing perception that the apparatus of the state would not tolerate trenchant criticism and demanded only obsequious affirmation. Time and again he found a sympathetic chord in literary forerunners: Dresden was his sad 'Elbflorenz', but instead of allowing himself to be pressured into foreign domicile, he chose to remain in the suffocating embrace of his homeland. Here, in this inner 'exile', he could continue to use literature as a sophisticated weapon to attack the distortions and back-slidings sanctioned by authority, and voice his disconsolate regret at the slow, erratic pace of socialist progress. Provocation was always his chosen mode for goading society out of inertia; it appeared in the title of his very first volume of poetry, *Provokation für mich* (1965), and has grown in virulence in recent years: 'Ich

weiß nur soviel: daß ich provoziere, die ich doch liebe, die Gesellschaft, und die Frau, daß ich sie verletze aus ungeduldiger Liebe,
und die Verletzte schlägt zurück oder umgekehrt ich oder' (VF, p.
152). The innate violence in this description echoes Braun's recurrent metaphor of the clinch for his relationship to the GDR: he feels
himself almost physically locked in the closest of encounters, a
static struggle particularly wasteful of energies that could be released productively by both antagonists.

   This impulsive aggression born of impatience can be traced
through Braun's work from his earliest play, *Die Kipper*, written
between 1962–65, but not performed until 1972. The energetic
dumper-driver Paul Bauch seeks to encourage his fellow-workers
to ever greater output, purely as a joyous feat, in his vision of an
untroubled Utopia: 'Wir stehn ganz am Anfang. Es wird ein
Überfluß an materiellen Gütern dasein, ein Überfluß an Gedanken
und ein Überfluß an Gefühlen[. . .] Ich sage, der Mensch des neuen
Jahrtausends wird leben wie es angenehm ist. Es gibt keine Sitten,
es gibt keine Normen. Es gibt nur den Tag, der ist immer neu' (K,
p. 47). In an interview on the play's première in France in 1979
Braun declared that there was no more important theme than that
of *Die Kipper*, namely that Marx's definition of society as the
realisation of the full potential of human beings fell far short of the
harsh reality of everyday life in the GDR:

> C'est une des plus violentes contradictions de la société socialiste. Ainsi,
> l'ensemble de la société tend vers la réalisation des aspirations, mais,
> pour un temps encore indéterminé, la réalisation de tâches matérielles
> exige que 40% de la population ait un statut de manoeuvre[. . .] La tâche
> principale, le but d'une société qui se prétend socialiste est de résoudre
> cette contradiction, insoluble dans l'instant. C'est dans cette difficulté
> que réside l'espoir.[3]

Braun described the rift 'entre les petits pas réels, concrets, et la
théorie' strikingly as 'une petite déchirure que l'on ne peut pas
cautériser. C'est comme une gerçure toujours ouverte'.[4] Nevertheless, the enthusiasm of Braun's youth had shone through in the
spontaneity and hopefulness of both theme and execution in his
earlier literary work; there was a quiet euphoria about the open
ends of revolution, optimism in the opportunities and underlying

---

3. 'Comme une gerçure toujours ouverte', interview with Volker Braun in *La
   Nouvelle Critique*, 121, 1979, p. 20.
4. Ibid., p. 21.

certainties of a nation seeking to create an egalitarian system.

During the 1970s Braun was gradually overcome with frustration at the halting pace of socialism and disillusion with the emergence of a ruling stratum of people in public life who became more and more detached from the ordinary citizen. His sombre diagnosis unambiguously informs the essay 'Büchners Briefe' (1977):

> Solange eine Gesellschaft, sie mag mittlerweile wie immer heißen, auf Gewalt beruht, nämlich solange es 'die da oben und die da unten' gibt, bedarf es der Gegengewalt, sie zu verändern. Zwar der Charakter dieser Gegengewalt mag sich modeln, er mag feiner werden: oder in sozialistischen Staaten gar freundlicher, aber mitnichten nachgiebiger. Es wird nicht der Hanf sein und die Laterne, nicht einmal der Streik und die Demonstration. Wo das Oben und Unten sich nicht mehr in der archaischen Gestalt von Klassen gegenübersteht, aber doch die verschiedene Stellung der Individuen in der Pyramide der Verfügungsgewalt anzeigt, geht der Kampf nicht mehr um den Platz an der Spitze, sondern um die Zertrümmerung der Pyramide. (VF, pp. 98–9)

Braun reiterated his critique in France:

> Il m'a fallu un certain temps pour me rendre compte que la division du travail dans la société socialiste n'est pas seulement horizontale mais aussi verticale; cette société reste hiérarchisée, pyramidale, avec des relations de subalternité; il n'y a pas de domination de classes sur des classes mais d'hommes sur des hommes.[5]

This image of the pyramid was to recur many times in Braun's subsequent writing, as was his classification of rulers and ruled into 'Herrscher' and 'Angeherrschte', with all the brutal militaristic overtones of the latter word.

The most insidious tactic employed by those in power to reinforce their position was to throttle independent initiative by arrogating to themselves the entire responsibility for all decision-making. The citizens were reduced to the state of 'Unmündigkeit' described so trenchantly by Immanuel Kant in his pamphlet of 1794, *Beantwortung der Frage: Was ist Aufklärung?*: 'Unmündigkeit ist das Unvermögen, sich seines Verstandes ohne Leitung eines anderen zu bedienen[. . .] Daß der bei weitem größte Teil der Menschen [. . .] den Schritt zur Mündigkeit, außer dem daß er beschwerlich ist, auch für sehr gefährlich halte: dafür sorgen schon jene Vormünder, die die Oberaufsicht über sie gütigst auf sich

5. Ibid.

genommen haben.' Braun felt the choking hand of authority almost physically, voicing his discomfort and anger in the complex poetic structures of *Training des aufrechten Gangs*. The prose poem 'Höhlengleichnis' alludes to Plato's cave and concludes with a gleam of hope: 'Darüber begannen wieder Jahrhunderte zu vergehn voll neuem Schutt, geplanten Kosten, Kunstersatz und normativem Gespeichel. Aber in dieser Zeit begann ein neues, härteres Training, des schmerzhaften und wunderbaren aufrechten Gangs' (T, p. 61). Despite these stirrings, the muzzling of critical voices, however constructive, continued unabated. It was later documented again by Braun in his 1985 essay in homage to Rimbaud, the mutinously impetuous poet of the Second Empire in France:

> Unsere Erzieherin aber – die Gesellschaft, strenge sorgend[. . .] Sie hat uns in ihre Obhut genommen, Gouvernante, die uns ihre Liebe verbarg. Sie hat uns ferngehalten von der harten Welt. Die Schule – nicht das Leben. Der Glaube – nicht die Widersprüche. Das Kollektiv – nicht die Gemeinsamkeit[. . .] Wir sollten rein bleiben, Muttersöhnchen des Sozialismus. Sie hat uns wie Kinder gehalten, als wir längst Männer werden wollten. Das muß zu einem Aufbegehren führen,[. . .] Scheißstaat, höre ich mich sagen[. . .] Was wir entbehrten, war Vertrauen. (VF, pp. 112–13)

The denial of maturity and trust was the motive force that drove much of Braun's writing in the 1970s. It finds its most reflective and devastating embodiment in the narrative *Unvollendete Geschichte* which, after an initial appearance in *Sinn und Form* (no. 5, 1975), was refused further publication in the GDR until 1989. In this story Braun penetrates to the core of the malaise in East German society. Unlike the three plays he wrote around the same time, *Guevara oder der Sonnenstaat* (1975), *Großer Frieden* (1976) and *Simplex Deutsch* (1978/9), which treat the problems of power, responsibility and revolution in abstract or metaphorical terms, and unlike the dialectical and linguistic coruscations of his poetry, *Unvollendete Geschichte* confronts with bitter bluntness the abuse of power over the individual in the everyday reality of the GDR.

The thread of the banal love story – loosely based on a true incident – encapsulates the theme of an over-solicitous state, mediated through authoritarian parents who succeed in totally alienating their child. Ideology ousts humanity. Karin, daughter of a high Party official and a successful woman journalist, is warned by her father to drop her friendship with Frank, a sometime 'Rowdy' who has already fallen foul of the police and is under suspicion of wanting to flee the country. Her father is also appalled by the prospect of his daughter becoming involved with someone of Frank's family background: 'diese Familie allein, das ist für uns untragbar' (UG, p.10).

This insensitivity to her feelings gradually estranges Karin from her parents. She moves in briefly with Frank and his mother, discovering a warmth in this somewhat slovenly household that is lacking in the chill and loveless atmosphere of her own privileged circumstances. Her eyes are also opened to the fact that humanity has little to do with ideological belief or commitment to political ideals. She perceives that Frank's family, for all its social disharmonies, is more real, genuine and human than her own kin:

> Die elterliche Informationspolitik hatte sie den Wechselfällen der Welt nicht unbedingt ausgesetzt, sie hatte nur eine Frage stellen gelernt: ist einer für uns oder ist er gegen uns. Jetzt lebte sie mit Leuten in einem Haus zusammen, die mal so und mal so redeten, die sich abschindeten auf Arbeit – und auf die Arbeit schimpften. Diese herzensgute Frau, die für sie sorgte – aber nicht zur Hausversammlung ging. Bei der Post war sie Aktivist geworden – und abends hockte sie vor dem Westprogramm. Es war so einfach gewesen, es war unglaublich. (UG, p. 72)

Under the pressures being put on his relationship with Karin and threatened with punishment for his suspected Western contacts, Frank attempts suicide. Karin meanwhile has become pregnant, and her heightened bodily sensations make her more than ever sensitive to the lack of human contact and communication with her parents and awaken her awareness that she is an object of ideological conformism:

> Ihr Vertrauen zu den Eltern war grenzenlos gewesen – sie waren *mehr* als Eltern, sie vertraten für sie den Staat. Den Staat, in dem fast alles gut ist oder gut geht. In dem man auf die andern hören kann, nur hören muß. Das hatten sie ihr erklärt. Es war ein schönes Märchen, das fast wissenschaftlich klang. Das konnte sie glauben, bis zur Gedankenlosigkeit. (UG, p. 71)

As the realisation dawns in Karin that human relationships are a necessity for individuals, her father too – though not her mother with her 'selbstbewußtes sicheres Gesicht' (UG, p. 82), who unfeelingly proposes an abortion – becomes aware of the distortions and devastation his blind ideological obedience has wrought in the lives of these two young people. First, the regional secretary

explains to him as they walk by the river the unnatural posturings
that keep the GDR on edge and prevent it from living in a relaxed,
humane manner: 'Wir sind nicht nur wir, wir sind wir und nicht
sie, wir gegenüber ihnen. Das ist die Spannung, die uns kribblig
macht, die Belastung, die uns jagt und hemmt. Diese Geschichte –
hat das ganze Land' (UG, p. 69). In disgust at himself, Karin's
father muses on the botched upbringing of his daughter: 'Die
Wachsamkeit, ja – aber was hatte er bewacht, wenn er ein Kind
verlor, und ein andrer wirklich draufging? Er hatte so sehr aufge-
paßt, daß er nicht aufpaßte, was wirklich passierte. Sein Mittel
vernichtete den Zweck, womöglich, die Sorge um den Menschen
brachte den Menschen um – oder um was, wer fragt schon *was*?'
(UG, p. 83). To his wife's alarm and incomprehension he takes to
seeking social contact in pubs, while Karin retreats into self-
absorption with her own intimate self and the child she is expecting. The story ends in a muted key, leaving Karin and Frank, who
has just left hospital, standing on the pavement in a mutually
supportive embrace, oblivious to and cut off from the swirl of life
around them.

In *Unvollendete Geschichte*, Braun has carefully geared his deployment of language to maximise the emotional as well as intellectual
power of the theme. To do this he reawakens the impact of such
fictional documents of alienation as Goethe's *Werther* and Büchner's
Lenz through allusion and direct quotation. One Sunday Karin
engrosses herself in Plenzdorf's *Die neuen Leiden des jungen W.* with
extreme empathy, but thinks nevertheless that Werther expressed
the dissonance of his world more sharply:

> Der stieß sich an ihrem Kern. W. stieß sich an allem Äußeren [. . .] Das
> Ungeheure in dem "Werther" war, daß da ein Riß durch die Welt ging,
> und durch ihn selbst. Und doch war auch in all dem Äußeren ein *Inneres*,
> W. drang nur nicht hinein, ein tieferer Widerspruch – den man finden
> müßte! Wie würde ein Buch sein – und auf sie wirken, in dem einer
> heute an den Riß kam . . . in den er stürzen mußte. (UG, pp. 45f.)

The words are both self-referent – *Unvollendete Geschichte* is this
book – and a sign-post to Büchner's Lenz, who sinks beyond hope
into the night of madness: 'die Welt, die er hatte nutzen wollen,
hatte einen ungeheurn Riß'.[6] The affinity with Lenz permeates

6. Georg Büchner, *Werke und Briefe* (Nach der historisch-kritischen Ausgabe
von Werner R. Lehmann), Munich and Vienna, 1980, p. 86.

Karin's experience. Dislocation of his troubled state of mind begins early in the story as she travels to M. on a wintry January day:

> [. . .] ihr war seltsam in Kopf. Es schneite stärker, die Dörfer wie zugehängt, die Bäume am Straßenrand rückten ganz fern und unwirklich weg. Sie fror. Sie hielt die Masten und Schneisen in ihrem Blick, das kam ihr nun alles zu, und konnte nichts halten, es flog alles dahin, alle Gewißheiten, alle Sicherheit.
> Vor M. schien Sonne, die Straße blendete, schnitt wie ein Schneidbrenner in die Brücken ein, der Fluß wie grauer Teig in den Mulden. (UG, p. 15)

Detachment from the world around, lack of communication, and incomprehension become keenly physical as her disjunction emerges in actual bodily sensations: 'Sie lag ins Kissen vergraben und fühlte ihr Bewußtsein aus dem Kopf strömen, ihr war als beule sich ihr leerer Schädel ein, zu einem harten Klumpen' (UG, p. 51). Or when she is finally waiting for Frank to emerge from the hospital gates: 'Die Sonne brannte: sie wußte nur, daß sie schwitzte. Da sie nichts Bestimmtes denken wollte, floß ihr alles wirr durch den Kopf; die Gedanken schmerzhafte langsame Würmer im Gehirn, wenn sie einen zerriß, krochen die Teile weiter. Es war gräßlich' (UG, p. 97). Frank, too, reacts with a physical susceptibility to hindrances and suspicions; he had tormented himself for days with the thought that Karin wanted to be rid of him: '[. . .] seine Gedanken wie ein Ausschlag, der ihn juckte, er mußte darin kratzen, keine Arbeit lenkte ihn ab, sein Gehirn nur eine Wunde. Er hätte sich den Kopf einschlagen mögen' (UG, p. 31).

Büchner's political pamphlet *Der hessische Landbote* also provides an emphatic quotation ('Was ist denn nun das für [ein] gewaltiges Ding: der Staat?')[7] to point up the correlation between oppressive societal demands on the individual in the GDR and the crushing of the human being through crude economic and political exploitation in Büchner's Hesse. In *Unvollendete Geschichte* the GDR comes perilously close to comparison with the heavy police state which Büchner fled.

Unvollendete Geschichte is a significant, though understated, piece of writing. Its intimate links with the German cultural perception of Büchner are paradigmatic for Braun's use of the literary tradition. From his earliest work he had engaged particularly with

---

7. Ibid., p. 212. Braun, in using this quotation (UG, p. 78), adds an 'ein' which is not in the original.

German writers in a two-way traffic of fructification and polemic, acceptance and rejection.[8] The context of a solid cultural and historical continuum gave credibility, legitimacy and resonance to specifically orientated East German themes. Within this framework Braun achieved a dialectic sharpness which measured the present by the dimensions of the past, and in turn probed and questioned the past with a fresh perspective. He describes the 'Stimmen der Toten als ganz bewußtes Kompositionselement' in GDR poetry, pointing to the dominant significance of Hölderlin and Klopstock in the 1960s.[9] As the years passed and Braun sensed the dead hand of oppressive political tutelage stifling freedom and the imagination he invoked the rebellious presences of Büchner, Kleist and Rimbaud; their work refracted through his serves the dual dialectic: 'das hat einerseits den Vorteil, daß da große Dinge bewahrt werden, und zum anderen, daß das Heutige in der Verwandlung plötzlich deutlicher wird, weil es auf der Folie von alten Abläufen oder Gedanken abrollt. Damit wird das Heutige verfremdet und zugleich vielleicht schärfer gefaßt.'[10]

In the last decade in particular Braun's consciousness of the tradition has intensified and broadened to range over a wide spectrum of significant historical movements and men that have moulded Western culture. His four most recent plays acknowledge direct inspiration: *Dmitri* (based on Schiller's *Demetrius*, 1982); *Die Übergangsgesellschaft* (an allusive reworking of Chekhov's *Three Sisters*, 1982); *Siegfried – Frauenprotokolle – Deutscher Furor* (incorporating salient elements of the Nibelungen saga, 1984); and *Transit Europa* (an adaptation of Anna Seghers' novel, *Transit*, 1988). The latest volume of poetry incorporates notes (reminiscent of T.S. Eliot's practice) with references to Catullus, Homer, Goethe, Klopstock, Lessing, Rimbaud, Hölderlin and other lesser names. Arriving early at an international conference in Pisa in 1987, Braun's first act was to catch a bus to the coast and sit in homage on the shore of the Ligurian Sea where the beach hut of Ezra Pound had stood when he composed *The Pisan Cantos*; his political convictions are far from those of Pound or Eliot, Dante or Goethe, but he accepts a solidarity 'wie zu Brüdern, die wir eigentlich an die Brust ziehen

---

8. See Christine Cosentino and Wolfgang Ertl, *Zur Lyrik Volker Brauns*, Königstein, 1984, for a detailed consideration of the 'Traditionsbeziehungen' in Braun's poetry.
9. 'Volker Braun und Christoph Hein in der Diskussion', in Chiarloni et al. (eds), *Die Literatur der DDR 1976-1986*, Pisa, 1988, p. 439.
10. Ibid., p. 440.

wollen, zugleich aber merken wir, daß wir ihnen auch auf den Kopf hauen müssen'.[11]

That ubiquitous Goethean figure, Faust, in a 'clinch' with his subversive mentor Mephistopheles, was from the start a productive influence in Braun's work; the two are cast in the roles of Hinze, the proletarian worker, and Kunze, party official and ideological leader, in the play *Hinze und Kunze* (1973 – a first version, in 1968, bore the title *Hans Faust*). The location is typically the work-place demanding rough, physical labour. Hinze, impatient for the new dawn of easeful living, is angered and frustrated by this demeaning work ('Gewaltiges Kriechen auf / Lahmen Knien in die neue / Zeit. Die alte Scheiße') and comes into direct confrontation with Kunze, the party secretary and representative of cumbersome central planning. He puts a brake on Hinze's Faustian impetuousness and counsels methodical, if slow, advances. In a reversal of Goethe's *Faust* at the close, Hinze is incensed that Marlies has chosen to abort his child in favour of her own career. But the two men achieve a final reconciliation as Hinze accepts the wisdom of Kunze's longer vision of the path to progress: 'Dachtest du, es sei ein Spaziergang, die rauhe Strecke zwischen Schutt und Zukunft!'

The collision between the planners of the party and the impulsive aspirations of the workers may have been averted in 1973 – and *Hinze und Kunze* also documents Braun's autodidactic effort to curb his own impatience – but a decade later, with the publication of *Berichte von Hinze und Kunze*, Braun hit upon a literary form that allowed him to distinguish the subtle nuances that governed the relationship of ruler and ruled in an equal society. If the play had identified the dissatisfaction of the worker with the role imposed on him of carrying out policies dictated from above (a theme surfacing in such paradigmatic heroes as the norm-breaker Hans Aehre in Claudius' *Menschen an unsrer Seite* and the dynamic brigade leader Balla in Neutsch's *Spur der Steine*), the *Berichte* dissect the complex attitudes and mental processes of these interdependent protagonists in a series of brief, anecdotal prose pieces written in aphoristic or parabolic style: 'Kunze und Hinze unterschied wenig. Das Gehalt, die Verantwortung, die Befugnisse – und daß Kunze den Unterschied für nicht aufregend hielt' (B, p.13). Though with a different political intent, the *Berichte* are strongly reminiscent of Brecht's *Flüchtlingsgespräche*, written largely in his Finnish exile in 1940/41 to express in a dialogue between the physicist Ziffel and the metal-worker Kalle Brecht's own views on world events and the individual's

11. Ibid.

predicament. Ziffel and Kalle represent that ever-present and trouble-some polarity in marxist thinking, the intellectual and the worker; but in *Flüchtlingsgespräche* they are in the same boat, both in flight from Nazi Germany. In Braun's *Berichte*, however, Hinze is subordinate to Kunze and it is only the discontinuous autonomy of the separate 'Berichte' that allows his voice equal status with Kunze's.

By the early 1980s Braun's bitter resentment at the impregnable self-complacency of the ruling cadres in the GDR precluded any conciliatory writing on his part pleading for participation from below in the decision-making processes; instead he reached for the only weapons available to a writer to challenge those in power – satire and the exposure of the language of lies masking the truth. Braun derives his ridicule from the everyday life of the GDR, for instance in 'Mängel, positiv formuliert':

> Wenn Kunze, ohnehin nicht oft, eine Arbeit öffentlich kritisierte, überlegte er sich seine Sätze. Er sagte nicht: Das ist nicht in Ordnung, er sagte: Daran ist weiter zu arbeiten. Er sagte nicht: Wir sind im Rückstand, er sagte: Wir müssen das Tempo erhöhen. Er sagte nicht: Da wurde ein Fehler gemacht, er sagte: Vorwärts zu neuen Erfolgen. – Warum nimmst du dir das Zeitungsblatt vor den Mund? fragte Hinze. Gemeckert wird genug, knurrte Kunze, wir orientieren nach vorn. Sehr freundlich, entgegnete Hinze, aber wer hört dir hinten zu? (B, p.6)

Hinze, the muzzled underdog in reality, is vouchsafed the upper hand in the fictional construct.

The *Berichte* led in 1985 to the appearance of a fully-fledged 'novel', *Hinze-Kunze-Roman*, which intensified and made more coherent Braun's virulent portrait of the condition socialism had been reduced to in the GDR. His despondency at the ever-widening gulf between power and the people drove him more deeply into the satirical mode which he admitted had become dominant in GDR literature, to his own 'Ärger und Unbehagen':

> [Die Satire] ist eine Erscheinung, die sich durch große Teile der DDR-Literatur zieht[. . .] Und die Stimmung, aus der die Satire kommt, ist nicht die erquicklichste und erfreulichste, so daß ich für mich eigentlich hoffe, ich könnte sie überwinden. Man muß aber auch sehen, daß uns die Wirklichkeit die Komik oder das Material der Satire an die Hand liefert. Natürlich schneidet die Wirklichkeit zuerst die Fratze, und die Literatur malt es ab. Man braucht nur einen nüchternen Blick, um die Wirklichkeit bei ihren eigenen Grimassen zu ertappen.[12]

12. Ibid., p. 445.

The apparent caricature proffered by satire is for Braun a faithful exposition of reality (it signifies 'einen Zugewinn an Realismus'),[13] and *Hinze-Kunze-Roman* is a densely-packed appraisal of the contemporary state of the GDR with its fragile and distorted socialism, the abuse of power, the supine docility and apathy of disregarded citizens, but also the plebeian strength latent in their sceptical debunking of authority.

The axis of the novel is the ambivalent relationship between Kunze, a high-ranking party official, and Hinze, his chauffeur, who drives him around the country from one engagement and one sexual encounter to another. Kunze is a short, thick-set, hairy man with a powerful physique and insatiable sexual appetite which he displays with brutal prowess in the pursuit of women. This callous reification rebounds on him in the account of his visit to the Hamburg brothel where, to his discomfiture, a black girl demands fixed payment for every item in their transaction: 'Er schloß die Augen, entblößte sein kräftiges Gebiß, preßte seine weiche, weiberhafte Hand auf das schwarze Gesicht und ging wütend vor. Die Frau bläkte erschrocken auf, hielt aber sofort die Luft an, und der Reisende, ein schäumendes, röchelndes, das Nord-Süd-Gefälle brutal nutzendes Schwein' (HKR, p. 90). Kunze's sexual degradation of women parallels his exploitation of all his fellow-citizens. Yet women do appear – like the busy workers in the linen-washing complex – who brush him aside. Hinze's spirited Berlin wife Lisa, in particular, similarly to Marlies in the earlier drama *Hinze und Kunze*, maintains the upper hand over Kunze's lust for her; indeed, though she beds indifferently with him and Hinze, she uses Kunze's interest to create a career for herself and ultimately rejects both their claims to 'ownership' over her new-born daughter.

The master-servant theme, immediately reminiscent of Brecht's Herr Puntila and his chauffeur Matti, allows Braun maximum latitude to deploy the intricate details of authority and submission. He is assuredly aware of the prolific literary tradition encompassing Don Quixote and Sancho Panza, Don Juan and Sganarelle, and not least Diderot's *Jacques le fataliste et son maître*, which is explicitly referred to by Braun and is a clear model in such formal aspects as the constant narratorial interventions, the interruption of the fiction by actual events, and self-comment by the author. Like his literary forerunners, Hinze is both menial and indispensable, always at his master's beck and call, but also a source of good counsel and hard sense. In equipoise, Kunze is nakedly authoritarian towards Hinze and yet

13. Ibid., p. 446.

often feebly dependent on him. Neither is to be admired, both are intrinsically pusillanimous – certainly in contrast to Lisa – in their acquiescence in the cumbersome, inflexible structures dominating the land; this may have prompted Braun's designation of his novel as 'dieses leider deutsche Buch'.[14] It is true that Hinze, in an excursus dominated by metaphors of battle that describe his previous employment as a factory lathe operator, does have a momentary intimation of the real struggle being enacted:

> Diese lebendigen Leute hier, Spitzendreher, Bestarbeiter, standen im Krieg gegen tote Dinge, die sich anhäuften, das Vergangne, das Erloschene, das sich wie Lava in die Halle wälzte[. . .] Aber zwischen ihnen, hinter ihnen, über ihnen stand etwas, wurde fest, geronnene, rostige Verhältnisse[. . .] Die Institutionen, Produkte langjähriger Arbeit von oben herab, die sich in der Landschaft festgesetzt hatten wie ägyptische Pyramiden, wehrten sich mit den alten plumpen Methoden, Tricks, zu denen ihre Mumien noch fähig waren[. . .] Er blieb im Clinch mit den gemachten, den vergangnen, den angehäuften Formen. Die herrschende, die angeherrschte Klasse[. . .] Aber alles deutete darauf hin, daß eine Entscheidung fallen mußte. So oder so; denn der Kampf hatte alles und jeden bis in die Fasern ergriffen. Entweder würden sie in den mächtigen eisernen Bedingungen verschwinden, oder sie müßten sie zerbrechen, wie der Falter die Larve sprengt. (HKR, pp. 83–6)

The final image, ironising the socialist realist mode, is of Hinze leaving the factory with his fellow-workers: 'Er schritt aus, den Kopf zur Seite gedreht, skeptischen Blicks nach hinten, seine Lippen fest aufeinander, die Mundwinkel eine Spur herabgezogen, die Stirn gefurcht, Gesichtsfarbe ungesund gelblichbraun, ein Krieger, der den Tod gesehn hat, am gestreckten Arm die Faust geballt um die Lohntüte' (HKR, p. 86). Here literature accurately foreshadows the headlong peripeteias of 1989 in the GDR: the crumpling of paper tigers and the prostration of the worker before affluence.

The corrosive satire of *Hinze-Kunze-Roman* targeted the sacred cows foisted for so long on the citizens of the GDR, and showed them in the actuality of everyday locations in work-place and home: filthy factory canteen and coal-mine, computer centre and training establishment, convalescent home and maternity hospital, public meeting and march past, Kunze's opulent bungalow and Hinze's dilapidated slum flat, all recreate the authentic milieu of the

---

14. In a dedication to the present writer.

contemporary GDR. This realism is reinforced by Braun's subtle differentiation of language, from terse, demotic idiom to canting phrasemongering:

[. . .] eine Rede, die in der gesprochenen Sprache (auch der Dialekte) wurzelt, die scheinbar mit deren Laxheiten läuft und dabei doch sehr bewußt Bedeutungsüberschneidungen und -verschiebungen produziert, die gläubige Wendungen und Vokabularlisten auf ihren Sinn befragt und ihren Unsinn zeigt. Das alles nicht bloß als 'Form', weil hier[. . .] Sprache in ihren hohl gewordenen Konventionen, Glätten, Verschweigungen zum Gegenstand gemacht, Sprachkritik geleistet wird.[15]

Official jargon embedded in the bureaucratic distortions of party meetings, speeches, slogans on walls and in newspapers, political discussions, resolutions, administrative decisions, are incisively parodied by Braun as they were in the *Berichte*. Empty phraseology is unmasked for what it is: a weapon to obstruct enlightenment and manipulate the subjected individual. Braun shows it to be akin to Newspeak in Orwell's *1984*.

The arrogance and insolence of power has so incensed Braun in recent years that his writing has barely managed to restrain his anger at 'die rabiat stumpfe Gläubigkeit der festen Position' (VF, p.145). Time and again he inveighs against the 'Deckgebirge der Verheißungen',[16] and in *Die Übergangsgesellschaft* – with all its resonances of the contemporary GDR – he puts a violent diatribe in the mouth of Anton, the writer:

Die Literatur hat nur einen Sinn, das wieder wegzureißen, was die Ideologen hinbaun. Das schöne Bewußtsein. Das uns so viel kostet. Solange diese Fachschaft jubelt, muß die Literatur gegenhalten. Unsere Arbeit ist die Zerstörung [. . .]
Ich esse das Blei der Zeit. Ich laufe in das Messer der Verhältnisse, um den Schmerz zu fühlen. Ich begebe mich in den Clinch, soll es mich zerreißen und ich will ihre Klauen zeigen, ihre Tyrannenfresse, ihre fürchterliche Macht[. . .] Es mag vorwärtsgehn, aber da ist kein Land für uns. Es ist besetzt, hier *schlägt sich an den Kopf* eine Kolonie. Wir zahlen Tribut, an die tote Zukunft. Ja, einmal war es richtig, es war alles richtig. Wir haben die Morgenröte entrollt, um in der Dämmerung zu wohnen.[17]

15. Dieter Schlenstedt, 'Anhang' to *Hinze-Kunze-Roman*, p. 202.
16. For instance, in Braun's Rimbaud essay (VF, pp. 112–13) and 'Diskussion'.
17. Volker Braun, 'Die Übergangsgesellschaft', in *Theater Heute*, 4, 1989, pp. 48–50.

That Anton speaks for Braun is not in doubt: Mascha reads from his book a poem published by Braun in *Langsamer knirschender Morgen*, 'Das Lehen': 'Ich bleib im Lande und nähre mich im Osten. / Mit meinen Sprüchen, die mich den Kragen kosten / In andrer Zeit: Noch bin ich auf dem Posten. / In Wohnungen, geliehn vom Magistrat / Und eß mich satt, wie ihr, an der Silage. / Und werde nicht froh in meiner Chefetage / Die Bleibe, die ich suche, ist kein Staat.' The poem continues with further hard-hitting lines not quoted in the play: 'Wie komm ich durch den Winter der Strukturen. / Partei mein Fürst: *sie hat uns alles gegeben* / Und alles ist noch nicht das Leben. / Das Lehen, das ich brauch, wird nicht vergeben' (LKM p. 49).

The virtual dismemberment of the SED following widespread public protest and unrest led to the rapid dissolution of the frozen structures of the state. Braun quickly spoke out on the elated but unstable freedoms newly found: the Stalinist party had embodied 'das Mißtrauen gegenüber dem Volk',[18] and should no longer have power but a more elevated function, 'als Instrument radikaler emanzipatorischer Interessen, als Organisator des Widerspruchs, der produktiven Konflikte'. The squabbles of a parliamentary system are already a great step forward from absolutist rigidity, but greater democracy would be achieved by a system of citizens' forums, people's committees, 'um schon unten an dem Text zu arbeiten, der oben geredet wird'; these would both enhance and modify their elected representatives as 'die massenhafte Autorität, die Regierung beauftragt oder ihr entgegentritt, die erworbene Autorität des Volkes'. Braun advocates a permanent process of political ferment: 'suchen wir die Staatsform, die ein Protestmarsch bleibt gegen die elenden Verhältnisse'; and he seeks to dissuade his fellow countrymen from embracing too eagerly a Western ethos: 'Wir sind die politische Kette los; binden wir uns nicht wieder an ans Gängelband eines falschen gesellschaftlichen Interesses, das im Kaufhaus des Westens zu haben ist. Wir kannten den Opportunismus der Macht: fürchten wir jetzt den Opportunismus der Freiheit.' Imaginative though these concepts may be, one must remain sceptical about the possibility of their ever being implemented in the new Germany which will emerge. Is Volker Braun fated to continue to play the role of the poetic voice, alone but for a handful of kindred spirits, in an ideological wilderness?

---

18. Volker Braun, 'Notizen eines Publizisten', in *Neues Deutschland*, 8 December 1989, p. 4. Remaining quotations are taken from this article.

Author's Note

The following editions and abbreviations are used for Braun's works:
G : *Gedichte*, Frankfurt am Main, 1979.
VF : *Verheerende Folgen mangelnden Anscheins innerbetrieblicher Demokratie*, Frankfurt am Main, 1988.
K : *Die Kipper*, in *Stücke 1*, Frankfurt am Main, 1975.
T : *Training des aufrechten Gangs*, Halle-Leipzig, 1979.
UG : *Unvollendete Geschichte*, Frankfurt am Main, 1977.
B : *Berichte von Hinze und Kunze*, Halle-Leipzig, 1983.
HKR : *Hinze-Kunze-Roman*, Halle-Leipzig, 1985.
LKM : *Langsamer knirschender Morgen*, Frankfurt am Main, 1987.

Suggested Further Reading

Other works by Volker Braun:
Wir und nicht sie. Gedichte, Halle-Saale, 1970.
Das ungezwungne Leben Kasts. Drei Berichte, Berlin and Weimar, 1972.
Gegen die symmetrische Welt. Gedichte, Halle-Saale, 1974.
Es genügt nicht die einfache Wahrheit. Notate, Leipzig, 1975.
'Kommt Zeit, kommt Räte', in Michael Naumann (ed.), *Die Geschichte ist offen. DDR 1990: Hoffnung auf eine neue Republik. Schriftsteller aus der DDR über die Zukunftschancen ihres Landes*, Hamburg, 1990, pp. 15–21.

Secondary Material

Gilbert Badia, 'über Volker Brauns Dramatik', in Chiarloni et al., (eds), *Die Literatur in der DDR 1976-1986*, Pisa, 1988, pp. 347–54.
Christine Cosentino. 'Volker Brauns Essay "Rimbaud.Ein Psalm der Aktualität" im Kontext seiner Lyrik', in *Studies in GDR Culture*, 7, pp. 171–84.
Ingrid Hähnel, 'Politische Poesie als Vorgang zwischen Menschen. Volker Brauns Gedichtband *Gegen die symmetrische Welt*' in Inge Münz-Koenen (ed.), *Werke und Wirkungen*, Leipzig, 1987, pp. 214–55.
Ulrich Profitlich, *Volker Braun. Studien zu seinem dramatischen und erzählerischen Werk*, Munich, 1985 (contains good bibliography).
Jay Rosellini, *Volker Braun* (Autorenbücher), Munich, 1983.

'Kulturerbe und Zeitgenossenschaft. Volker Braun and Georg Büchner', in *German Quarterly*, 60, 1987, pp.600–16.

Gisela Shaw, 'Die Landschaftsmetapher bei Volker Braun' in *GDR Monitor*, No.16, 1986/87, pp.105–39.

Arrigo Subiotto, 'Volker Braun, Rimbaud und die DDR', in Chiarloni et al. (eds), *Die Literatur der DDR 1976–1986*, Pisa, 1988.

Hans-Jürgen Timm, 'Geschichte als Erfahrungsraum. Zu Aspekten der Dramatik Volker Brauns', in *Weimarer Beiträge*, 35, 1989, pp. 1506-30.

Ian Wallace, *Volker Braun: Forschungsbericht*, Amsterdam, 1986 (contains an essay on 'Tendenzen und Probleme der Braun-Forschung' and a comprehensive list of primary and secondary literature up to date of publication: an indispensable volume).

—— 'Volker Braun: Hinze-Kunze-Roman' in Chiarloni et al. (eds), *Die Literatur der DDR 1976–1986*, Pisa, 1988, pp. 159–68.

Ilse Winter, '*Dmitri* versus *Demetrius*: zu Volker Brauns kritischer Adaption von Friedrich Schiller', in *German Quarterly*, 60, 1987, pp. 52–67.

-14-

Reading Christoph Hein

J.H. Reid

Of all the GDR's authors to emerge in the 1980s Christoph Hein is the one who has made the greatest impact, in the West as well as in the East. His 1982 novella *Der fremde Freund*, published in the Federal Republic under the title *Drachenblut*, received almost unanimously enthusiastic reviews in over twenty newspapers and journals, and since then each succeeding publication has been accorded the attention usually reserved for writers such as Christa Wolf. In the upheavals of 1989 it was Hein who, beside the older generation's Wolf and Stefan Heym, was the author most heavily involved, whether addressing demonstrators or being interviewed for the media.

Because of the overwhelming impact of *Der fremde Freund* it is often overlooked that Hein had already been writing for a good ten years previously, mainly plays, few of which were performed or published, although he had even been awarded the prestigious Heinrich Mann prize. In 1987 he spoke bitterly about the obstacles which confronted East German writers who tried to adopt contemporary topics for the stage, advising prospective dramatists to turn to fiction instead.[1] Some years earlier, recognising that the GDR's theatre was 'an inspiration for fiction',[2] he had taken his own advice and published a first collection of short fiction, *Einladung zum Lever Bourgeois*. The public nature of theatre has always imposed considerable constraints on the GDR writer. Although Hein has returned to the theatre again and again, most successfully with *Die wahre Geschichte des Ah Q*, it is his fiction that gives him his international reputation, and it is on it that I intend to concentrate here.

---

1. In *X. Schriftstellerkongreß der Deutschen Demokratischen Republik*, ed. Schriftstellerverband der Deutschen Demokratischen Republik, Berlin/Weimar, 1987, vol. 2, p. 242.
2. 'Ein Interview', in *Öffentlich arbeiten*, p. 101.

J.H. Reid

Hein's commitment to socialism has never been overt. Unlike most of his older colleagues he has never been a member of the SED. In his works orthodox Party members tend to be negative figures. In the story 'Der Sohn' the initially conformist son of a Party functionary becomes a rebel, asking provocative questions at school and repeatedly attempting to defect to the West. Since each time his father's influence saves him from the punishments which less privileged teenagers would have experienced, in the end he resigns himself to conformity once more. The play *Lassalle* lampoons one of the founding fathers of German socialism, contrasting the lofty words of his political speeches with his actual treatment of his senile mother. Hein's most recent play *Die Ritter der Tafelrunde* is a thinly-veiled satire on the men of the GDR's Politbüro, who appear as the aged knights of King Arthur's court, out of touch with ordinary humanity and filled with doubts as to whether the Holy Grail of socialism is attainable, or even exists at all. Earlier the play *Cromwell* had taken up the topic of Stalinism, transposing it to seventeenth-century England and paralleling the fate of the socialist revolution with that of the English Revolution, its betrayal by Stalin with that by petty bourgeois Cromwell; the trotskyite Levellers are mercilessly machine-gunned to death on Cromwell's orders – this and other anachronisms suggest a parallel with the fate of the anarchists in Spain.

Stalinism has been the main target of Hein's critique of 'actually existing socialism'. It is a theme which dominates his fiction. Since the advent of Mikhail Gorbachev a major difference between the Soviet and GDR governments had been the degree to which they were prepared to admit the crimes committed in the name of socialism under Stalin. In 1987 Hein defended the Soviet film *Repentance*, which had been attacked by the GDR's conservatives for its 'pessimism' and 'nihilism'. His words reveal both a commitment to socialism and a determination to expose its past failings: 'so unerbittlich genau und unbeirrt kann nur ein Künstler arbeiten, der trotz der Verbrechen der Stalinzeit die Hoffnung auf den Kommunismus als einzige humane Alternative nicht aufgab'.[3] At a meeting of the Berlin branch of the Writers' Union in September 1989 he accused the GDR authorities in general and the Party newspaper *Neues Deutschland* in particular of continuing to trivialise Stalinism and of failing to rehabilitate its victims. Even at that late date his words could be published only in the West.[4] Just over two months

3. In *X. Schriftstellerkongreß*, p. 237.
4. 'Die fünfte Grundrechenart', in *Die Zeit*, 6 October 1989, pp. 65–6.

later, however, it was Hein who gave the opening address when the victims of Stalin were remembered at a public meeting in East Berlin.[5]

Hein, however, is primarily a writer, not a journalist. *How*, as much as *what* he writes, must be our preoccupation, not least because he himself has on a number of occasions challenged us to do so, criticising, for example, reviewers who concentrate on content to the exclusion of form,[6] and accusing academic scholars of being unable to deal with contemporary literature, which they invariably assess in terms of what they already know rather than of the novelty which is being offered.[7] Central to Stalinism is the subjection of the individual to the dictates of the Party. The literary equivalent of this is the socialist realist requirement that the reader be guided by an authoritative, not to say authoritarian narrator. By contrast, Hein has spoken of his reader as his 'partner'. He expects 'einen aktiven Leser, der die Dinge, wo ich aufhöre zu sprechen oder nur wenig mitteile, um ihm einen Freiraum zu lassen für seine Erfahrungen, auch zu Ende führen kann.' He is in favour of 'das dialogische Prinzip in der Literatur' – it cannot be coincidence that one of the catchphrases in the autumn of 1989 was the need for 'dialogue', one between the Party and the people. In the nineteenth century the author had been 'diese große, weise Figur [. . .], die dem Volk sagen kann, wo lang es zu gehen hat.' He himself was more modest: 'Ich bin so unberaten wie mein Publikum. Ich kann ihm nur etwas über den Weg sagen, den wir gegangen sind.'[8] An important influence on Hein has been Walter Benjamin, whom he quotes directly on a number of occasions and whose fate is the theme of the play *Passage*. In these words there is more than an echo of Benjamin's 1930 essay 'Krisis des Romans': 'Die Geburtskammer des Romans ist das Individuum in seiner Einsamkeit, das sich über seine wichtigsten Anliegen nicht mehr exemplarisch ausspre-chen kann, selbst unberaten ist und keinen Rat mehr geben kann.'[9]

5. See *Neues Deutschland*, 6 December 1989, p. 1.
6. In *X. Schriftstellerkongreß*, pp. 236–7.
7. 'Lorbeerwald und Kartoffelacker. Vorlesung über einen Satz Heinrich Heines', in *Öffentlich arbeiten*, p. 19.
8. Krzysztof Jachimzak, 'Gespräch mit Christoph Hein', in *Sinn und Form*, vol. 40, 1988, pp. 347–9.
9. Reprinted in Eberhard Lämmert et al. (eds), *Romantheorie. Dokumentation ihrer Geschichte in Deutschland seit 1880*, Cologne, 1975, p. 176. This source prints 'keinem' instead of 'keinen', although in a later version of the same passage it prints 'keinen' (p. 253).

These points touch on a debate which has been going on since the mid-1970s. Kurt Batt had contrasted East and West German fiction. The latter had 'executed' the narrator; it was monological, 'dem Verstummen nahendes Vor-sich-hin-Sprechen'. The former was dialogical, 'Aussprache, die des Gegenübers bedarf'.[10] This thesis was seized on in 1983 by Wolfgang Emmerich as his starting-off point for an essay on the GDR's contemporary fiction. Admitting that it was essentially accurate up to about 1972, he denied that it applied to the 1970s overall; the GDR's literature had now become 'contemporary' with West European literature in general, having undergone the process which the latter underwent between 1910 and 1930, the process called 'modernism'. Quoting Benjamin, he claimed that the GDR's literature was no longer 'dialogical': ' . . . wer "selbst unberaten ist und keinen Rat geben kann", hat, willentlich oder nicht, das dialogische, kommunikative Erzählen aufgekündigt, ist beim "stummen Vorsichhinsprechen" angekommen . . .'[11] In 1986 Rüdiger Bernhardt in turn took issue with Emmerich's thesis. Admitting that it had some validity as far as the younger and middle generation were concerned, he repudiated it as a general statement, finding on the contrary an increasing tendency towards 'auktoriales Erzählen' in contemporary fiction. Bernhardt stresses the 'social function' of the narrator, whose reader is a 'partner'. Although the similarity with Hein's words is striking, Bernhardt's conception of partnership is not one between equals: the narrators in the novels he discusses become 'Autoritäten', a position which Hein rejects.[12] Bernhardt's 'partner', unlike Hein's, is really a Lukácsian teacher.

Although neither Emmerich nor Bernhardt mentions Hein in this connection, his own poetics invite consideration of his fiction in this light. That he is as well known in the West as in the East might indicate the convergence between the two German literatures detected by Emmerich. Hein himself has repudiated this: the literature which was being written in the West by authors of his generation, Botho Strauß, Franz Xaver Kroetz and Lothar Baier, was 'entirely different' from that of his own country.[13] He has

10. See 'Realität und Phantasie', in Kurt Batt, *Schriftsteller, Poetisches und wirkliches Blau. Aufsätze zur Literatur*, Franz Fühmann and Konrad Reich, (eds), Hamburg, 1980, p. 322.
11. 'Der verlorene Faden. Probleme des Erzählens in den siebziger Jahren', in P. U. Hohendahl and P. Herminghouse (eds) *Literatur der DDR in den siebziger Jahren*, Frankfurt am Main, 1983, p. 157.
12. 'Die Hoffnung der Erzähler. Beobachtungen zur Rolle des Erzählers in Prosa-Neuerscheinungen', in *Weimarer Beiträge*, vol. 38, 1986, pp. 675–83.
13. To Jachimzak, 'Gespräch mit Christoph Hein', pp. 358–9.

distanced himself from West German cultural fashions on a number of occasions, most outspokenly in his review of Peter Sloterdijk's *Kritik der zynischen Vernunft*, which he saw as symptomatic of the crisis of the West German left.[14] A few weeks before the Berlin Wall was opened, he bitterly attacked the West German government, accusing it of 'colonialism' with regard to the GDR, of using its greater economic strength to entice the GDR's doctors and skilled labour across the frontier.[15] In this interview he was as politically explicit as he has ever been. Although the GDR's 'actually existing socialism' had been discredited by its association with Stalinism, nevertheless, unlike the mood prevailing in Poland and Hungary, there was still a consensus that what was needed was a form of socialism, a 'Sozialismus, der wirklich den Namen verdient' (Ö, p. 30). Whether his fiction is 'monological' or 'dialogical', however, requires a detailed investigation of its narrative techniques.

The dimension of community created by the authoritative narrator postulated by Bernhardt is entirely lacking in Hein's fiction. Many of the shorter stories in *Einladung zum Lever Bourgeois* are Kleistian in their narrative stance: their narrators are covert and not altogether reliable, refrain from making judgments, but through the use of irony evidently expect an active, alert reader who, as Hein suggests, is prepared to reach his or her own conclusions. The two most substantial pieces, the first, which gives the collection its title, and the last, 'Die russischen Briefe des Jägers Johann Seifert', are worth examining in more detail.

'Einladung zum Lever Bourgeois' focusses on the playwright Jean Racine. It is early in 1699, a few weeks after his fifty-ninth birthday. He is preparing to depart to attend the morning levée of Louis XIV. Two episodes from his past preoccupy him, one public, one personal. The first is his failure to investigate an atrocity committed by French officers during the sack of the Netherlands, when as official court historian he had the opportunity to do so. The second was his opportunistic abandoning of his real love, the actress Marie de Champmeslé, to marry the pious Catherine de Romanet. The theme of betrayal, one of Hein's most important motifs, is central to both: the man's betrayal of the woman, the intellectual's betrayal of his mission.

The text may be read as interior monologue. The narrative focus

14. 'Linker Kolonialismus oder Der Wille zum Feuilleton', in *Öffentlich arbeiten*, pp. 135–53.
15. '"Die DDR ist nicht China". SPIEGEL-Gespräch mit dem DDR-Schriftsteller Christoph Hein', in *Der Spiegel*, 23 October 1989, p. 31.

is almost entirely that of Racine, the narrator remaining unobtrusive and refusing to comment. The question of dialogue, however, is made thematic. Racine left Marie the day he resolved to end his work for the theatre, having suddenly discovered that it had 'keinen Adressaten' (E, p. 18), an oblique reference to the scandal over *Phèdre*, whose premiere was sabotaged by rivals. Hein's own situation is implied here. Thwarted in his ambition to write for the theatre, the dialogical art par excellence, the social art with an audience, he has turned instead to the more private and perhaps monological art of fiction. 'Einladung zum Lever Bourgeois', however, *has* an addressee, implied in the deictive narrative present, so characteristic of traditional GDR fiction and a tense which Hein does not use in his later works, but more significantly in the text's title. Racine has been invited to attend the royal levée; the reader is invited to attend Racine's 'bourgeois' levée, an occasion not of pomp and ceremony but of physical human frailty, with a constipated old man trying to move his bowels. We, like Racine, are courtiers, placemen, sycophants. We are also voyeurs, an important motif elsewhere in the story, when Racine remembers his excitement watching caged tigers fight over the meat that was thrown to them. Like him, we see what we want to see. Most of us, too, would refuse to 'open the barndoor' for fear of the horrors that lie behind it.

'Die russischen Briefe des Jägers Johann Seifert' consists of twenty-four fictitious letters to his wife from Alexander von Humboldt's manservant, accompanying his master on his travels through Russia in 1829. Having been used as lining paper for a flat in Berlin, they are found and published with a preface and occasional comments by an 'editor'. The language, a pastiche of early nineteenth-century German, itself makes some considerable demands of the reader.

The dual narration conveys a number of provocative ambiguities. The primary first-person narrator Seifert is addressing his wife Ludmilla. The letters are love letters, full of yearning, but also of jealousy and suspicion that she may be unfaithful. It is poignant that, as it turns out, she never received the letters, which were intercepted by the German secret police. Again and again Seifert laments her failure to reply, the lack of resonance, complaining how difficult it is to write in such a vacuum. As with Racine and with Hein himself, the 'dialogue' has been interrupted. However, although the Seiferts cannot know this, the letters do in the end find a recipient, the twentieth-century reader, thanks to the editor 'C.H.'. Ultimately the truth will be revealed in spite of dictatorial attempts to suppress it. This optimism is undermined by the character of C.H. himself, a fanatical, pompous scholar, who is not in the least interested in the individuals concerned and is even prepared to destroy private homes in order to obtain more letters which he suspects may be concealed behind the wallpaper. That Hein has chosen his own initials for this scholar is an irony which encourages the reader to engage in dialogue with the text, to question the function of writing in general, to find answers to questions which the author himself is unsure of.

Both texts therefore thematise the acts of writing and reading. In the former we are confronted directly with a professional writer, writing under circumstances which are not dissimilar to those of the GDR writer of 1980. Racine has attempted to make good his earlier failures by publishing an anonymous pamphlet on 'the misery of the people'. The King himself is highly indignant and anxious to prosecute its perpetrator. In a Stalinist state this may be the only path open to the writer. But at the same time Hein is suggesting that it is self-indulgence. Racine is presented as more than slightly senile, muttering and chuckling to himself in his carriage; he is at least as pleased at having personally outwitted Louis as at having done something to alleviate popular distress. In 'Die russischen Briefe', too, there are numerous parallels with Honecker's GDR: travel diaries are popular because people cannot travel themselves, both the Russian and the Prussian secret services are active, Humboldt has to give assurances that his journey is purely scientific and that he will not engage in political activities. Under such circumstances writers, we learn, both in Russia and in Germany, have to resort to parables in order to criticise – just as Hein appears to be doing through the historical costume. It is a position which the text itself calls in question. Humboldt regards 'aesopian language' as opportunist; a free man ought to have the courage of his convictions and speak out directly (E, pp. 161–2).[16] History in 'Die russischen Briefe' is therefore more than a mask. Hein is suggesting, here quite in keeping with Georg Lukács, that the nineteenth century was the 'prehistory of the present', that the unhappy condition of the contemporary GDR is a product of an earlier opportunistic, unheroic age, not the least of whose characteristics was the anti-semitism embodied in Seifert himself.

Both 'Einladung zum Lever Bourgeois' and 'Die russischen

---

16. In his essay 'Waldbruder Lenz' Hein condemns aesopian language as 'eine – unausgesprochene – Übereinkunft mit den Herrschenden' (*Öffentlich arbeiten*, p. 71).

J. H. Reid

Briefe' have a historical setting. Hein's next work of fiction, *Der fremde Freund*, is set in the GDR's present, and for that reason had a much greater impact. The allusion to the introduction of summer time in the GDR, which occurred in the spring of 1981, allows the events described to be almost exactly dated.[17] Claudia, a hospital doctor, forty years old, is narrating the story of her relationship with Henry Sommer, who entered her life in April or May 1980, in spite of their intimacy remained, in the words of the title, a 'stranger', and died a year later in a brawl with some teenagers. It is a gloomy picture of GDR society that is furnished by Claudia, one almost entirely lacking in idealism or sense of direction. Her apartment flat is in a large shabby block, whose occupants either are elderly and spend their time spying on one another or else change so frequently that neighbourliness cannot develop. Her colleagues are motivated by professional rivalry, sexual relationships are dominated by sadism and exploitation, family ties are a sham and the young find fulfilment in alcohol and violence. The title implies the paradigmatic status of Henry, a man who, explicitly regarding life as meaningless, loves fast, dangerous driving and whose death is as 'absurd' as his life was – the parallels to Albert Camus's *L'Etranger* are numerous.[18]

If the text's content appears to contradict the facile optimism of traditional socialist realism, its narration is equally challenging. To the absence of the community invoked by the early GDR novel[19] corresponds the absence of a relation between narrator and reader. Claudia is writing six months after Henry's funeral (F, p. 206). Why she is writing or for whom is nowhere made explicit. Like the numerous photographs which she takes as a hobby but shows to no one, her text is dialogue with herself – monologue. For this reason, as Hein himself pointed out, it is open to varying interpretations: according to their own personal experiences of life some readers regarded it as pessimistic, others as optimistic.[20] It is no coincidence that Rüdiger Bernhardt, with his authoritarian view of the proper relation between narrator and reader, was most uneasy

17. See Klaus Kändler's contribution to 'Für und wider: "Der fremde Freund" von Christoph Hein', in *Weimarer Beiträge*, vol. 29, 1983, p. 1639.
18. They are pointed out by Bernd Schick and by Ursula Wilke in their contributions to 'Für und wider: "Der fremde Freund" von Christoph Hein', pp. 1651–2; see also Gisela Shaw, 'Christoph Hein: The novelist as dramatist manqué,' in *Literature on the Threshold. The German Novel in the 1980s*, Oxford, 1990, p. 98.
19. Dennis Tate, *The East German Novel. Identity, Community, Continuity*, Bath, 1984.
20. To Jachimzak, 'Gespräch mit Christoph Hein', p. 349.

–220–

about this text, finding that his students, all too ready to identify with Claudia's view of the GDR, were not mature enough to adopt the necessary distance.[21] He may have felt himself vindicated when Claudia's final nihilistic words turned up as the spoken text to a piece by one of the GDR's 'alternative' rock bands.[22]

However, *Der fremde Freund* does not entirely ignore the presence of an external reader. Its title is already a provocation, an oxymoron demanding to be resolved. The awareness that the author is a male while his narrator is a woman encourages critical distance. But it is mainly the numerous contradictions between her words and her actual behaviour which invite the reader to question Claudia's narrative and to become like Claudia's mother, scrutinising her daughter's photographs for clues to her character. Claudia's words are those of a cynic; in practice she is kind and helpful. She claims to have bathed in 'dragon's blood' – hence the West German title – and to have become emotionally invulnerable; unlike Siegfried, however, she betrays her vulnerability throughout, whether in her hysterical reaction to the news that Henry is married or in her yearning for Katharina, her childhood friend – or, indeed, in her writing the text itself. Her final word, 'Ende', even implies a recipient, perhaps the radio buff who picks up signals from afar, as Claudia signs off her desperate message to the outside world.

If Claudia is addressing herself, we must ask why she is doing so. One reason might be self-justification, implying an awareness that her text may be read. More obviously, it is self-analysis. Claudia rejects psychoanalysis as unhelpful: repressions are a defence mechanism, bringing them to the surface defeats their original object (F, p. 115). Paradoxically, the intrusion of the 'alien' Henry into her life prompts her, possibly unconsciously, to explore her own past. The crucial chapter of the text describes a visit to the town of G., where she spent her childhood. Although the physical encounters are unfruitful, the memories which the episode provokes are highly revealing, at least to the reader. That she cannot bring herself to spell out the name of the town in full, although all other places, Berlin, Magdeburg, Wörlitz, are named, suggests that what occurred here remains undigested. And here the true importance of the text's chronology becomes evident. The years at G. were a time when she suffered traumatic personal disappointments, the arrest of

21. In his contribution to 'Für und wider: "Der fremde Freund" von Christoph Hein', p. 1637.
22. 'Der Expander des Fortschritts', recorded on *Parocktikum* (Amiga 056409). My thanks are due to Martin Watson for pointing this out.

a favourite uncle for collaborating with the Nazis, an insensitive sex education, above all her own betrayal, under pressure, of her friend Katharina, a committed Christian. They were the years 1953–7, equally traumatic years for the GDR, in which the uprising of 17 June occurred and Claudia learned not to ask questions about it. Destalinisation failed to take place. Hein is implying that Claudia's repression of her own past has made her the distorted person she now is, and that the same applies to the GDR's society in general.

These same years are the setting of the novel *Horns Ende*, begun before *Der fremde Freund* but completed later.[23] Disgraced in 1953 for succumbing to 'bourgeois ideology', the historian Horn was forced to move from Leipzig to the small town of Bad Guldenberg; there his refusal to interpret history according to the dictates of the Party led to further hounding and his eventual suicide. The novel, however, is not the story of Horn but of German society from the 1930s to the present day, epitomised in Guldenberg itself, a place of informers, who betray to the Nazis the hiding place of a mentally retarded girl so that she may be taken away to be put down, or to the communists the heresies of a Horn, a place of intolerance to outsiders such as the gypsies who survive the Third Reich but are driven out in 1957, a place of petty and philistine materialism, in which women are usually the victims, exploited or raped by their menfolk. Like *Der fremde Freund* the text implies that it is easy enough to change political institutions, much less so to change individuals. Horn, as one of his chief adversaries admits, was done a personal injustice but in the name of a higher principle, the historical necessity of realising socialism (H, p. 83). This, too, was Stalinism.

The narrative present, however, is the early 1980s. For Hein, history is a means of understanding today.[24] *Horns Ende*, its eight chapters divided into a total of thirty-nine sections, has five separate narrators. Each chapter is prefaced by a brief passage of dialogue between what appear to be the dead Horn and Thomas Puls, one of the narrators, in which Horn is insistently urging Thomas to 'remember'. There are some indications that Thomas is therefore interviewing the other four narrators in order to obtain their versions of the past, or else collating their 'evidence': although he does not doubt that the events of these years can be 'reconstructed',

23. See Françoise Barthélémy-Toraille, 'Rencontre avec Christoph Hein', in *Connaissance de la RDA*, 25, 1987, p. 18.
24. 'Anmerkungen zu CROMWELL', in *Öffentlich arbeiten*, p. 117, also to Jachimczak, 'Gespräch mit Christoph Hein', p. 351.

Kruschkatz, the former mayor of Bad Guldenberg, refers to 'the whole enterprise' as 'questionable' (H, pp. 25–6), while Dr Spodeck, we learn, is writing a chronicle of Guldenberg (H, p. 161), a diatribe reminiscent of Thomas Bernhard's polemics against Salzburg. Horn may have chosen Thomas as his mouthpiece because he is the youngest of the persons involved: born in 1945, he is entirely of the post-Nazi generation (and almost exactly as old as the author himself); there is also a certain appropriateness inasmuch as the young Thomas had imposed himself on Horn. These, however, are speculations. Kruschkatz is convinced that the affair is one without an 'addressee' (H, p. 26), Spodeck assumes that his chronicle will be destroyed after his death and one of the narrators, the mentally retarded Marlene Gohl, could not possibly be interviewed and indeed appears to be 'speaking' in 1957. Alone of the narrators, Marlene is addressing a specific individual, her mother – but her mother is dead. Ostensibly *Horns Ende* consists of five monologues, interrupted by a 'dialogue' with a dead man. It is a 'modernist' novel, whose narrative technique resembles that of the West German Gerd Gaiser's *Schlußball* of 1958 or even the 'epic' scenes of Max Frisch's play *Andorra* of 1961, in which the citizens of Andorra take turns to step forward and justify their actions or failure to act on behalf of the murdered Jew.

The implications of this narrative technique are multiple. By introducing a variety of voices Hein has created a 'dialogical' novel in a different sense, that of Mikhail Bakhtin. If Hein is a 'dramatist manqué', as Gisela Shaw suggests, this is one way in which drama and the polyphonic novel converge.[25] Like Uwe Johnson's *Mutmaßungen über Jakob* and Ulrich Plenzdorf's *Die neuen Leiden des jungen W.*, *Horns Ende* is a text in which the reader is invited to come to an independent decision on the accuracy of the various versions provided. Surprisingly, although we are invited to see him as a victim of Stalinism, none of the witnesses has anything good to say about the dead Horn and the act of remembering which he enjoins on Thomas seems to backfire on him. Against this there speaks the friendship he struck up with Kruschkatz's wife Irene, who in Kruschkatz's memory was entirely angelic. Beyond this, however, there is the implication that history knows no heroes, that victims, too, may be awkward and unpleasant.

The reader's attempt to make sense of the evidence is reflected in

---

25. Gisela Shaw, 'Dramatist manqué', pp. 91–105; Tzvetan Todorov, *Mikhail Bakhtin: The Dialogical Principle*, translated by Wlad Godzich, Manchester, 1984, p. 68.

the narrators' interpretations of what they see. This is especially
true of the boy Thomas, to whom Irene appeared as a prostitute
and who placed the most fantastic, Hoffmannesque interpretations
on his father's collection of pornography. But the most important
function of the narrative technique is the link it makes between the
individual and the social in their relations to the past, memory and
history respectively. Horn, Kruschkatz and Spodek are all in their
own ways historians but with diverging views of history.[26] Socialist realism taught that literature should 'reflect' historical reality.
Spodeck relates how Shuftan's mirror can be used even to falsify
historical photographs. History is unreliable, individual memory
no less so. The painter Gohl shows Thomas how the cunning use of
perspective can create the illusion of reality. Hein's text, with its
multiplicity of narrators, suggests once more that truth is a matter
for the individual reader to determine.

Hein continues his investigation of the GDR's Stalinist past in his
latest novel, *Der Tangospieler*. Whereas *Horns Ende* furnished a
panoramic view, however, here he concentrates on a single protagonist, Hans-Peter Dallow. The 1950s have been replaced by the
1960s. Dallow, another historian, was arrested in 1966 for having
accompanied on the piano a satirical sketch by students which
mocked Walter Ulbricht, the elderly head of state. Asked to step in
at the last moment he had not even read the texts he was to
accompany. The novel begins with his release from prison in
February 1968 and ends shortly after the invasion of Czechoslovakia by the Warsaw Pact troops in August of that year.

Unlike the previous two texts *Der Tangospieler* is a third-person
narrative told by an extradiegetic narrator, who restricts himself,
however, almost entirely to the point of view of Dallow himself.
Once again there is no omniscient narrator, no 'signpost' to guide
the reader in the correct direction, no overt narratee. There is not
even any reference to the present day, as there was in *Horns Ende* –
nobody here is looking back from a superior vantage point.
Nonetheless, *Der Tangospieler* is less hermetic than the previous
two texts. The reader is continually invited to find parallels between the inconsistencies in the GDR's politics in 1968 and twenty
years later. Published at a time when the Soviet Union was initiat-
ing reforms which it had earlier suppressed in Czechoslovakia, it
assumes the reader's familiarity with subsequent events. This is
especially true of the ironic ending. When Jürgen Roessler, a

26. See Phil McKnight, 'Ein Mosaik. Zu Christoph Heins Roman "Horns
Ende"', in *Sinn und Form*, vol. 39, 1987, pp. 415–25.

former colleague of Dallow, is told by his students that the Warsaw Pact armies have invaded Czechoslovakia, he dismisses the news as Western propaganda: the invasion would contradict all the assurances given to the 'brother country', and in view of the earlier guilt of the Germans with regard to the Czechs it was unthinkable that the GDR could be involved in any such invasion. His failure to read correctly the Party's mind leads to his dismissal and replacement by Dallow himself. The novel ends with Dallow watching televised scenes of the invaders being welcomed with flowers and friendship, pictures which the 1989 reader knows to be false.

What distinguishes *Der Tangospieler* from simple satire is the character of Dallow himself. A historian whose very specialism is Czech and Slovak history, he is entirely indifferent to the conversations on 'Dubcek and Prague' which are going on around him. Like Henry Sommer, he is mainly interested in sex and his car. Why he is as he is is left to the reader to decide. He has been alienated from society by the injustice of his prison sentence; although not prepared to collaborate with the secret police in order to be reinstated, he has no qualms about taking over Roessler's post. Nobody has a future who does not have a past, he reflects (T, p. 38), and his past is now the prison cell. But life in prison had been one of comfortable irresponsibility on which he looks back with some nostalgia. There are indications that even before his arrest his social commitment had been less than complete.

Appropriately, in view of the role played by the Kafka debates during the Prague Spring, the allusions to Kafka's novels, especially *Der Prozeß*, are numerous. Müller and Schulze, the two men from the state security office, who interrogate Dallow in anonymous offices and on his own doorstep, are kafkaesque, as are his encounters with the judge who presided over his trial. The technique of narrative focalisation, too, is that employed by Kafka in his novels. While contributing to the 'modernism' of the novel, these echoes shed further light on the character of Dallow. Like Joseph K., he is an ambiguous figure. Is he innocent or guilty? While it is clearly absurd and unjust that he should have been imprisoned for playing the music to a text which he had not read, we may question the moral status of someone who by failing to read the text avoided having to make a conscious, democratic choice. Once again the act of reading is thematised. Hein's readers cannot avoid this choice. What they choose is up to them, but choose they must.

In conclusion we may ask ourselves whether Hein's fiction is truly monological in Emmerich's sense, whether it does indeed belong to a pan–German modernist heritage. In Hein's own terms it is clearly 'dialogical'. While its *narrators* may well be soliloquising, the *texts* imply a reader who is not merely 'eavesdropping' but is being challenged to engage in dialogue with them. One feature of Hein's work which distinguishes it from that of a Botho Strauß, although not from that of an earlier West German writer such as Heinrich Böll, is the premise that contemporary reality cannot be understood without reference to the past. Moreover, this assumption that reality *can* be understood places Hein in the Enlightenment tradition which many of his West German colleagues have abandoned. In spite of his own denials, Hein is essentially a moralist.[27] The insistence that his readers make moral choices is a fundamental aspect of the dialogue.

Author's Note

The following editions and abbreviations are used for Hein's works:

E : *Einladung zum Lever Bourgeois*. Mit einer Nachbemerkung von Günther Drommer, Berlin/Weimar, 1980.
(West German edition: *Nachtfahrt und früher Morgen. Prosa*, Hamburg, 1982. 'Der Sohn' is omitted and 'Einladung zum Lever Bourgeois' and 'Die russischen Briefe des Jägers Johann Seifert' transposed.)

F : *Der fremde Freund. Novelle*, Berlin/Weimar, 1982.
(West German edition: *Drachenblut. Novelle*, Darmstadt/Neuwied, 1983. English version: *The distant lover*, New York, 1989.)

H : *Horns Ende. Roman*, Berlin/Weimar, 1985.
(West German edition, Frankfurt am Main, 1985.)

Ö : *Öffentlich arbeiten. Essais und Gespräche*, Berlin/Weimar, 1987.

T : *Der Tangospieler. Erzählung*, Berlin/Weimar, 1989.
(West German edition: *Der Tangospieler. Roman*, Frankfurt am Main, 1989.)

---

27. To Jachimczak, 'Gespräch mit Christoph Hein', p. 347.

Suggested Further Reading

Other works by Christoph Hein:

Cromwell und andere Stücke. Mit einem Nachwort von Rudolf Münz, Berlin/Weimar, 1981.

Das Wildpferd unterm Kachelofen. Ein schönes dickes Buch von Jakob Borg und seinen Freunden, Berlin, 1984.
(English edition: *Jamie and his friends,* London, 1988.)

Die wahre Geschichte des Ah Q. Stücke und Essays, Darmstadt/Neuwied, 1984.

Schlötel oder Was solls. Stücke und Essays, Darmstadt/Neuwied, 1986.

Passage. Ein Kammerspiel, Frankfurt am Main, 1988.

Die wahre Geschichte des Ah Q. Passage, Berlin, 1988.

Die Ritter der Tafelrunde. Eine Komödie, Frankfurt am Main, 1989.

Die fünfte Grundrechenart. Aufsätze und Reden, Frankfurt am Main, 1990.

Secondary Material

'Volker Braun und Christoph Hein in der Diskussion', in Chiarloni et al., (eds) *Literatur der DDR 1976–1986,* Pisa, 1988, pp. 439–47.

Jörg Bilke, 'Drachenblut', in *Neue Deutsche Hefte,* 1983, no. 4, pp. 833–35.

Brigitte Böttcher, 'Diagnose eines unheilbaren Zustands', in *Neue Deutsche Literatur,* 1983, no. 6, pp. 145–9.

Fabrizio Cambi, 'Jetztzeit und Vergangenheit: ästhetische und ideologische Auseinandersetzungen im Werke Christoph Heins', in Chiarloni, Sartori, Cambi (eds), *Literatur der DDR 1976–1986,* Akten Pisa, 1988, pp. 79–86.

Bernhard Greiner, 'Bürgerliches Lachtheater als Komödie in der DDR: J.M.R.Lenz' "Der neue Mendoza" bearbeitet von Christoph Hein', in Chiarloni et al. (eds), *Literatur der DDR 1976–1986,* Pisa, 1988, pp. 329–345.

Antonia Grunenberg, 'Geschichte und Entfremdung: Christoph Hein als Autor der DDR', in *Michigan Germanic Studies,* 8, 1982, 1/2, pp. 229–51.

Ursula Heukenkamp, 'Die fremde Form', in *Sinn und Form,* 35, 1983, pp. 625–32.

Phillip S. McKnight, '*Alltag.* Apathy, anarchy: GDR everyday life as a provocation in Christoph Hein's novella *Der fremde Freund,* in *Studies in GDR Culture,* 8, 1988, pp. 179–90.

Timm Menke, 'Der Literat als Politiker: zur Vorwärtsverteidigung der Kunst in den Essays von Christoph Hein', in *The Germanic Review,* 64,

1989, pp. 177–81.

Jiri Munzar, 'Die Dramen Christoph Heins und einige Gattungsprobleme der jüngeren Dramatik der DDR', in *Brücken*, 1986/87, pp. 148–55.

Janice Murry, Mary-Elizabeth O'Brien, 'Interview mit Christoph Hein', in *New German Review*, 3, 1987, pp. 53–66.

Jirina Saavedrova, 'Christoph Hein: Horns Ende. Versuch einer kommunikativ-pragmatisch orientierten Stilanalyse', in *Brücken*, 1986/87, pp. 106–114.

'Volker Braun? – Da kann ich nur sagen, der Junge quält sich . . .'

New Voices in the GDR Lyric of the 1980s

Ingrid Pergande

RUMPELSTILZ

für braun

heißest du hinz? heißt du kunz? heißest du siegfried?
heißest du etwa volker? – das hat der teufel dir gesagt!
so spricht er und stampft mit dem fuß daß die erde sich spaltet,
mit dem einen bein schon im abgrund, zerfallen mit seiner
besseren hälfte, die verse voll grimm und hölderlin, zerrissen
der autor statt seiner fotografie: das kindergesicht
zur faust geballt (fauste kommt auch vor), losungen gegen
– losungen, nur keine lösung in sicht – ach königin müllers
tochter die frau auf dem plakat muß helfen: stroh zu gold!
WAS LEBENDES WÄRE MIR LIEBER. mir auch. nur nicht das
was uns blüht
wenn leblos ideen gedichte bevölkern: hoffnung
die aussieht wie eine preußischblauende blume.

(Manuscript)

Volker Braun as a character from a fairy tale, as Rumpelstiltskin: tiny, cunning, stubbornly challenging the child of the miller's daughter; but then also prepared to compromise, irascible and finally outwitted . . . the irreverent confrontation of a young woman poet with one of the GDR's outstanding writers, a figure of international reputation and the controversial political and philosophical leader of a whole generation of lyric poets in the GDR. Is this stance adopted by the young and still virtually unknown poet

Barbara Köhler characteristic of the attitude of those who have begun to write in the last five to ten years?

The General Background

From around the middle of the 1970s the literary landscape of the GDR had been increasingly shaped by young authors and new names. This process was particularly marked in the field of lyric poetry, a genre traditionally associated with the vanguard of literary historical developments. It was very noticeable that the number of poets making their literary debuts with DDR publishing houses in the last ten years had been significantly higher than in any comparable period previously. Since the middle of the 1970s, authors such as Uwe Kolbe (b.1957), Hans-Eckardt Wenzel (b.1955), Steffen Mensching (b.1958), Thomas Böhme (b.1955), Richard Pietraß (b.1946), Thomas Rosenlöcher (b.1947) and Lothar Walsdorf (b.1951) had, along with some others, published two or more volumes of poems – albeit in relatively small editions. In view of the tight restrictions on printing paper in the GDR, as well as the effect of the censorship mechanisms, this was no small achievement. The possibilities for young poets to give public readings had greatly increased. They had also had access to very popular established series as well as new publishing outlets – for instance, *Poesiealbum, Auswahl, Edition Neue Texte, Die Schublade* and, to give the most recent example, *Außer der Reihe*. Literary journals such as *Neue Deutsche Literatur, Sinn und Form* and *Temperamente* also provided a regular outlet for new texts.

In tandem with this a number of young writers and graphic artists – with lyric poets setting the tone here – created forms of publication available to only a small circle of readers which were independent of the regular publishing system and book market. They published privately and in very small editions (25 to 100 copies) magazines produced for the most part on typewriters or word processors and containing a variety of texts, photographs and graphics. These magazines were based in various towns throughout the GDR and had titles such as *ariadnefabrik, Bizarre Städte, Schaden, Mikado, Verwendung, Undsoweiter, Anschlag, Zweite Person.* In other countries – the Federal Republic for instance – it is quite normal for private, and in part local, publishing enterprises of this sort to exist alongside the established publishing firms. They have the function with respect to new literature of sorting the wheat from the chaff, of giving genuine talent an initial helping hand and the opportunity to prove itself. Hitherto in the GDR there had been no appreciable tradition of this form of publication. This reason alone helps to explain the nimbus of the forbidden, of being part of an 'underground' movement, which always surrounded the activities of these young authors. There is the additional factor that the texts which were printed in these magazines – and we are referring now to the field of poetry – were frequently of a kind which for various reasons, but often because of their unsparing criticism of social shortcomings in the GDR, had been rejected by the official publishing houses.

But the activities of these young authors cannot be explained solely by the lack of, or being denied, the possibility of publication. There were other important factors involved such as the need to articulate their concerns amongst a small and intimate circle of friends and kindred spirits as well as in forms which differed from those which were usual and accepted in the GDR. Of equal importance here, in the motivation of what they did, was to be able to experiment, to attempt and to explore new approaches. For them and other young writers, cutting themselves off from everything which might be associated with the socialist *Literaturbetrieb* was essential to their political and poetological self-image.

A handful of young poets had, in recent years, published volumes of poems in the Federal Republic or, temporarily or permanently, moved there to continue their life and work in the other German state. The personal and poetic changes in the literary landscape of the GDR which had come about since the expatriation of Wolf Biermann had also left their mark on recent lyric poetry. It is clear that the move of young poets from East to West was as much a matter of political as of literary decision. If at the end of the 1970s and beginning of the 1980s it was relatively easy for young poets to publish their work in the Federal Republic and, thanks to it having been stamped as literature which had been suppressed in the GDR, for them to immediately acquire the accolade of literary 'quality', things would become much more difficult for them at the end of the 1980s. The situation of individual poets was very varied and would require separate investigation from case to case.

From the mid 1980s on, there appeared in the Federal Republic three very different anthologies of recent GDR literature which sadly made it very clear what consequences accrue when young and talented writers are either denied an audience in their own country or are severely restricted in what they may publish or perform there. These were Sascha Anderson and Elke Erb's *Berührung ist nur eine Randerscheinung. Neue Literatur aus der DDR;*[1] *Mikado oder Der Kaiser ist nackt. Selbstverlegte Literatur in der DDR* , an anthology including all three genres which was edited by Uwe Kolbe, Lothar Trolle and Bernd Wagner;[2] and Egmont Hesse's anthology of poetry and interviews *Sprache & Antwort. Stimmen und Texte einer anderen Literatur aus der DDR.*[3] These anthologies drew attention to several important new developments in GDR lyric poetry in recent years, some of which will be discussed in what follows. They are worthy of critical scrutiny – particularly the one edited by Anderson and Erb – inasmuch as they lay claim, in their role as the so-called 'other' literature, to be the real literature of the GDR.

Writers making their literary debut with lyric poetry are generally much younger than beginners in other genres. The poets who are the subject of these observations were all born in the 1950s or early 1960s. Despite the differences which give each of these authors a distinctive profile, they nevertheless have a number of biographical co-ordinates in common which influence the role which writing has in their individual development and which also shape their understanding of the function which literature has in society. Along with school, military service, professional training or studying, it is the first years of work which form their view of the world. In addition there are experiences with the opposite sex as well as the first taste of bearing responsibility for a family and children of their own. It is characteristic of a great number of the lyric poets born in the 1950s and 1960s that, at a relatively early age, they turn their backs on the prospect of pursuing any other career and opt instead to become full time writers. This could cause certain problems. Hardly any young writer, and least of all a lyric poet, could live exclusively from his work, from what he earned from publishing poems. This element of insecurity – admittedly of their own choosing – along with a relatively narrow horizon of practical social experience, was in the long term not necessarily of benefit to many writers. It was noticeable for instance in recent years that a whole series of young authors had made themselves outsiders and cultivated a feeling of not being needed. On the other hand, the rigour of the questions and views articulated in the most recent

1. Sascha Anderson and Elke Erb (eds), *Berührung ist nur eine Randerscheinung. Neue Literatur aus der DDR*, Cologne, 1985.
2. Uwe Kolbe, Lothar Trolle and Bernd Wagner (eds), *Mikado oder Der Kaiser ist nackt. Selbstverlegte Literatur aus der* DDR, Darmstadt and Neuwied, 1988.
3. Egmont Hesse (ed.), *Sprache & Antwort. Stimmen und Texte einer anderen Literatur aus der DDR*, Frankfurt am Main, 1988.

lyric poetry is precisely a product of that readiness to take risks which is implicit, in any one particular author, in concentrating on writing as *the* form of existence.

Volker Braun as a symbolic figure in the work of Uwe Kolbe, Steffen Mensching and Hans-Eckardt Wenzel

As we can see by observing literary developments in very different historical epochs every new generation of writers may also be moulded by an especially close and even frequently polemical relationship with the preceding generation. It is therefore not surprising that since the 1980s the name of Volker Braun should repeatedly crop up in so many of the lyrical and theoretical utterances of young poets. In a relationship which is marked by feelings of both solidarity and distance, Braun is a symbol as it were of that new generation of poets whose literary debut at the beginning of the 1960s caused such a stir. As no other poet of his generation, he turned his attention to the *political* landscape of the GDR. It is for this reason that those who saw themselves in relation to him also had to grapple with the concept of a politically interventionist literature. This applies not only to writers, but also to literary criticism and to public discussion about lyric poetry where comparisons with Braun were a frequent occurrence. It is significant in all this that Braun was presented as a figure of undisputed stature, was held up to young writers as a model of political engagement whom they were of course expected to emulate. What appears to have been forgotten here is the extent to which Braun's own early poetry was subject to stringent critical discussion. The vociferous lyrical 'We' of many of Braun's poems at the beginning of the 1960s was the expression of a fresh attitude to life, an approach to the achievements of socialism which differed in important respects from that of the preceding, older generation of poets. Braun's appeal: 'Kommt uns nicht mit Fertigem! Wir brauchen Halbfabrikate . . . Hier wird täglich das alte Leben abgeblasen . . .'[4] is representative of this new attitude. It also, however, has to be said that it did not meet with universally friendly approval. Günther Deicke who was born in 1922 later described very vividly how this approach of then young writers in the 1960s was often at odds with the social reality of the time:

4. Volker Braun, *Provokation für mich. Gedichte*, Halle, 1965, p.10.

Volker Braun und seine Altersgenossen wuchsen bereits in dieser
Welt auf – und wo wir uns noch vornehmlich mit der Vergangenheit
auseinandersetzten, fanden sie in dieser ihrer Gegenwart bereits ihre
Reibungsflächen, entdeckten, wo wir Fortschritt sahen, schon Un-
vollkommenheiten, sie griffen ein, stritten sich mit ihresgleichen und
Gleichgesinnten und demonstrierten in der Praxis, was wir erst
mühsam theoretisch begreifen mußten: die Schärfe und Härte und
Lösbarkeit der nichtantagonistischen Konflikte.[5]

Let us now juxtapose this quotation, initially without comment,
with statements by two representatives of the young generation of
today. The almost unknown Fritz-Hendrik Melle (b.1960), who
contributed poems to the *Berührung ist nur eine Randerscheinung*
anthology, wrote in 1985 of Braun:

Hoffnung, die enttäuscht wird, Erwartung, die von der vorhergehenden
Generation übermittelt wird: Uwe Kolbe hat gesagt, wir werden in eine
Erwartung geboren. Jeder hat doch sein Kainsmal, das, woran er krankt.
Bei Uwe waren viele Gedichte beschäftigt mit diesen getäuschten Er-
wartungen, mit denen ich nichts mehr zu tun habe. Nichts mehr? – Da
war ich so 14, 16, als das klar wurde. Volker Braun? – Da kann ich nur
sagen, der Junge quält sich. Dazu habe ich keine Beziehung mehr. Ich
bin in einer frustrierten Gesellschaft schon aufgewachsen. Diese
Enttäuschung ist für mich kein Erlebnis mehr, sondern eine Voraussetzung.[6]

While Leonhard Lorek (b.1958) had the following to say:

auf mich haben mal, mit sechzehn, siebzehn, volker brauns gedichte sehr
suggestiv gewirkt. vor allem wegen dem, scheinbar selbstverständ-
lichen, benutz der vokabel genosse. ein eigentlich gar nicht so wichtiges
wort. aber diese gedichte haben dem genossen eine eigenständige existenz, außerhalb des staatsbürgerkunde und blaulicht romansprachenge-
brauchs ermöglicht. nur steht braun für ne andere generation von
poetern.[7]

The title of Uwe Kolbe's first volume of poetry, *Hineingeboren*,
published in 1980, gives us the key to what characterised the nature
of the relationship of the young generation of writers to socialism

5. Günther Deicke, 'Auftritt einer neuen Generation. Schriftsteller über
   Schriftsteller', in Annie Voigtländer (ed.), *Liebes- und andere Erklärungen*,
   Berlin and Weimar, 1972, pp. 36ff.
6. In Anderson and Erbe, *Berührung*, pp. 151ff.
7. Ibid., p.123.

in the GDR: the fact of having been born into a society where the foundations for socialist development had been created and in which its future path already seemed to have been mapped out. School and professional training, the first spheres of autonomous social experience provided the knowledge required to reinforce this view and were supposed to provide the ideological conviction to match. But this process had its contradictions and inconsistencies, produced various approaches to life and, in retrospect, elicited very different responses from individual young writers. All however had to come to terms with an 'angelernte[s] Sozialismusbild' (Jutta Schlott at the 9th Writers Congress) which was all too frequently at odds with the day to day realities of socialism. The search for a place in society, for recognition and a feeling of being needed was fraught with crisis for many young writers. The consequences which accrued from this for their literary activity had varying effects on different members of the group. From the outset it was impossible to bring the young poets under one denominator since they were anything but an homogenous group. A basic difference between them and the Braun generation who appeared on the scene in the 1960s was that any sense of belonging together or of group feeling existed only intermittently and then always on a very small scale, as for instance through a connection with one of the magazines already mentioned. The theme and sense of this essay will become clearer as, on this very point of the relationship of younger authors to Volker Braun, we begin to see a quite marked parting of the ways (Mensching and Wenzel for instance on the one hand, and Melle and Lorek on the other); or rather as stages in the development of individual authors begin to emerge such as those we can identify in the work of the poet Uwe Kolbe. The following poem is from the early phase of his writing:

Zweite, überschüssige Legitimation

Ich bin aufgehetzt worden
Im Verlauf einiger Jahre
meiner eng befristeten Existenz.
Bin aufgestöbert worden
von einer Frau in einem dunklen Zelt,
von einer kleinen Hand in der Schulbank.
Die ersten Wünsche, der erste Begriff
von Unerfüllbarkeit,
brachten mich auf.
Alle Systematik und Rüstung in mir

flimmerte umschauert, rostete
sekundenschnell und brannte durch,
verfiel in Starre und Dunkel.
Ich trauerte, atmetete tief, las
und erlauschte uns,
brachte die Schulgenügsamkeit heraus,
vermengt mit Kot und Schleim.
Verkostete Expressionismus, quirlte
formal mein graues Hab
und das Gute durch und um.
Ich band mich fest und zeugte
ein Kind am Rande der Dichtung
– so hart wurde ich, so
begann ich zu reden –
Es pulste Gift durchs Innre mir,
die bürgerliche Dichtung, Trakl,
Benn und Rilke, Whitman und Pessoa,
die stets genannten Schwierigen.
Ich kam zur Stellung Schreibender
zu ebensolchen Irren,
zur Frage des Genies.
Ich wurde aufgehetzt von jedem Atemzug,
von jeder langen Weile, von Blicken
blasser Mädchen hier am Band.
Ich wurde schwatzhaft von dem Vodka
in der Mittagspause, schrieb
die Flüche auf des dicken Herbert
und das Lallen seiner dicken Frau.
Ich bin gehetzt von dieser Zeitansage
durch das neue Telefon,
angekratzt von der Verflachung
meiner Sinne und der Bilder drinnen.
Jeder Weg macht mich wirr,
jeder Schritt erinnert mich
an den größten Anspruch bei Braun
und bei mir.

Ich bin aufgehetzt worden.
Die Geschwindigkeit nimmt zu.
Ich finde unser Bild nicht mehr scharf.
Wir vervielfachen uns
in der Bewegung, unaufhaltsam,
– für mein Auge,
wenn es kreist und aufschreit.[8]

8. Uwe Kolbe, *Hineingeboren. Gedichte von 1975–1979*, Berlin, 1980, pp.92–4.

Whereas these first years of an 'eng befristeten Existenz' are presented in the work of other young poets in an exclusively negative
light as an age of deformation, Kolbe's poem 'Zweite überschüssige Legitimation' confronts us with a somewhat different
state of affairs. Of moment here is the gesture of restlessness, of
disturbance, of an early, inner uncertainty which will be a dominant feature of the lyrical voice – in varied form of course –
throughout all his subsequent work (he has meanwhile published
two further volumes of poetry: *Abschiede und andere Liebesgedichte*
(1981)[9] and *Bornholm 11*, (1986)[10]. The invocation of Volker Braun
in this context yields further profound and complex insight. It
emerges for instance in the solidarity implicit in comparing his own
'größten Anspruch' with that with which Braun's name is identified, namely the claim to be a vital part of a community of
like-minded spirits in which one's intellect has a critically challenging philosophical contribution to make. It is of essential moment
for the identification with Braun that at this very point in the poem
the 'Ich' of the first person monologue should suddenly intensify
into 'Wir'. The use which Kolbe makes of pathos here is noticeably
similar to that of Braun's early poems. Admittedly the pathos in
Kolbe is interrupted and carried along by very contradictory emotions. It also harbours a polemical dimension with respect to Braun
which is not immediately recognisable. In Braun's third volume of
poetry *Gegen die symmetrische Welt* (1974) we find a two-lined
poem, something more akin to an aphorism:

Jeder Schritt, den ich noch tu,
                    reißt mich auf[11]

The Braun phrase 'reißt mich auf' is the expression of a painfully
activist stance. In Kolbe's reference to it the emphasis is somewhat
different. There we read: 'Jeder Weg macht mich wirr'. A lyrical
'Ich' takes shape which is looking for orientation, which has tasted
uncertainty and made its first tentative, probing and partly painful
experience of the world. Kolbe's poem constitutes an act of self-
clarification rooted in the tensions between what he has actually
experienced (and the Volker Braun of the 1960s is a part of that
experience), and the elevated demands made of life and the happiness it supposedly brings – all of which are constantly subject to a

9. Uwe Kolbe, *Abschiede und andere Liebesgedichte*, Berlin and Weimar, 1986.
10. Uwe Kolbe, *Bornholm II. Gedichte*, Berlin und Weimar, 1986.
11. Volker Braun, *Gegen die symmetrische Welt. Gedichte*, Halle, 1974, p.22.

disillusionment which can, in turn, be put to varyingly productive use.

Kolbe's theoretical utterances reveal – in marked contrast to all other young poets – that, in the course of the years he has, as it were, historicised his relationship to Braun's tone and style. In 1979, in a round table conversation with other young poets, he commented: 'Meine Generation hat die Hände im Schoß, was engagiertes (!) Handeln betrifft. Kein früher Braun heute.'[12] In 1985 in the anthology *Berührung ist nur eine Randerscheinung* he acknowledged his early affinity to Braun: 'Vermutlich habe ich doch verschiedenen Grammatiken angehört im Laufe der Zeit, z.b. der Volker Brauns . . .', whereby by 'Grammatik' he understood a 'Grammatik des Denkens' which, 'sich zwischen bestimmten Begriffen bewegt, die '"Versatzstücke des Denkens" sind, und an denen man hofft, Sinn zu pumpen'.[13]

Whereas for Kolbe lyric poetry in the style of early Braun is no longer possible, the texts of two other poets who have won themselves a considerable reputation and have made an original contribution to developments in the recent GDR lyric reveal a quite different stance. Steffen Mensching and Hans-Eckardt Wenzel are both very versatile authors, actors, comedians and singers. As poets they both seek to intervene directly in social processes, to draw attention to areas of conflict in society and to contribute to their resolution. As in Volker Braun's early poetry, the lyrical 'Ich', or the 'Wir' in Mensching's poem 'Vollgas', for instance, veers between declaration and address.

Vollgas

In den historischen Autos,
Mit Kippen, Flaschen, rissigen Fahnen,
So eilig, immer, so haltlos
Schlittern wir über die Autobahnen
Und lassen das Haar wehn,
Verliebt ineinander, einander verhaßt,
Mit Zähnen, Fingern und Zehn
Gekrallt in die knatternde Unrast.
Ach, so laut, ohne Rollgurt,
Singen wir unsre elegischen Lieder,

12. 'Ohne den Leser geht es nicht. Ursula Heukenkamp im Gespräch mit Gerd Adloff, Gabriele Eckart, Uwe Kolbe, Bernd Wagner', in *Weimarer Beiträge*, 25, 1979, no.7, p.46.
13. *Berührung*, p.38.

Doch im Vollgas, im Endspurt
Rolln wir die Jammerkatzen nieder –
Dann platzen die Reifen
Und schleudern die Freunde ums Leben –
Wir treten die Bremsen, sie keifen
Bis schlotternd am Asphalt wir kleben.
Wir müßten uns, so sagen wir,
Verbiegen, verbieten oder erschlagen,
Hätten wir weniger, hier,
Sagen wir, zu leben, oder zu sagen.[14]

In an article, the author himself has described the basic posture of many of his poems, and this would certainly include 'Vollgas', as follows: 'Ich appelliere an niemanden, sondern versuche meine Fragen zu formulieren – und auch diese nicht manifestartig-erklärend, sondern durch konkrete, prosaische Vorgänge, die, seltsam skurril gelegentlich, auf etwas verweisen, das nicht als verbal festgemachte Aussage, Botschaft in ihnen steht . . . Ich versuche so, Handlungen aufzeigend, Haltungen vorzustellen, zu denen sich der Leser/Hörer in Beziehung setzen kann.'[15]

The emphasis in the poem 'Vollgas' is on a dynamic thrusting forwards to forge a powerful sense of community. The description of a youthfully reckless motorway drive at breakneck speed conveys, in its images of excess, elements of ironic self-criticism: 'verliebt ineinander, einander verhaßt', 'singen wir unsre elegischen Lieder', 'Jammerkatzen' etc. On the one hand, the last four lines emerge from the image which has been set up in the first sixteen lines, but can also, on the other hand, stand on their own: 'Wir müßten uns, so sagen wir, / Verbiegen, verbieten oder erschlagen, / Hätten wir weniger, hier, / Sagen wir, zu leben, oder zu sagen.' It is astonishing – particularly in comparison with other young poets – how in this poem Mensching succeeds in conveying, virtually intact and, as it were, without any historical distance, an attitude to life which is the basis of the activist lyrical pathos of Volker Braun at the beginning of the 1960s.

The reference to the 'Freunde' as a community of like-minded spirits, of similarly impatient contemporaries, was characteristic of much of the early poetry of Volker Braun. In this context his celebrated poem 'Ilmtal' springs immediately to mind. In Mensching

14. Steffen Mensching, *Erinnerung an eine Milchglasscheibe. Gedichte*, Halle-Leipzig, 1984, p.7.
15. Steffen Mensching, 'Grenzwertberechnung', *Neue Deutsche Literatur*, 32, 1984, no.5, p.45.

and Wenzel we find a very similar mode of address from within, or to, a group – as for instance in the following untitled poem by Wenzel:

IN MEINEM KOPF, das da, sperrt sich,
Gegen, was es braucht, Strom, also Ufer;
Gegen, das es schlägt, ein Meer, Land.
Mein kreditwürdiges know-how loben Dispatcher.
Fremd gehe ich fremd.

Schmuggler, Ohren und die anderen
Sinne, die mich beliefern, sattfüttern
Mit Staatsgeheimnissen, den alten
Weisen, Bleioxid, machen mich
Gegen mich aufsässig.

Jeder hat Recht. Wie nur ein Mann,
Energisch, stehn viele Männer
Vor dem Infarkt, im Wohngraben,
In der allergischen Epoche. Volker hört
Die Signale. Wer ist Volker? Fragt Volker.

Auf und ab, in historischen Kleidern
Gehn meine Freunde, Sklerosen im Anzug, und hoch
Die gekräuselte Füllung der Köpfe, Aldehydgruppen spalten
Sie hoffnungsgeladen, reden mir
Ein und aus die Entscheidungen.

In meinem Kopf, aber das, gegenwärtig,
Verhornt, verballhornt, das da, das
Schmerzt, dauernd, das sich sperrt,
Gegen, was es braucht, Ufer also Fluß,
Gegen, das es schlägt, ein Mehr, Land.[16]

This poem of Wenzel from the volume *Lied vom wilden Mohn* (1984) is one of a group of 'Sechs Gedichte für Hölderlin' which are entitled 'Grenzen'. At first one is reminded that Volker Braun in his early poems also displayed a strong affinity with Hölderlin. The subject of Wenzel's Hölderlin poem is contradictory everyday experience in an age which – as Braun and Mensching would say – is not yet the *real* one. In the third stanza Wenzel uses his own coining, the 'allergische Epoche', and then continues: 'Volker hört die Signale. Wer ist Volker? Fragt Volker.' The sentence 'Volker

16. Hans-Eckardt Wenzel, *Lied vom wilden Mohn. Gedichte*, Halle-Leipzig, 1984, p.58.

hört die Signale' is richly evocative: it immediately yields an association with the revolutionary appeal of the *Internationale*; 'Völker hört die Signale, auf zum letzten Gefecht . . .'. Apparently by accident, out of carelessness, 'Völker' becomes 'Volker' and an appeal becomes a statement, namely; 'Volker hört die Signale'. Anyone who has not yet noticed what a subversive game the author is playing with the mutated vowel will be either completely irritated, or be put in the picture by the subsequent 'Wer ist Volker? Fragt Volker'. Twenty years after Braun's early impatient and critical signals from the daily world of socialism, Wenzel is taking them for his own. In contrast to Braun's booming tone at the beginning of the 1960s (we need only think of his poem 'Kommt uns nicht mit Fertigem'), Wenzel's poem takes on an elegaiac note. the 'Signale' – to remain with the image – of a Volker Braun were barely audible; the last battle, the construction of a genuinely socialist society worthy of the name, proved to be a longer and much more difficult task than had been anticipated.

In what has been discussed so far one vital point has been neglected – Braun's characteristic use of language and the extent to which young poets today have been influenced by this or not. Both the poems by Mensching and Wenzel have elements in the handling of language which point to a direct and deliberate connection to Braun. This reveals itself above all in the particularly close relationship to everyday language and the spoken word, in the use for instance of colloquial expressions: in Mensching's poem, 'über die Autobahn schlittern', 'schlotternd am Asphalt kleben', or 'Verballhornt' in Wenzel's. Games are played with language as a way of shattering intellectual lethargy. 'Fremd gehe ich fremd' we read in Wenzel; 'Und schleudern die Freunde ums Leben' we find in Mensching.

A further point is that Mensching and Wenzel's texts – placing them consciously in the Braun tradition – are written specifically to be recited to an audience. This means that by punctuation and a positioning of commas which helps to organise the rhythmic sequence of thought, sentences and turns of phrase are frequently broken up in such a way that the full impact of a poem comes only when it is read aloud. We can see this in the last four lines of the Mensching poem: 'Wir müßten uns, so sagen wir, / Verbiegen, verbieten oder erschlagen,/ Hätten wir weniger, hier,/ Sagen wir, zu leben, oder zu sagen.'

Bert Papenfuß-Gorek - Turning away from Braun?

To relate the intense preoccupation of a number of young poets in the 1980s with the linguistic constitution of their poetry directly to Volker Braun would be somewhat misleading. On the contrary, those young poets – Bert Papenfuß-Gorek (b.1956) is a prime example – to whom we now turn our attention, are the very ones (see the remarks of Lorek and Melle already quoted) who have not only distanced themselves from, or even totally rejected Braun's poetry, but who have repeatedly vilified in unseemly and uncivilised manner those such as Mensching and Wenzel who see themselves as the heirs to Braun's tradition of writing.

It has to be said that the sad fate of Bert Papenfuß-Gorek's poems in the literary landscape of the GDR in the 1980s is typical of numerous works by young writers who were largely denied a public audience in their own country because of narrow-minded cultural and political regulation and control. When, in 1988, his *dreizehntanz* was finally able to be published by Gerhard Wolf in the Aufbau-Verlag, Papenfuß-Gorek already had fifteen years as a writer behind him and had produced six volumes or collections of poetry which had appeared either in the Federal Republic or which he had published himself. The volume published in the GDR gives only a very inadequate notion of the development of the various intellectual and poetic phases which he had gone through and in part rejected.

To return to Volker Braun's poetry for a moment, we can see that Papenfuß offers some points of comparison: he too deploys everyday, colloquial language as points of reference. But whereas Braun often makes use of everyday expressions from the sphere of political and ideological propaganda, Papenfuß frequently has recourse to jargon, to emotive catchwords which, in a poem, will always offend conservative sensibilities. In very similar fashion to Braun, Papenfuß is concerned that his poetry should question and criticise language, should unsettle routine concepts and expressions which daily use has polished into meaningless clichés. He works with words in a way which makes them lose their established meaning, changes them, gives them a fresh conceptual context. Whereas for Braun this process is bound up principally with the recitability of the poem, with Papenfuß one finds two main differences in approach. On the one hand he is frequently more interested in the *How*, the way in which a poem is made, than in the *What*, the content of what is being expressed. One of his central theses, for instance runs as follows: 'In normalen zwischenmenschlichen

Kommunikationen da läuft alles viel diffuser ab, du achtest auf die Gestik, Mimik, daraus erfährt man mehr als aus dem, was gesagt wird. Also aus dem *Wie* erfährt man eigentlich viel mehr als aus dem *Was*'.[17] The second difference lies in the central role played by the appearance of the poem on the page. Papenfuß firmly believes that one cannot have an adequate impression of the poetic text – what he has called 'sichtbar gemachte Sprachbewegung' – until it is actually printed. The poem 'jede uhr isn zeitzuender' gives clear demonstration of what this might mean in practice:

jede uhr isn zeitzuender

```
ich hab mich
              fon der zeit
                            ferspottet gefuehlt

jede zeit ferspottet jeden augenblikk
    jede zeit ferspottet jede uhr
        jede uhr ferspottet jeden augenblikk

jede uhr isn zeitzuender
    zeit is mir                    nichts
        jedes ich ferspottet jedes  nichts

im rechten augenblikk
    das linke zu tun
        & rechtzeitig zu gehn

jede uhr ferspottet jede zeit
    jede uhr ferspottet jeder zeit den
```

This poem, which is one of the author's relatively easily interpretable texts, is only comprehensible when its visual form on the page is taken into account. The poet's relationship to standard, or rather standardised grammar, semantics and orthography is extremely ambivalent. By arranging and organising the words and letters of a poem in a way which is completely new for the GDR lyric,

17. In Hesse, *Sprache und Antwort*, p.217.
18. Bert Papenfuß-Gorek, *dreizehntanz*, Berlin and Weimar, 1988, p.32.

Papenfuß is attempting to express his feelings by literally *depicting* them before they can coagulate into abstract, fixed concepts and constructions. Words, so to speak, are to be taken at their word; it is a matter – quite literally – of showing what is in them. In his way of arranging the words and the text there lurks, as Karl Mickel has put it: 'um jedes Wort ein mehr oder weniger großes Rudel anderer Bezeichnungen . . .'[19] In this respect, Papenfuß is the most consistent of all the young writers who have been representative of this trend in recent GDR lyric poetry.

The initial mistrust in principle which one finds in Papenfuß and other young GDR poets – further examples would be Stefan Döring (b.1954), Rainer Schedlinski (b.1956) and Eberhard Häfner (b.1941) – of everything handed down to them in linguistically fixed form is not only rooted in the biographical and ideological factors already mentioned, but also corresponds to interests of a philosophical kind. The strong and also theoretically motivated attention which young poets pay to the cognitive and communicatory function of language does not deny its intellectual point of contact with the discussions of modern bourgeois philosophers such as Habermas, Foucault and Wittgenstein. Their philosophical findings about a disturbed relationship between language and reality as the expression of growing alienation in modern society *tout court*, appear, in the context of much contemporary poetry, as the philosophical and theoretical correlate to the crisis experiences of young poets in the socialist society of the GDR. Gerhard Wolf who is very knowledgeable about young poets today and has done much to help and encourage them (just as Franz Fühmann did while he was still alive incidentally) has described them and the particular qualities of their work in the following terms:

> Ihre Psychogramme sind noch nicht geschrieben, aber daß diese Generation der um die Mitte der fünfziger Jahre Geborenen einen Konflikt aufreißt, der oft geleugnet wird, indem sie die Verhältnisse nicht aus ihren Realitäten, sondern aus ihren Äußerungen und Verlautbarungen heraus konstatieren, die geläufigen Wörter für sich neu buchstabieren – es wird an ihren Arbeiten sichtbar. Man mag sie leugnen, mißachten, als Dichtung verwerfen, als Warnung überhören. Ihre Zeichen – sprachlich, graphisch und musikalisch intoniert, oft in seltener Kommunikation miteinander – sind authentisch; mit ihnen kündigt sich eine andere Seh-, Empfindungs- und Denkweise an, um so dringlicher, je weniger sie sich in Lamento oder Larmoyanz verlieren.[20]

19. Karl Mickel, 'Aussagen über Papenfuß' in *Sinn und Form*, 1986, no.6, p.1230.
20. Gerhard Wolf, 'Wortlaut Wortbruch Wortlust. Papenfuß und andere. Zu

In conclusion, by drawing attention, if only briefly, to Volker Braun, it should be pointed out that the processes which have been illustrated with reference to recent lyric poetry are not restricted solely to the authors of the younger generation. He too in his poetry from the end of the 1970s and the 1980s has experimented with different lyrical techniques, text structures and modes of poetic address – as, for instance, can be seen from various of his 'Material' – texts in the volume *Langsamer knirschender Morgen* (1987). This is testament to the fact that over the years, and prior to the collapse of the system in November 1989, Braun too had distanced himself more and more from, and criticised increasingly sharply, earlier certainties and attitudes with respect to the social system of the GDR and the concept of socialism represented by the Party and state leadership.

Translated by Martin Kane

Suggested Further Reading

Useful anthologies of GDR poetry which set the historical and literary context from which poets writing today have emerged, are:

Uwe Berger and Günther Deicke (eds), *Lyrik der DDR*, Berlin and Weimar, 1970.

Ursula Heukenkamp, Heinz Kahlau and Wulf Kirsten (eds), *Die eigene Stimme. Lyrik der DDR*, Berlin and Weimar, 1988.

Secondary Material

Christine Cosentino, Wolfgang Ertl and Gerd Labroisse (eds), 'DDR-Lyrik im Kontext', in *Amsterdamer Beiträge zur neueren Germanistik*, vol.26, Amsterdam, 1988.

John L. Flood (ed.), *Ein Moment des erfahrenen Lebens. Zur Lyrik der DDR*, GDR Monitor Special Series no.5, Dundee, 1987.

---

einem Aspekt neuer Lyrik' in *Wortlaut Wortbruch Wortlust. Dialog mit Dichtung. Aufsätze und Vorträge*, Leipzig, 1988, p.366.

Ingrid Pergande

Christel and Walfried Hartinger, '"Ich sehe das Land nicht als Provinz". Gespräch mit Steffen Mensching', in *Positionen 2. Wortmeldungen zur DDR-Literatur*, Halle–Leipzig, 1986, pp.65–81.

Ingrid Hähnel (ed.), *Lyriker im Zwiegespräch. Traditionsbeziehungen im Gedicht*, Berlin and Weimar, 1981.

Karin Hiridina, '"Überhaupt montiere ich Zitate". Zu Texten von Hans-Eckardt Wenzel', in Siegfried Rönisch (ed.), *DDR-Literatur '84 im Gespräch*, Berlin and Weimar, 1985, pp.293–9.

Klaus Krippendorf, 'Unruhestiftender Lärm oder Weltentwurf? Die Anfänge zweier Lyrikergenerationen', in Hans Richter (ed.), *Generationen, Temperamente, Schreibweisen. DDR-Literatur in neuer Sicht*, Halle–Leipzig, 1986.

Dieter Schlenstedt, '"Wo bist du, Nachdenkliches?" Notizen zu Wenzels Gedichten und zur Literaturkritik', in *Neue Deutsche Literatur*, 34, 1986, no.8, pp.92–110.

Notes on Contributors

Agnes **Cardinal**: Honorary Research Fellow, the University of Kent at Canterbury. Her book *The Figure of Paradox in the Work of Robert Walser* was published in 1982 and an edition of Christa Wolf's *Der geteilte Himmel* in 1987.

Margy **Gerber**: Professor of German, Bowling Green State University, Ohio. Editor of *Studies in GDR Culture and Society* and author of numerous articles on cultural policy and practice in the GDR.

Reinhard **Hillich**: Research Fellow, Akademie der Wissenschaften, Berlin (East) and the co-author of *Erwin Strittmatter. Analysen, Erörterungen, Gespräche*, 1984. His other publications include translations of several Arthur Conan Doyle novels and stories into German, several articles on East German detective fiction, a new edition of Friedrich Glauser's *Wachtmeister Studer* and, as editor, *Tatbestand. Ansichten zur Kriminalliteratur in der DDR 1947–1986*, 1989.

Walter **Jens**: Emeritus Professor of Rhetoric, Eberhard-Karls University, Tübingen. Classical scholar, novelist and essayist, Walter Jens is one of West Germany's most prolific cultural critics. Publications include *Hoffmansthal und die Griechen*, 1955; *Die Götter sind sterblich*, 1959; *Zur Antike*, 1978; *Republikanische Reden*, 1979; *Der Mann der nicht alt werden wollte. Herr Meister*, 1987; *Statt einer Literaturgeschichte*, 1988. Dates indicate most recent editions.

Martin **Kane**: Senior Lecturer in German and European Studies, University of Kent. Publications include *Weimar Germany and the Limits of Political Art: A Study of the Work of George Grosz and Ernst Toller*, 1987 as well as various articles on East and West German literature.

Brian **Keith-Smith**: Senior Lecturer in German, University of Bristol. Has written widely on many aspects of nineteenth- and twentieth-century German literature, is the author of *Johannes Bobrowski*, 1970, and the editor of *Essays on contemporary German literature* 3rd edn., 1972.

Moray **McGowan**: Professor of German, University of Sheffield. Publications include *Marieluise Fleißer*, 1987 ('Autorenbücher') and numerous articles on German literature of the twentieth century, in particular of the 1970s and 1980s.

Malcolm **Pender**: Senior Lecturer in German, University of Strathclyde. Has written widely on German-Swiss literature. Publications include *Max Frisch: His Work and its Swiss Background*, 1979; *The Creative Imagination and Society: The German-Swiss 'Künstlerroman'*, 1985; *Max Frisch: Biedermann und die Brandstifter*, 1988.

Ingrid **Pergande**: Research Fellow, Akademie der Wissenschaften, Berlin (East). A former editor of *Weimarer Beiträge*, she has written widely on GDR literature.

Notes on Contributors

Editor, as Ingrid Hähnel, of *Lyriker im Zwiegespräch. Traditionsbeziehungen im Gedicht*, 1981.

H.J. **Reid**: Professor of Contemporary German Studies, University of Nottingham. Publications include *Heinrich Böll: Withdrawal and Re-emergence*, 1973; *Heinrich Böll: A German for his Time*, 1987; *The New East German Literature: Writing without Taboos*, 1990, as well as numerous articles on postwar East and West German literature.

Hans **Richter**: Professor of German Literature at the Friedrich-Schiller-University, Jena. He has written widely on many aspects of German literature. His most recent works are *Werke und Wege. Kritiken, Aufsätze, Reden*, 1984; *Generationen Temperamente Schreibweisen. DDR-Literatur in neuer Sicht* (ed.), 1986; *Verwandeltes Dasein. Über deutschsprachige Literatur von Hauptmann bis heute*, 1987.

Ricarda **Schmidt**: Lecturer in German at the University of Sheffield. Has published articles on E.T.A. Hoffmann, Christa Wolf, Angela Carter and on aspects of feminist literary criticism. Also, *Westdeutsche Frauenliteratur in den siebziger Jahren*, 2nd edition, 1990.

Arrigo **Subiotto**: Director of the School of Modern Languages, Saint David's University College, University of Wales. Has written widely on aspects of nineteenth- and twentieth-century German literature. Publications include *Bertolt Brecht's adaptions for the Berliner Ensemble*, 1975; *Hans Magnus Enzensberger*, 1985.

Dennis **Tate** is Senior Lecturer in German Studies at the University of Bath. His publications include *The East German Novel: Identity, Community, Continuity*, 1984; (as co-editor), *European Socialist Realism*, 1988; an edition of Günter de Bruyn: *Märkische Forschungen*, 1990. He has also written numerous articles on literature in the GDR.

Index

Index

Index

Index

Index

Index

Lorbeer, Hans, 3
Lorek, Leonhard, 234, 242
Louis XIV, 217
Louis XV, 157
LPG. 49
Luchterhand Verlag, 30
Lukács, Georg, 15, 34, 216, 219
Luxemburg, Rosa, 143

Manger, Philip, 174
Mann, Heinrich, 1, 4, 30
Mann, Thomas, 1, 10
Marchwitza, Hans, 1
Marcuse, Herbert, 140
Maron, Monika
    Flugasche, viii
Marx, Karl, 36, 130, 139, 151, 183,
    198
    Zur Kritik der politischen ökonomie,
    128
May 1968, 148, 149, 150, 154, 158
McCarthyism, 62, 64
Meitner, Lisa, 188
Melle, Fritz-Hendrik, 234–5, 242
Mensching, Steffen, 230, 233, 235,
    241
    Erinnerung an eine Milchglasscheibe,
    239n14
    'Grenzwertberechnung', 239n15
    'Vollgas', 238–9
Mickel, Karl, 244
Mikado, 230
Moog, Christa, 92
Morgner, Irmtraud, x, 147–61, 179,
    184
    Amanda. Ein Hexenroman, 148, 150,
    153, 155–9
    *Die cherubinischen Wandersfrauen: ein
    apokrypher Salmanroman*, 148
    *Leben und Abenteuer der Trobadora
    Beatriz nach Zeugnissen ihrer
    Spielfrau Laura*, 148, 150, 152–5,
    156
Moscow trials (1937), 113
Mozart, Wolfgang Amadeus, 79
Müller, Heiner, 125–46
    Der Auftrag, 142
    Der Bau, 126, 130
    'Der glückloser Engel', 143
    Der Horatier, 126–7
    Der Lohndrücker, 126, 127, 130, 131
    Die Hamletmaschine, 126, 135, 139,
    140, 141, 142
    Die Korrektur, 126, 130

Die Schlacht, 136
Die Umsiedlerin, 130
Germania Tod in Berlin, 126, 133,
    136, 138, 141
Herakles 5, 126
Kentauren, 140
*Leben Gundlings Friedrich von
    Preußen Lessings Schlaf Traum
    Schrei*, 126, 133, 136, 137
Philoktet, 126, 131, 132, 133, 134,
    142
*Verkommenes Ufer Medeamaterial
    Landschaft mit Argonauten*, 126,
    133, 142
Wolokolamsker Chausee, 127, 138, 140

National Socialism (and Nazi), xi, 4,
    26, 27, 30, 32, 33, 34, 44, 63, 66,
    79, 112, 113, 167, 188, 206, 222
naturalism, 135
Neubauer, 44
Neue Deutsche Literatur, 230
Neues Deutschland, 214
Neutsch, Erik,
    Spur der Steine, 205
Nibelungenlied, 91, 204
Nietzsche, Friedrich, 11, 137
Ninth Writers' Congress, 235
Nobel Prize, 126
Noll, Dieter
    Kippenberg, x
November 1989 (also refs. to autumn
    1989), vii, xi, 55, 62f., 70, 141,
    144, 176, 195, 208, 213, 215, 245
November Revolution 1918, 2

Odyssey, 102
Orwell, George,
    1984, 209

Papenfuß-Gorek, Bert,
    dreizehntanz, 242
    'jede uhr isn zeitzuender', 243
Pessoa, Fernando, 236
PEN, West German, 28
Pietraß, Richard, 230
Pinthus, Kurt,
    Menschheitsdämmerung, 2
'Planer-und-Leiter-Literatur', 51
Planck, Max, 188
Plenzdorf, Ulrich, *Die neuen Leiden
    des jungen W.*, 202, 223
Poesiealbum, 230
Politbüro, 214